ALTERNATIVE MODELS OF
FAMILY PRESERVATION:
FAMILY-BASED SERVICES IN CONTEXT

ABOUT THE AUTHORS

Kristine E. Nelson, D.S.W., is Associate Professor at the University of Iowa School of Social Work and Director of Research at the National Resource Center on Family Based Services. She has been the Principal Investigator on several federally-funded studies of family-based services and child neglect, and has taught research and family policy at The University of Iowa since 1979. Dr. Nelson has been a contributing author to several texts on family preservation and has published articles in *Social Service Review, Child Welfare,* and *Children and Youth Services Review* among others. Dr. Nelson earned her doctoral degree at the University of California at Berkeley, and holds an M.S.W. from Sacramento State University and a B.A. from Stanford University.

Miriam J. Landsman, M.S.W., is Senior Researcher at the National Resource Center on Family Based Services, University of Iowa School of Social Work. She has been working on federal and state-funded research and program evaluation in child welfare and family-based services since 1983. Ms. Landsman holds an M.S.W. from the University of Iowa and a B.A. from The University of Delaware.

ALTERNATIVE MODELS OF FAMILY PRESERVATION: FAMILY-BASED SERVICES IN CONTEXT

By

KRISTINE E. NELSON, D.S.W., M.S.W.
MIRIAM J. LANDSMAN, M.S.W.

National Resource Center on Family Based Services
School of Social Work
The University of Iowa
Iowa City, Iowa

With a Foreword by
Cecelia E. Sudia

C H A R L E S   C   T H O M A S   •   P U B L I S H E R
Springfield • Illinois • U.S.A.

Published and Distributed Throughout the World by

CHARLES C THOMAS • PUBLISHER
2600 South First Street
Springfield, Illinois 62794-9265

© *1992 by* CHARLES C THOMAS • PUBLISHER

ISBN 0-398-05810-5

Library of Congress Catalog Card Number: 92-13534

With THOMAS BOOKS *careful attention is given to all details of manufacturing
and design. It is the Publisher's desire to present books that are satisfactory as to
their physical qualities and artistic possibilities and appropriate for their particular
use.* THOMAS BOOKS *will be true to those laws of quality that assure a good
name and good will.*

Printed in the United States of America
SC-R-3

Library of Congress Cataloging-in-Publication Data

Nelson, Kristine E.
    Alternative models of family preservation : family-based services
in context / by Kristine E. Nelson, Miriam J. Landsman.
        p.   cm.
    Includes bibliographical references and index.
    ISBN 0-398-05810-5
    1. Family services—United States.   2. Problem families—
Counseling of—United States.   I. Landsman, Miriam J.   II. Title.
HV699.N44   1992
362.82′0973—dc20   92-13534
                                                                  CIP

Dedicated to Our Families:

Ruth K. Nelson	*Estelle F. Landsman*
Nels Y. Nelson	*Jerome J. Landsman*
Paul L. Adams	*Steven P. Horowitz*
Sarah K. Adams	*Veronica Landsman Horowitz*
	Jacob Landsman Horowitz

FOREWORD

I am very pleased to have the opportunity to recommend this major report on family-based services from the National Resource Center on Family Based Services and the School of Social Work at The University of Iowa. Given the preeminence of Iowa and of this University in the development of these services, I was planning to give them credit for the original idea. However, I recently reviewed a history of the U.S. Children's Bureau (Bradbury, 1962), which noted that in 1923, the Bureau issued "Foster-Home Care for Dependent Children" which the author characterized as a publication that was far ahead of its time. She noted that all of the ten agencies studied were moving from a strong emphasis "on adoptions and free-home permanent placements" to "stressing the preservation of family ties."

Rather more recently, a 1960 report from State Charities Aid Association in New York described ten programs throughout New York state that addressed the multiproblem family. In Chemung County, services were directed toward the permanent rehabilitation of families with especially difficult, long-standing problems. In Syracuse, services were characterized by active, even aggressive, reaching out to families in trouble with 75 percent of services in the home, an emphasis on the neighborhood relationships of the family, and a special effort to reach fathers including at home and at his work, during evenings and weekends. Services were considered expensive, with Monroe County reporting an average length of activity of three months, at $345 per case. In Erie County, a specialist worker was paid an annual salary of $7500. One is tempted to search the Sumerian archives from 2000 BC to see if they recommended in-home services to families.

Nevertheless, FAMILIES, INC. of West Branch, Iowa, shares honors with the Mendota Mental Health Institute in Madison, Wisconsin, the Lower East Side Family Union in New York City, and Homebuilders in Tacoma, Washington for rediscovering the value of a family and community-based approach to social services. However, only in Iowa did the provision of these services become a movement early on. Iowa established programs statewide, and started the first state association for home-based services. Gradually, the idea spread in the Midwest with the inception of similar services in neighboring states of Minnesota, South Dakota, and Illinois. The most recent Directory of the Center lists nearly 400 programs, many of them now statewide (National Resource Center on Family Based Services, 1991).

In the middle 1970s the University of Iowa was funded to develop a clearinghouse on in-home services, which has been in operation under various names ever since that time, providing training, technical assistance, consultation, newsletters, and most especially, research and evaluation studies.

A signal difficulty, reflected in the 1960 New York project reports and almost all studies since then, are the questions of effectiveness and cost. Everyone likes the programs, families appreciate and use the services, workers feel that they really make a difference. Everyone involved understands their value. But we live in an era when cost questions are regularly asked and programs must be justified by carefully planned studies which document accomplishments and cost-effectiveness, usually within the year. Such cost accounting ignores the lifetime costs to society of not providing the service, but legislatures fund a year at a time. It also carries a message that the public is not willing to assist families in trouble unless it is to their immediate economic advantage. Surely this is a devaluation of the worth of our troubled families and children, and quite at odds with the empowerment message the services are supposed to carry.

The current volume is a major contribution to the development of the field. It provides much needed information on the range of the programs, how they work with families with various social ills of our time: child neglect, physical abuse, sexual abuse, and problem youth. While individual programs have frequently been evaluated, and found to be successful, the studies have not usually gone beyond reporting a "black box" effect; the services "fixed up" all types of families and problems, with no information on how they worked with particular types of families or particular child and family problems or what variations might be due to the community setting. This study addresses many of these issues and surely provides the field with a range of much needed information—for administrators selecting the most appropriate type of program, for program managers implementing and managing the services, and for family workers as they connect with the family. We are very pleased that it is now available to the field.

CECELIA E. SUDIA
Family Services Specialist
Children's Bureau, A.C.Y.F.

PREFACE

Family-based services designed to provide an alternative to avert the out-of-home placement of children have expanded rapidly since the late 1970s, with efforts to evaluate and explain the effectiveness of these services following close behind. Caught up in the enthusiasm which these programs have generated among administrators, practitioners, and client families, research has focused largely on documenting their effectiveness in preventing unnecessary placements. Relatively little attention has been paid to understanding the different client populations served in the variety of settings in which these programs have emerged.

In this volume, we have sought to focus on these issues. We begin by briefly reviewing the history of family-based services and tracing the development of the existing research base. We then turn to describing specific client populations and modes of service delivery, based on data collected by the National Resource Center on Family Based Services' federally-funded multistate study. In this book we examine 454 cases drawn from nine family-based service programs, looking at case outcomes for different client populations and service delivery settings. Complementing the statistical models for each analysis are descriptive case studies of the programs, families, and the social workers who served them. While the study findings cannot be considered representative of all family-based programs in the country, this research is important in beginning to look at underexplored issues in family-based services.

Families experiencing such diverse problems as child abuse, neglect, sexual abuse, and delinquency/status offenses are examined in separate chapters, as are programs based in rural locales, providing in-office services, and operating under public and private auspices. Our primary purposes are to bring important questions about service effectiveness with different populations and in different service settings to the forefront of research in family-based/family preservation services, and to offer practitioners, program planners, and policymakers empirically-based information which can be applied to providing and improving services to families at risk of placement.

ACKNOWLEDGMENTS

We would like to express our appreciation to a number of individuals and agencies instrumental in helping us carry out the original study and in completing this manuscript.

First, we thank the project staff of the OHDS-funded study (Grant # 90-CW-0732) which provided the data for this book: Arthur Emlen, Co-Investigator, Regional Research Institute for Human Services at Portland State University; Janet Hutchinson, the original Project Director; Anne Zalenski, Carla Marcus, and Carol Inskeep, Research Assistants at the National Resource Center on Family Based Services, University of Iowa School of Social Work; Richard Black, Research Assistant at Portland State University; and Patrick Leung, Statistical Consultant. At the Department of Health and Human Services, two Federal Project Officers, Alice Fusillo and Soledad Arenas, provided guidance and advice throughout the course of the study.

We would also like to acknowledge the efforts of the key staff at the eleven study sites. These individuals contributed a great deal of time and effort to this project, helping to develop the data collection instruments, selecting the samples, and monitoring data collection activities: Ruth Anderson, Supportive Child/Adult Network, Inc. of Philadelphia; Tony Bibus, Dakota County Human Services Department (MN); Larry Boven, Boulder County Department of Social Services (CO); Vince Lindgren and Val Broste, Lutheran Social Services (MN); Steve Davis, Adolescent Day Treatment Program (CO); Gloria Gray, Donell Lloyd, and Linda Ross, Iowa Children and Family Services (IA); Selma Harrison, Franklin County Children Services (OH); Rolly Hartley, Oregon Children's Services Division; Julie Plekan and Jim Smith, Albertina Kerr Center (OR); Richard Moore and David Stout, Iowa Department of Human Services.

We are especially grateful to several individuals who reviewed the manuscript and offered useful suggestions for its improvement: Richard Barth of the Berkeley Child Welfare Research Center, University of California at Berkeley; David Stout of the Iowa Department of Human

Services, who was the key contact person from the Ottumwa District Office in the original study; and Cecelia Sudia, Family Services Specialist at the Children's Bureau, Administration for Children, Youth, and Families, who has been a source on ongoing assistance and support since the inception of the original study.

Several individuals reviewed and corrected our descriptions of the agencies for this manuscript, and we are grateful for their assistance: Larry Boven, Boulder County Department of Social Services; Laura Murphy, Children and Families of Iowa (formerly Iowa Children and Family Services); Jack M. Donahue, Franklin County Children Services; Jack Tovey, Intensive Family Services, Multnomah County; Jim Nice and Bill Showell, Oregon Children's Services Division; and Mark Bronson, Lutheran Social Services of Minnesota. The authors, of course, are solely responsible for any errors remaining in the text.

Finally, we would like to acknowledge Marcia Culver of The University of Iowa for editing this manuscript and Debbie Black of the National Resource Center on Family Based Services for her assistance in typing both text and tables.

CONTENTS

LIST OF TABLES

ALTERNATIVE MODELS
OF FAMILY PRESERVATION:
FAMILY-BASED SERVICES IN CONTEXT

Chapter One

THE DEVELOPMENT OF
FAMILY-BASED SERVICES

A revolution is taking place in the field of child welfare. Like all revolutions, it has grown out of ideas and discontents which long preceded it and which are now being transformed in the process. The idea of family-based services has roots deep in the history and traditions of social work in the United States. Prototypical family-based programs began to emerge as early as the 1950s. But it was only with the passage of P.L. 96-272, The Adoption Assistance and Child Welfare Act of 1980, that the process of replacing the old system of child welfare practice with a new model of family-centered social services began on a national level.

What is revolutionary about the family-based services movement is its rejection of a world view which blames families for their failures in child rearing and sees foster care or institutional placement as the best way to save children. In place of this old world view, the family preservation movement holds forth a new vision: one which sees that *families* are worth saving, as well as children. Indeed, we have begun to recognize that the best and often the only way to save children is through their families.

This change in perspective has profound implications for social work policy and practice. The new model of child welfare differs from the old paradigm in valuing families' strengths and respecting their needs and views, even in the face of serious child maltreatment. Family-based workers recognize that an essential part of their job is to instill hope and engage families in a process of change which is both goal-oriented and time-limited. And while preventing placement is most frequently seen as the primary goal of family-based services, families, workers, and agencies all know that this can only be achieved through improvement in family functioning, social, material, or psychological, which allows children to remain *safely* in their own homes.

BACKGROUND TO THE STUDY

Family-based services have evolved over the past twenty years as a means of helping families who had, in essence, been abandoned by the existing child welfare system. The earliest family-based programs reported impressive results in averting out-of-home placement. When in the 1970s an explosion in the number of children in out-of-home care coincided with a growing awareness of the limits of foster care, the success of these first family-based programs offered a ray of hope (Goldstein, 1973; Hutchinson, Lloyd, Landsman, Nelson, & Bryce, 1983). Soon, a growing number of preplacement prevention programs were developed to divert families judged to be at high risk of placement into special units within public agencies or into private programs established specifically to avert placement and to reunify families who already had a child removed.[1]

The success of these early family-based programs contributed in 1980 to the passage of a federal law, P.L. 96-272, which requires all public child welfare agencies to demonstrate that they are making "reasonable efforts" to prevent out-of-home placement in order to continue receiving federal funds for child welfare services. Although the record of early successes shaped this law and led to widespread replication of family-based placement prevention programs in both public and private child welfare agencies, these results had not been empirically tested or validated. Also, as interest in the family-based approach grew, questions arose concerning the minority of families who did not seem to benefit from these services.

Thus, in 1984 the Office of Human Development Services (OHDS) requested proposals for research that would provide information on families in which placement was not averted, information that would lead to the development of better criteria for case management and planning. In response, the University of Iowa School of Social Work's National Resource Center on Family Based Services in conjunction with Portland State University's Regional Research Institute for Human Services, an early leader in the permanency planning movement, fielded a study of eleven different family-based service programs in six states. This book is an attempt to chronicle the efforts and achievements of nine of these programs. Although individual programs and cases are profiled in order to give a realistic picture of family-based services in action, the practices highlighted are those that were found to be important to the success of services across agencies.

FAMILY-BASED SERVICES DEFINED

Family-based services developed within the child welfare system as a means of preventing unnecessary out-of-home placements and keeping families intact whenever possible, through intensive work with families of children at imminent risk of placement. A variety of terms have been used interchangeably with family-based services: home-based services, family-centered services, in-home services, and most recently, family preservation services. Despite differences among individual programs in such areas as theoretical orientation (Barth, 1988; Nelson, Landsman, & Deutelbaum, 1990) and program features (e.g., length and intensity of service), most family-based programs share the following fundamental assumptions:

1. The family has a powerful influence on children and should be maintained and supported whenever possible.
2. Children need continuity and stability in their lives, and most children are better off with their own families than in substitute care.
3. Separation has detrimental effects on both parents and children.
4. The first and greatest investment should be in preplacement services, and society should be willing to spend at least as much on attempting to keep families together as it does on placement.
5. Time-limited, intensive and comprehensive services including therapeutic, concrete and supportive services should be provided in accordance with the needs and priorities of each family (Bryce, 1982; Bryce & Lloyd, 1981; Nelson et al., 1990; Nelson, Emlen, Landsman, & Hutchinson, 1988; Stroul, 1988; Whittaker & Tracy, 1988).

Operating on the theory that the family is a social system and the behavior of one member influences and is influenced by all others, family-based programs focus on the family as a unit, rather than on an individual's problems. Services are usually delivered in the families' homes and communities, although some of the relatively less intensive programs also use office settings for treatment (Nelson et al., 1990; Whittaker & Tracy, 1988). In keeping with a commitment to empowering families, family members are involved in setting treatment goals and parents are in charge of treatment (Bryce, 1982; Bryce & Lloyd, 1981). Goals common to many family-based service programs include: (1) protecting children; (2) preserving family integrity and preventing unnecessary placement; (3) promoting family reunification where placement has been necessary; (4) stabilizing crisis situations; (5) improving family relationships; (6) increasing families' coping skills and competencies; and (7) facilitating families' use of appropriate formal and informal helping resources (Stroul, 1988; Whittaker & Tracy, 1988).

AN HISTORICAL PERSPECTIVE

Although in many ways family-based services represent a new approach in child welfare, they have methodological and ideological roots in early social work practice and in late nineteenth- and early twentieth-century public policy (McGowan, 1988; Wells, in press). The earliest and most direct antecedent of family-based services was the Charity Organization Societies' practice of sending friendly visitors into the homes of poor families to offer advice and to serve as role models for parents. The first professional caseworkers, like these earlier volunteers, also did most of their work with families through home visits (McGowan, 1988).

In 1909, the first White House Conference on Children lent support to the principle that children should not be removed from their homes due to poverty alone (McGowan, 1988). And, although Conference participants favored the use of funds from private charities to help families, subsequent legislation authorized states to provide public funds for parents without other income in order to enable them to support their children in their own homes.

Beginning in the 1930s, however, the psychoanalytic movement contributed to an individualistic treatment approach in social work practice and a shift away from the social context of family problems. From this point of view, problems were defined as internal to the child or parent and treated accordingly. Thus, despite early movement toward a family-centered approach to child welfare, out-of-home placement remained the primary method by which public agencies dealt with problem children and families in crisis (McGowan, 1988).

Family-based services as we know them today began in 1949 with the St. Paul (Minnesota) Family Centered Project (Bryce, 1982; Hutchinson & Nelson, 1985; Stroul, 1988; Wells, in press). This project documented the disproportionate use of existing social welfare services by "multi-problem families" and demonstrated that home-based, family-centered programs were effective in preventing child placement and increasing the competencies of troubled families. Although the results of the St. Paul project were encouraging and suggested a shift from an emphasis on out-of-home placement to a family-based approach, the program was not widely or carefully replicated (Wells, in press). Out-of-home placement remained the most widely available option among child welfare services.

While evidence about the long-term effects of foster care is inconclusive, there is no doubt that unnecessary out-of-home placement is unfair to children and their families, as well as costly to the state. Maas and Engler's study *Children in Need of Parents* (1959) offered the first major critique of the foster care system. These authors found that few efforts were ever made to keep children at home and that, once children were placed in foster care, 75 percent were unlikely to return home. Yet the impact of this study was slow to be felt. Federal legislation such as the 1971 amendments to the AFDC Foster Care sections of the Social Security Act and the Child Abuse Prevention and Treatment Act of 1974 continued to support placement rather than family-centered work and, intentionally or not, offered few or no incentives to keep families intact (McGowan, 1988). Although agencies in the private sector continued to experiment with family-centered work, public agencies generally developed categorical, child-focused services (Hutchinson & Nelson, 1985).

In the 1960s and 70s, however, some broad changes in the social and cultural climate began to turn the tide away from conventional strategies of removing children from their homes. At the same time that concern about the number of children in placement was becoming more widespread and urgent, a new willingness to question and challenge existing institutions and practices was beginning to reach into the social service establishment as well. Concepts like "deinstitutionalization," and "least restrictive environment" began to be applied to the treatment of status offenders and delinquent youth (McGowan, 1988).

During this period, public as well as private agencies began to implement programs to provide preventive or reunification services to families, although the earliest versions of these programs tended to focus on the mother rather than on the family as a whole, and thus cannot be strictly classified as family based (Nelson et al., 1988). In the projects studied by Jones, Neuman, and Shyne (1976), for example, there was an average of seventeen in-person contacts with the mother and only three with the father if he was in the home. "Intensive" services involved an average of two in-person contacts a month, and services extended over a lengthy time period, often more than a year (Magura & DeRubeis, 1980). Throughout the 1970s, however, a family-based placement prevention approach began to be applied to a variety of situations in which children were at risk of out-of-home placement in mental health, juvenile justice, and child welfare agencies (Maybanks & Bryce, 1978).

At about the same time, the Oregon Permanency Planning Project addressed the problem of "foster care drift" by stressing children's need for stability and the responsibility of child welfare agencies to establish a permanent home for each child. The Oregon Permanency Planning Project produced materials for foster care workers which were disseminated nationally. A follow-up study of the Oregon project, as well as studies of other programs which implemented these techniques, showed that with careful planning and effort, many children who were living in substitute care could be reunified with their families, adopted by their foster parents or others, or placed in long-term "permanent" homes (Lahti et al., 1978; Wiltse, 1985).

A FIELD EXPANDS

The passage of P.L. 96-272, The Adoption Assistance and Child Welfare Act of 1980, signified a return at the federal level to a focus on families, and has been the primary legislative force in the development and spread of family-based service programs since 1980. It should be noted that several states, including New York, California, Maryland, Pennsylvania, Washington and Colorado, had passed legislation prior to 1980 that encouraged efforts to prevent placement and maintain families while assuring the safety of children. However, the federal legislation is important in requiring *all* states to ensure that "reasonable efforts" are made to prevent out-of-home placement, to reunite families where placement has been necessary, and to provide permanent homes for children for whom reunification with their own families has not been possible (McGowan, 1988; Nelson et al., 1988; Stroul, 1988; Whittaker & Tracy, 1988).

From their earliest forms, family preservation programs have evolved in terms of therapeutic focus, target populations, and cost containment. Most contemporary programs subscribe to either family systems or behavioral approaches, although interventions are individualized and eclectic. As the programs have matured, they have imposed fewer exclusions and eligibility requirements on client families and have begun to deal with a broader range of presenting problems, for example, substance abuse. Thus a wider client population is being served today than in the past. In their efforts to contain costs, however, programs have moved toward shortened treatment duration and away from teaming of family service workers.

Interest in family-based services continues to grow, perhaps in response to an increase in child maltreatment, poverty, and single-parent households in the 1980s. In a survey on the status of placement prevention and family reunification programs conducted by the National Resource Center on Family Based Services (Tyler, 1990), most of the thirty-five responding states reported that programs were either meeting or exceeding expectations; that placement rates were either declining or increasing at a lower rate than would have been expected in the absence of these services; and that family-based services were generally being expanded.

While the Children's Bureau of the U.S. Department of Health and Human Services promoted family-based services throughout the 1980s, a growing number of other organizations are now also advocating this approach, including the Edna McConnell Clark Foundation, the Child Welfare League of America, the National Association for Family-Based Services, the Center for the Study of Social Policy, the National Conference of State Legislatures, the American Public Welfare Association, and the National Governors' Association.

A CONCEPTUAL BASE: THREE MODELS OF FAMILY-BASED SERVICES[2]

Although family-centered programs share basic characteristics such as a commitment to maintaining children in their own homes whenever possible, to focusing on entire families rather than individuals, and to providing comprehensive services that meet families' therapeutic, supportive, and concrete needs, programs vary considerably with respect to their auspices (public or private), theoretical orientation (behavioral or systemic), target population and identified problem (child maltreatment or juvenile offenses), and primary location of service (home or office). Programs also vary dramatically in terms of intensity (from more than twenty hours to less than one hour of direct contact per week), duration of services (from thirty days to a year or longer), caseload size (from two to more than twenty families), and teaming with other professionals or paraprofessionals (Nelson et al., 1988; Stroul, 1988). These structural characteristics to a large extent determine the program's productivity in terms of the number of cases a worker serves in a year and, along with salary levels and other related expenses, the cost of the service per family.

The expansion and diversification of family-based services has prompted several authors to develop typologies of family-centered programs in an effort to achieve further definition and clarity about these services. Stroul (1988, pp. 10–11) has categorized programs according to the duration and intensity of the services they provide, ranging from short-term crisis programs (up to three months), through midrange, brief treatment programs (three to six months), to long-term programs for multiproblem families (six months to three years or more). Frankel (1988) classifies programs according to their objectives, either as crisis intervention programs that stabilize the situation so other services can become involved or as family treatment programs that aim to reduce or eliminate the need for further service. Barth (1988) emphasizes the theories employed by different programs, describing crisis intervention, family systems, social learning, and ecological theories and evaluating the empirical support for each one. None of these typologies, however, captures the full range of variation among family-centered services or links program characteristics to theoretical orientation.

Nelson et al. (1990) describe three family-centered program models which have been widely replicated and studied: the crisis intervention model, the home-based model, and the family treatment model. Conceptualizing family-based programs within this typology allows for an understanding of program characteristics in relation to the underlying theoretical base and client population. In the following pages, prototypical programs within each model are described with respect to their history, theory base, program structure, and practice methods.

The Crisis Intervention Model

This model was developed by the Homebuilders program in Tacoma, Washington, which began in 1974 with funding from Catholic Community Services and the National Institute of Mental Health (see Table I–I). Originally designed as an "intensive family crisis program" to provide an alternative to foster care and psychiatric hospitalization (Haapala & Kinney, 1979), the program has expanded over the years both in funding sources and in service populations. Since 1982 it has been operated by an independent agency, the Behavioral Sciences Institute, with primary funding from the state of Washington to serve four counties (Kinney, Haapala, Booth, & Leavitt, 1988). The Homebuilders model has also been widely disseminated outside Washington through the support of the Edna McConnell Clark Foundation.

The Homebuilders program is based on crisis intervention theory, which holds that families are most open to change during periods of crisis when typical coping patterns can no longer maintain family stability and independence. To take advantage of this opening, the program provides intervention within twenty-four hours of referral, around-the-clock availability of therapists, low caseloads (maximum of three), and brief services (30 to 45 days). Services are delivered primarily in the home to provide outreach and accessibility, more accurate assessments, opportunities to model behavior in a realistic setting, and maximum self-determination for families seen "on their own turf" (Kinney et al., 1988).

Social learning theory, which stresses the importance of expectations, behavior modification, and skill development, provides the theoretical base for the interventions most frequently employed in Homebuilders programs. Thus, therapists emphasize psychoeducational services such as tracking behaviors, reinforcement, environmental controls, parent-effectiveness training, and self-management training (Kinney et al., 1988). Like all family-centered programs, crisis intervention programs also borrow strategies from other schools of thought, such as values clarification, active listening, cognitive restructuring, hypnosis, reframing, and paradox. Following Rogerian principles, treatment goals are set according to the family's priorities and their perception of the problem, and therapists are encouraged to create interventions that fit each family's needs and perceptions (Haapala & Kinney, 1979).

The provision of concrete and supportive services is also very important in the crisis intervention model and may include transportation, homemaker services, financial aid, housing assistance, day care, and shopping or cleaning with the family. In one study, parents and children both identified concrete assistance as the most helpful service they received (Fraser & Haapala, 1987–1988).

Table I-I

CHARACTERISTICS OF ELEVEN FAMILY-CENTERED PLACEMENT PREVENTION PROGRAMS

Model/Agency	Program	Year Initiated	Auspices	Staff Education	Primary Treatment Approach	Concrete Services Provided by
Crisis Intervention						
Behavioral Sciences Institute, WA	Homebuilders	1974	Private	MS in Soc Science A Few BA	Behavioral/Social Skills	Worker
Utah Dept. of Social Services	Family Preservation Services	1982	Public	MSW	Behavioral/Social Skills	Worker
Hennepin Co. Child Welfare, MN	Specialized Home Based Units	1985	Public	MSW with Family Therapy Training	Structural Family Therapy	Staff Specialist
Home-Based						
FAMILIES, INC., IA	Family-Based Services	1974	Private	MSW/MA A Few BA	Family Systems/Therapy	Worker
Iowa Children & Family Services (ICFS)	In-Home Family Counseling	1980	Private	BA	Family Support Counseling, Advocacy	Worker
Lutheran Social Services of Minn. (LSS)	Intensive In-Home Treatment Program	1981	Private	MSW/MA/BA/ BSW	Family Systems/Therapy	Worker
Franklin Co. Children Services, OH	Home-Based Family-Centered Services	1983	Public	MSW/BA Team	Casework Individual/Family Counseling	Family Specialist

Family Treatment

Iowa Dept of Human Services Ottumwa District (IDHS)	Family Therapy Unit	1974	Public	BA or MA in Social Science	Family Systems/ Brief Therapy	Case Manager
Intensive Family Services Multnomah Co., OR	Intensive Family Services	1980	Private	MSW/MA A Few BA	Family Systems/ Multiple Impact	Case Manager
Children's Services Division OR (CSD)	Intensive Family Services	1982	Public	MSW	Family Systems/ Multiple Impact	Case Manager
Dakota Co. Human Services Department, MN	Intensive Services Program	1981	Public	MSW/MA BSW	Systemic Family Therapy	Case Manager

The Home-Based Model

The home-based model, which was initiated in the mid-seventies in the Midwest, displays many of the same characteristics as the crisis intervention model but includes longer-term interventions based on family systems theory. The prototypical home-based program is FAMILIES, INC., which originated in West Branch, Iowa, with a contract from the Iowa Department of Social Services. Along with the School of Social Work and the University of Iowa Institute of Child Behavior and Development, FAMILIES, INC. was an original sponsor of the National Clearinghouse for Home-Based Services that began in 1977 (Maybanks & Bryce, 1978). In 1981, with a grant from the Children's Bureau of the Department of Health and Human Services, the Clearinghouse became the National Resource Center on Family Based Services.

The FAMILIES, INC. program was originally designed to provide an alternative to the out-of-home placement of adolescents. Focusing on the family as the locus of change, services are provided in the family's home for many of the same reasons cited by advocates of crisis intervention programs: more accurate assessment, the opportunity to model behaviors in the environment in which they must be adopted, and increased family empowerment (Leverington & Wulff, 1988). In a rural state like Iowa, home-based services also provide greater accessibility to services. Therapists are assigned to families by county and work from their own homes. Half-day staff meetings are held every two weeks for support and case consultation, and informal consultation is continual. Although families were initially seen for an average of seven months, FAMILIES, INC. therapists currently carry a caseload of ten to twelve and see families for an average of 4.5 months.

Family systems theory, the basis for assessment and intervention in the home-based model, focuses attention on the family as a whole, on subsystems within the family, and on the family's interaction with the community (Lloyd & Bryce, 1984). Families actively participate in the assessment of their situation and the setting of treatment goals. Originally, all FAMILIES, INC. cases were assigned two therapists in order to provide flexibility in working with subsystems, but funding restrictions have since dictated the use of a single therapist in about half the cases. The primary focus on working with the family and other systems in the community has not changed, however, with a goal of improving linkages, perceptions, and relationships between the family and its environment.

Family systems theory encourages the use of a wide range of interventions, including genograms to clarify intergenerational patterns and boundaries, structural techniques, reframing and paradox, and homework to improve communications skills, as well as more behaviorally-oriented interventions such as parent training and fair fighting (Hartman, 1978; Hartman & Laird, 1983; McGoldrick & Gerson, 1985; Minuchin, 1974; Minuchin & Fishman, 1981; Satir, 1982). Concrete and supportive services such as transportation and advocacy are provided directly by FAMILIES, INC. therapists, who also coordinate services provided by others, including day care, financial assistance, housing, and health care.

The Family Treatment Model

The family treatment model differs from the other two models in its emphasis on therapeutic interventions and its lower level of involvement in the direct provision of concrete and supportive services (Tavantzis, Tavantzis, Brown & Rohrbaugh, 1985). Generally, it is a less intensive model that may be deployed in an office or home setting. One of the first programs to stress the family treatment component of family-based services was the Intensive Family Services (IFS) program of the State of Oregon's Children's Services Division.

IFS was started in 1980 to provide an alternative to substitute care for families in crisis when a child was about to be removed from the home. Services were initially purchased from private providers for demonstration projects in four counties. By 1982, services had been expanded to an additional seven counties through purchase-of-service agreements and to another five counties, where no private provider was available, through direct provision by the Children's Services Division. All IFS programs must meet the same contract requirements which specify that, on average, programs maintain a ninety-day service period, caseloads of eleven, and a 75 percent success rate in preventing placement during the treatment period.

The IFS program is also based on family systems theory, which views one person's behavioral problems as reflecting other problems within the family (Carter & McGoldrick, 1980; Napier & Whitaker, 1978). Treatment is focused on the family as a whole and is designed to help family members meet their needs in more functional and satisfying ways (Janzen & Harris, 1986; Minuchin, 1985). The treatment process employs a variety of approaches such as structural, strategic (Stanton, 1981), brief (de Shazer, 1985 & 1988), and communications-based family therapy (Satir, 1982; Watzlawick, 1974). The initial phase often includes a structured family interview in which the family's structure, communication patterns, and decision-making skills are assessed. Therapeutic interventions are provided directly by the IFS staff and are complemented, when appropriate, by case management, parent training, homemakers, and other services provided by other units in the agency. About 15 percent of the families participate in an initial multiple impact intervention (Balmer, Kogan, Voorhees, Levin-Shaw, & Shapiro, 1979) in which two to four therapists work with the family in a treatment session lasting several hours, with weekly follow-up sessions for three to five and one-half months. In about half of IFS cases co-therapists provide services to the family, with one of the therapists taking primary responsibility. The remaining 36 percent are seen by a single therapist.

Comparison of the Three Models

A previous analysis of data from three different studies including a total of eleven programs (AuClaire & Schwartz, 1986; Nelson et al., 1988; Fraser, Pecora, & Haapala, 1989) compared these three models of family-based services (Nelson et al., 1990) (see Table I–II). This analysis found that the crisis intervention and family treatment programs studied tended to serve children who were somewhat older than children in the home-based programs (average ages of 13, 14, and 11, respectively). The most dramatic differences between the models, however, were in caseloads, length of service, and placement rates. Crisis intervention programs had the shortest service periods (one to two months) and the lowest caseloads (2 to 6 at one time). Family treatment programs served families for three to four months and had the highest caseload range (5 to 25). Two of the family treatment programs saw a substantial proportion of cases in the office, which decreased travel time and allowed for larger caseloads. Home-based programs served families the longest, four and one-half to eight months, and had the lowest average annual caseloads (8 to 28 cases per worker over the course of a year). (Annual caseloads were computed by dividing 365 days by the average length of service and multiplying by the average caseload, adjusted to a per-worker caseload when cases were teamed.)

Placement prevention rates at termination also differed substantially among the models. In these studies, crisis intervention programs had the highest average prevention rate at termination (94%). However, it should

Table I-II

FAMILY AND SERVICE CHARACTERISTICS

| | | Crisis Intervention Programs | | | | Family Treatment Programs | | | Home-Based Programs | | | |
		WASH	UTAH	HENNEPIN	IDHS	MULTNOMAH	CSD	DAKOTA	FAMILIES	ICFS	LSS	OHIO
No. in Family	m	4.3	4.7	3.2	3.8	3.9	4.0	4.0	5.6	4.2	4.3	3.6
Age												
Child I[a]	m	11.9	14.0	14.3	13.3	15.3	14.3	14.5	11.7	10.2	14.5	7.9
Primary Caretaker	m	35.0	38.2	32.0	36.4	37.5	38.4	39.4	37.0	30.9	36.8	29.3
Single Parent	%	36.7	36.9	53.4	45.7	49.6	51.6	45.4	48.9	48.3	31.8	54.3
Minority	%	18.3	13.5	29.3	8.3	17.2	4.1	1.7	10.0	5.0	0.0	17.3
Prior Placement	%	26.6	34.3	40.0	22.8	68.1	28.5	26.7	33.0	17.5	35.1	27.0
Intact at Intake	%	87.9	87.4	37.9	97.4	87.7	98.4	89.7	85.0	91.8	91.6	86.3
Length of Service (days)	m	30.2	62.8	37.4	154.2[b]	158.9[b]	128.1	87.1	136.0	231.3	149.4	214.0[b]
Teamed	%	5.0[c]	5.0	100.0	0.0	41.0	17.6	48.0	50.0	0.0	0.0	100.0
Caseload	m	2	4-6	4[d]	25.6	10.7	10.0	4.9[d]	10.6	6.6	5.5	10.0[d]
Annual Caseload	m	23.6	28.3	19.5	60.6	24.6	28.5	15.5	28.4	10.4	13.4	8.5
Prevention Rate[e]	m	94.2	92.9	NA	88.2	84.6	88.7	79.3	85.0	81.0	77.7	75.0

[a] Average age of oldest child served.
[b] Mean much higher than median; medians = IDHS (95); MULTNOMAH (109); OHIO (172).
[c] Agency average.
[d] Teamed cases are counted in each worker's caseload.
[e] Percent of families intact at termination, includes relative placements.

be noted that this reflected a smaller "window of opportunity" for placement due to much shorter periods of service. Family treatment programs had lower prevention rates (85%), while the home-based programs had the lowest rates (80%), in part because they saw families longer and more often placed children with relatives. Caution is warranted in comparing prevention rates since the proportion of children who would have been placed in the absence of family preservation services is unknown. It should also be noted that the lack of a common definition and inability to verify risk of placement as well as wide variation in presenting problems and eligibility criteria (including whether reunification cases were included in the sample) preclude drawing conclusions about program effectiveness or comparing programs solely on the basis of placement rates.

In all three program models, social workers generally agreed that believing most children to be better off in their own homes is important to effective family-based services. There was also considerable agreement about the importance of asking clients to identify and prioritize their own treatment goals. Consistent with the structure of their programs, however, workers in crisis intervention programs considered time-limited service, 24-hour availability, and scheduling appointments at the convenience of the family as more important than workers in family treatment programs.

Implications of the Three Models

The greatest differences among these three models occurred in program structure and treatment approach, while the greatest similarity lay in a shared commitment to placement prevention and family empowerment. Differences in program structure and treatment approach may reflect underlying differences in theory and program goals. Although largely untested (Barth, 1988), crisis intervention theory implies a need for immediate, accessible, short-term services, most closely matched by the crisis intervention programs studied, both in terms of program structure and treatment philosophy. While the other two models also deal with a family's precipitating crisis, their systems theory base focuses interventions on problem resolution and addresses the underlying patterns and needs that the crisis is believed to reflect. This theoretical approach lends itself to a more flexible program structure with respect to treatment setting (home or office) and caseload size. Home-based programs use family therapy techniques in the context of the family's home and community with direct provision of concrete and supportive services, while family treatment programs focus primarily on therapeutic interventions. This theoretical approach also enables more flexibility with respect to length of service, which is determined more by the needs of the client population than by the dictates of the model.

The similarities among the three models suggest that each may be employed in a variety of contexts. On the basis of differences found among the programs in these three studies, such as in the average age of the children served, it may be hypothesized that the crisis intervention and family treatment models are particularly suited to families with older children and the home-based model to families with younger children.

Although due to variations in sampling frames and target populations the data from these three studies cannot address each model's relative effectiveness, they do shed light on the productivity of each model. In terms of annual per capita caseloads, on average, crisis intervention and family treatment programs in these three studies served the most families and home-based programs served the fewest. It should be noted, however, that the two home-based programs with the lowest annual caseloads served low-income, single-parent families with young children at risk of physical abuse and neglect for whom brief services may not have been appropriate (Nelson et al., 1988). Shorter-term home-based programs served families with adolescents and, when caseloads of ten were maintained, saw as many families in a year's time as most family treatment and crisis intervention programs.

SUMMARY

This chapter has provided a definition and brief history of the development and expansion of family-based placement prevention services. The typology of three models of family-based services: crisis intervention, home-based, and family treatment, is useful in sorting out the wide variety of programs that continue to emerge under the rubric of "family-based services," "family preservation," or other similar program titles.

Chapter Two will review the current state of knowledge in family-based services research, including studies of all three models, and will introduce the methodology of the study which informs the remainder of this text. Chapters Three through Nine use data gathered from the National Resource Center's study of four home-based and five family treatment programs to analyze a number of special issues in detail: child abuse and neglect; work with juvenile offenders; rural and urban comparisons; public and private auspices; and in-home and in-office delivery of services. Since no crisis intervention programs were included in this research project, the crisis intervention model is not represented in Chapters Three through Nine. However, there are a number of studies of crisis intervention programs, and these are described in the following chapter. Detailed case studies of home-based programs and cases they served are presented in Chapters Three, Four, Seven and Eight. Descriptions of family treatment programs and their clients can be found in Chapters Five, Six, Eight, and Nine.

Endnotes

1. The authors wish to acknowledge Margaret Tyler's contribution to this portion of the manuscript: "A Brief History of Family Based Services," National Resource Center on Family Based Services, 1989.
2. Portions of this section are reprinted by special permission of the Child Welfare League of America from CHILD WELFARE, Volume 69, No. 1, 1990, pp. 3–21.

Chapter Two

STATE OF THE ART
IN FAMILY-BASED SERVICES RESEARCH

The research on family-based services is best understood from a developmental perspective. Three generations of studies on family-based placement prevention programs can be identified, each characterized by an increasing level of sophistication. The earliest studies of intensive placement prevention services were implemented largely for the purpose of supporting the expansion of family-based services. These first-generation studies were usually very limited in scope and modestly funded. For the most part they did not involve outside evaluators, studied relatively small numbers of cases, and did not compare outcomes with those of similar families receiving other kinds of services. Outcome measures typically included placement, which was infrequent, and cost savings, which were spectacularly high, calculated on the assumption that all families in treatment would have experienced placement had they not received family-based services (Hutchinson, Lloyd, Landsman, Nelson, & Bryce, 1983).

The second generation of studies enjoyed significantly increased funding. With support from the Children's Bureau of the U.S. Department of Health and Human Services, two studies initiated in 1985 analyzed larger numbers of cases in multiple states (Fraser, Pecora, & Haapala, 1989; Nelson, Emlen, Landsman, & Hutchinson, 1988). While these studies were largely descriptive, they used multiple outcome measures and began to address the issue of the effectiveness of family-based services with different client populations. In addition to these two federally-funded studies, several programs implemented research projects using quasi-experimental designs (e.g., AuClaire & Schwartz, 1986; Pearson & King, 1987).

Responding to the need for more rigorous testing of the effectiveness of family-based services, the third generation of studies introduced the use of randomly assigned control groups (Feldman, 1991; Yuan, McDonald,

Wheeler, Struckman-Johnson, & Rivest, 1990). Unfortunately, it is difficult to conduct sound experimental studies in practice environments.
For example, in the studies cited, the referral criterion of "imminent risk
of placement" was not adhered to by referring workers. In addition,
comparable measures of family functioning and of service provision
were not available for the control groups (Nelson, 1990).

The following overview applies this developmental perspective to
studies of placement prevention conducted prior to the emergence of
family-based services *per se,* and also to each of the three major models of
family-based services: crisis intervention, home-based, and family treatment, followed by a summary of the current state of knowledge about
factors associated with success and failure in family-based services, and a
discussion of some issues currently under debate in family-based services research. This chapter concludes with the methodology of the
National Resource Center's study of eleven family-based service programs.

PRE FAMILY-BASED SERVICES RESEARCH

Studies of placement prevention services prior to the family-based
services movement show that these earlier services differed from later
family-based services in intensity, time limits, and family focus. Perhaps
the best known of these early studies of placement prevention and
reunification was the New York State Preventive Services Project (Jones,
Neuman & Shyne, 1976). Compared to contemporary standards of service intensity, this project and other early placement prevention programs included considerably fewer contacts between worker and family
and longer service periods, often more than a year (Lawder, Poulin, &
Andrews, 1984; Magura & DeRubeis, 1980; Yoshikama, 1984). In several
projects, two-thirds or more of the cases were still open by the study's
end (Halper & Jones, 1981; Jones et al., 1976; Magura & DeRubeis, 1980;
Yoshikama, 1984). Randomly assigning families to experimental (preventive services) and control groups (standard agency services), the New
York Preventive Services Project found that a smaller proportion of
children from the experimental group were placed in out-of-home care
and that placement was delayed for a longer period of time for the
experimental group (Jones, 1985).

In the early 1980s, Wald, Carlsmith, and Leiderman (1988) conducted
a quasi-experimental two-year study in northern California. This study
compared a small group of abused or neglected children who were

treated in their own homes (n = 19) with children in a different county who were placed with relatives or in family foster care (n = 13), and with a larger group of children who had not been abused or neglected (n = 42). Although the findings support the hypothesis that there is no difference over time between children served in their own homes and those placed in foster homes, differences between the original samples in type and severity of family problems raise questions concerning the validity of some of the study's conclusions, which stress the positive aspects of foster care (Nelson, 1989). Due to imbalance in the original groups, it was also necessary to exclude black families from most of the analyses.

CRISIS INTERVENTION PROGRAMS

First-Generation Studies

Crisis intervention programs have been evaluated more extensively than the other models. First-generation evaluations of the Homebuilders program reported high rates of placement prevention both at termination of services and at six- to twelve-month follow-ups. Initial findings concluded that 90 percent of potential removals were avoided during treatment and that 97 percent of these children remained with their families for at least three months following treatment (Kinney, Haapala, Madsen, & Fleming, 1977). Data collected since 1982 indicate a 92 percent placement prevention rate, excluding placements with relatives and those lasting two weeks or less (Stroul, 1988). Caution should be exercised in interpreting these findings since without randomly assigned control groups, it is not possible to assess true prevention rates, specifically, how many children who would have been placed under normal circumstances remained with their families because they received family preservation services. This caution applies to prevention rates reported in uncontrolled studies of home-based and family treatment programs as well.

Other projects based on a crisis intervention model have also reported generally high success rates in preventing placement, although some have had mixed results. Projects in Florida (Paschal & Schwahn, 1986) and Utah (Callister, Mitchell, & Tolley, 1986) report placement prevention rates of 95 percent of 196 children and 85 percent of 192 children at termination and, in Florida, of 84 percent at a twelve-month follow-up.

Another study of five programs in Maine found the model equally effective with "crisis" cases and with those "in a 'chronic' state of maladaptive behavior" (Hinckley, 1984). Placement prevention rates at termination for a total of 167 families varied from 82 percent to 95 percent in the five programs, and families demonstrated substantial decreases in verbal and physical violence (Hinckley & Ellis, 1985).

More recently, an evaluation of intensive family preservation pilot projects in Iowa found that out of 747 families for whom complete data were available, 69 percent were intact at the end of service, and 66 percent remained together at a twelve-month follow-up (Thieman, Fuqua, & Linnan, 1990). An analysis of 367 families served by the Emergency Family Care Program, Children's Home Society of California (San Francisco and Oakland) found that 96 percent of the families were intact at termination, 90 percent six months later, and 88 percent at the 12-month follow-up (Berry, 1990).

Second-Generation Studies

The second generation of research on the crisis intervention model is represented by three quasi-experimental studies of the Homebuilders program with comparison groups composed of families who could not be seen because caseloads were full, as well as quasi-experimental studies of other crisis intervention programs. The studies of Homebuilders found prevention rates among status offenders of 73 percent for the treatment group and 28 percent for the comparison group (families who could not be served because caseloads were full), and prevention rates for mental health cases of 80 percent for the treatment group and zero for the comparison group (Kinney, Haapala, Booth, & Leavitt, 1988). Haapala and Kinney (1988) also report an 87 percent success rate at a twelve-month follow-up interview in a project involving 678 status offenders.

A study of a Homebuilders project in the Bronx, New York (Mitchell, Tovar, & Knitzer, 1989), which compared 45 families who received intensive family preservation services with 12 families who could not be served because the program was full, found no differences in officially-recorded placements at a twelve-month follow-up.

A quasi-experimental study of intensive family preservation programs, including the Homebuilders program in Washington and a similar program in Utah (Fraser et al., 1989) reported that in Washington 94 percent of the children in the families receiving family preservation services were not placed out of the home at case termination; in Utah the rate was 91 percent. Follow-up at twelve months indicated that of the 342 children who could be located (out of the original study group of 581), 70 percent in Washington and 59 percent in Utah remained at home. In another component of this study, cases from an overflow comparison group that received traditional child welfare or mental health services were matched (by child variables including race, gender, previous inpatient placements, substance abuse, and school attendance, and family characteristics such as income, structure, and size) with families receiving intensive family preservation services in Utah. At the twelve-month follow-up, the overflow group had experienced a placement rate of 85 percent, compared to 44 percent for families who had received intensive family preservation services.

A quasi-experimental study of a crisis intervention program based on systems theory which was conducted in Hennepin County, Minnesota (AuClaire & Schwartz, 1986), involved families with adolescents who were awaiting or in court-approved placements. Families receiving the family preservation service (n=58) were compared with a randomly selected sample of 58 families who could not be served due to the limited capacity of the program. While no differences were found between the groups in number of placements, the family preservation group did spend fewer days in placement.

Third-Generation Studies

Szykula and Fleischman (1985) studied two projects in Oregon which, although not crisis intervention programs, were based on social learning theory, as are most programs in the crisis intervention model. One achieved a 100 percent placement prevention rate in child abuse cases at a twelve-month follow-up. The other project divided the sample into two levels of difficulty and used an experimental design with random assignment to treatment and control groups. Among the 26 less difficult cases (defined as having fewer than three reports of abuse, no serious problems with housing or transportation, and child conduct as the major problem), significant differences in prevention rates were found between the treatment (92%) and control groups (62%). Among the 22 multiproblem families, placement prevention services provided to the treatment group did not yield better outcomes than those obtained by the control group.

Two third-generation studies of crisis intervention programs have been published in the past two years (Feldman, 1991; Yuan et al., 1990). These studies have generally found that family preservation services did not result in a decrease in agency-recorded child placements six to twelve months after the termination of services when compared with a similar group of families who received other services.

Feldman's experimental study (1991) randomly assigned 183 families assessed as at risk of placement (using a risk protocol) either to intensive family preservation services or to a traditional child protective services program. Improvement on the composite and parental disposition scales of the Child Well-Being Scales, but not on the child or household scales, was significant for the experimental group only. While the experimental families had proportionally fewer placements and a slower rate of placement during the study period, by a twelve-month follow-up significant differences between the two groups had disappeared.

Yuan et al. (1990) studied 709 families referred to eight California demonstration projects. The third year of the evaluation included random assignment of 304 families assessed as being at imminent risk of placement by a referring worker to the intensive family preservation programs or to the regular child welfare services offered by the agencies. Eight months after the termination of intensive family preservation services, no statistically significant differences in placement rates between the experimental and comparison groups were found, nor were intensive family preservation services found to be more cost-effective.

HOME-BASED PROGRAMS

First-Generation Studies

In contrast to the number of studies of crisis intervention programs, research on home-based programs is less abundant. Representing the first generation of research, a study of the 150 cases seen by FAMILIES, INC. therapists during its first three years found 97 percent intact at the time of the follow-up interview (Bryce, 1978). In a comprehensive home-based program in Nebraska, 86 percent of the 21 families who had completed treatment remained together or were reunified at the end of five months of service (Leeds, 1984). In Virginia, a study of fourteen placement prevention projects (Virginia Department of Social Services, 1985) found that 93 percent of the children served remained at home at the end of the study period and 69 percent of the 391 families improved in overall functioning.

In another study of 331 families served by fourteen diverse placement prevention projects in Wisconsin (Landsman, 1985), 82 percent of the children deemed at risk of placement remained with their families at the end of the data collection period, and families were assessed by their social workers as having improved significantly in such areas as mental health of the parent, discipline of children, family communication, marital relationships, children's mental health and behavior, and school performance. Socioeconomic characteristics of the families did not change a great deal.

Second-Generation Studies

In a second-generation quasi-experimental design conducted in Maryland, Pearson and King (1987) studied 80 families who received home-based intensive family services (IFS) from a professional/paraprofessional team and a comparison group of 180 families who received traditional child protective services (CPS). They found placement prevention rates of 82 percent for the IFS group and 67 percent for the CPS group. IFS cases also improved in employment, housing, protection of the child from the perpetrator of abuse, and support for the primary caretaker.

Reid, Kagan, and Schlosberg (1988) compared 31 placement cases in Albany, New York, with a random sample of 55 cases from more than 400 families who remained intact, matched by the year of termination. Most of the families (80%) received some type of family therapy, but individual or group counseling for parents and/or children was also common. Placement cases had a considerably lower degree of goal achievement, missed a greater number of appointments, and demonstrated a lower level of engagement in services after six months of service. At a two and one-half-year follow-up, they also expressed less satisfaction with services.

In the only study of a home-based program using an experimental design, Lyle and Nelson (1983) randomly assigned 74 families in Ramsey County, Minnesota, to home-based services or to traditional child protection services. The researchers reported that the experimental group was more successful in averting placement and that when children were placed, they spent less time in out-of-home care.

FAMILY TREATMENT PROGRAMS

As with home-based programs, research on family treatment programs in the context of placement prevention has been less abundant than that on crisis intervention programs. Nevertheless, there is evidence of the effectiveness of this service model with certain families at risk of out-of-home placement.

Outcome studies of the State of Oregon's Intensive Family Service program report that the program has been successful in keeping families together. In one study of 261 families 88 percent of children approved for placement did not experience any out-of-home placements during the three-month treatment period, and 66 percent remained with their families without any placement episodes one year after the termination of services (Showell, 1985). In a later study of 999 families served by IFS, therapists judged that nearly half the families had good to excellent clinical success, and that 65 percent had a good to excellent likelihood of avoiding placement in the future. Services were most successful with disrupted adoption and sexual abuse cases and least successful with neglecting families (Showell, Hartley, & Allen, 1988).

Related studies of family therapy and family-centered services for juvenile justice and child protective cases have found similar success rates. Lantz (1985) studied the use of functional family therapy (see Alexander & Parsons, 1982) in 21 cases with adolescents at risk of placement and found a prevention rate of 82 percent three months after the project had ended. Combining principles of structural and systemic family therapy with home-based services, Families Work in Schenectady, New York, had a success rate of 84 percent with 57 adolescents at risk of placement. Nearly three-quarters (72%) of the families remained together at a six-month follow-up (Tavantzis, Tavantzis, Brown, & Rohrbaugh, 1985).

Reviewing the results of three studies, Barton, Alexander, Waldron, Turner, and Warburton (1985) found functional family therapy effective in reducing recidivism and placement when delivered by workers of different educational levels, and with previously incarcerated delinquents as well as status offenders. One study compared outcomes of 63 cases before and after workers received training in functional family therapy with 216 cases served by workers who were not trained in these techniques, and reported significantly lower rates of foster care placement for the experimental group posttraining. Another of the three studies used a quasi-experimental design in which seriously delinquent adolescents incarcerated in a state training school were provided functional family therapy. A control group matched by age, ethnicity, socio-economic status, education, and number and severity of offenses received an alternative treatment, a group home and case management services. This study reported lower recidivism rates and fewer offenses in the experimental group.

Gordon, Arbuthnot, Gustafson, and McGreen (1988) report on the effectiveness of in-home non-time-limited family therapy with families of disadvantaged juvenile delinquents which used a combined behavioral/family systems therapy approach. A quasi-experimental design with non-random assignment compared 28 families of high-risk juvenile offenders who received in-home service with 27 lower-risk juveniles who received probationary, but no other counseling services. The study found significant differences in recidivism over a two and one-half-year follow-up between the two groups: 11 percent for the experimental group, and 67 percent for the control group.

FACTORS RELATED TO CASE OUTCOME

The National Resource Center's study of eleven family-based service programs was not designed to assess the effectiveness of family-based services in preventing placement, but to identify differences between cases in which families remained together and those in which children were placed. The initial analysis found that the outcome of service was associated primarily with family characteristics and history. Family characteristics which were related to a case outcome of placement or nonplacement were (1) characteristics of the child, such as prior placements, age, behavior at home, relationships with other family members, school status and attendance, and delinquency; (2) the number and severity of family problems; and (3) characteristics of parents, including their motivation, engagement and cooperation with services, and affection and attachment to their children. Service factors which were found to be related to case outcome included goal achievement, improvement in family functioning, involvement of family members in services, and specific interventions such as teaching skills and teaming workers (Nelson et al., 1988).

In their study of Homebuilders projects in Washington and Utah, Fraser et al. (1989) identified several characteristics measured at intake that were associated with an outcome of placement. Combining the samples from both sites, they found that placement was associated with parental attitudes and child behavior. Measures taken at termination found differences between the placement and nonplacement groups in mental health, parenting, motivation to solve problems, attitude towards placement, and cooperation with services. Child measures distinguishing failures from successes included mental health, school adjustment, and delinquent behavior. Families for whom treatment was successful were assessed as having made significant positive change on 38 of the 51 items in the Family Risk Scales compared to 13 items for families for whom treatment failed.

Yuan et al. (1990) identified a number of family and child characteristics associated with placement and placement prevention. Specifically, they found that caretakers and children who experienced placement were more likely to be disabled, to receive public assistance, to have had previous out-of-home placements, to be referred again for child abuse and/or neglect after receiving intensive services, and to have lower scores on the Child Well-Being Scales both at intake and termination of services. Families in which placement did not occur had received more intensive services than those who eventually had a child placed.

CURRENT DEBATES IN FAMILY-BASED RESEARCH

One debate in the family-based services field centers around the limitations of placement as an outcome measure. Studies differ in their definition of placement. Some count as placements any out-of-home living situation, such as informal placements with friends or relatives, while others rely exclusively on officially-recorded placements involving the public child welfare agency. There is a growing interest in using outcome measures such as improvement in child and family functioning in addition to placement, in order to better assess the effectiveness of family-based services. (See Appendix A for a full discussion of placement as an outcome measure in this study.)

There is also discussion about how long a program should be held accountable for placement prevention. That is, at what point is it reasonable to measure case outcomes: at case termination, six months or twelve months after termination? How long should a crisis intervention program of four weeks duration, for example, be expected to maintain a family's stability, and how should the effects of services received after termination from the family-based program be assessed?

The difficulty in using risk of imminent placement as a criterion for referral to family-based services has already been noted. Programs have applied this criterion in different ways, some very broadly to families with a child at some risk of being placed, others more systematically, using a risk protocol or a placement review committee. Whatever the method, it is apparent that many families assessed to be "at imminent risk" of placement never actually experience placement, whether they receive family-based or other services.

There is also a growing interest in increasing knowledge about the effects of specific services or interventions on case outcome. Perhaps client characteristics emerge as the most important predictors of outcome because measures of family characteristics are more refined and more reliable than service measures. Little is known about which components or qualities of family-based services increase their effectiveness with different client populations.

THE NATIONAL RESOURCE CENTER'S STUDY

The information on programs described in the following chapters is from the National Resource Center's study of eleven family-based service programs, funded by the Children's Bureau from 1985 through 1987. The primary goal of this study was to provide empirically-based guidelines for the further development of family-based child welfare services by identifying service and client characteristics that contributed to success or failure in preventing placement. It was not an objective of this study to determine whether family-based services actually reduced placement compared to other types of service families might have received. Some general information about the programs selected for the study, the methodology, definitions of key terms, and data analysis techniques are provided to serve as a guide in understanding the findings presented in subsequent chapters.

The Programs

The research project studied eleven family-based service programs including public and private agencies, rural and urban areas, in-home and in-office services, and family problems ranging from child maltreatment to juvenile offenses. Programs were selected for the study to exemplify a broad range of family-based placement prevention services. All of the programs were established between 1975 and 1983 and thus are examples of stable programs that could provide a minimum of 50 closed cases for the sample. Efforts were made to include one public and one private agency program in each state, and this was achieved in four states. In the other two states, one private program (Pennsylvania) and one public program (Ohio) which served similar populations participated in the study. The programs are not representative of the totality of family-based programs, but they serve as examples of the types of programs which were in place in the mid-1980s. Because the data were derived from case records from the first half of the decade, certain issues which received greater attention later in the decade, in particular substance abuse, were not noted as problems in a large proportion of the cases in this study. Since these programs were neither selected at random nor are presumed to be representative of all family-based programs, caution is warranted in generalizing from these findings.

Nine of the original eleven agencies studied are included in the analyses presented in this volume (see Table II–I). Two of the eleven have been excluded because they served populations atypical of family-based placement prevention programs: one served a population clearly not at imminent risk of placement; the other was an adolescent day treatment program. The nine agencies, which are described in greater detail in subsequent chapters, are briefly introduced below.

Home-Based Programs

Iowa Children and Family Services (ICFS). This private agency used a home-based model to provide intensive services to families referred by the Iowa Department of Human Services whose needs were more extensive than those served by the office-based family therapy program. Referred families had usually been through the system before, lacked the motivation for office-based services, and needed more intensive services. Based in rural Iowa, ICFS workers often performed paraprofessional tasks in addition to counseling.

Lutheran Social Services of Minnesota. This private agency program, originally serving a sixteen-county rural area, was one of the first four intensive in-home programs established in the state of Minnesota. Based on family systems theory, the program employed family therapy tech-

Table II-I
CHARACTERISTICS OF AGENCIES IN THE STUDY

Model, State and Agency	Auspices	Primary Geographic Location	Primary Referral Problem	Primary Location of Service
Home-Based				
Iowa				
Iowa Children & Family Services	Private	Rural	Child Maltreatment	Home
Minnesota				
Lutheran Social Services	Private	Rural	Juvenile Offenses	Home
Ohio				
Franklin County Children Services	Public	Urban	Child Maltreatment	Home
Pennsylvania				
Supportive Child/Adult Network (SCAN)	Private	Urban	Child Maltreatment	Home
Family Treatment				
Oregon				
Intensive Family Services, Multnomah County	Private	Urban	Juvenile Offenses	Home
Children's Services Division	Public	Suburban	Juvenile Offenses	Office
Colorado				
Boulder County Department of Social Services	Public	Suburban	Child Maltreatment	Office
Iowa				
Iowa Department of Human Services	Public	Rural	Child Maltreatment	Office
Minnesota				
Dakota County Human Services	Public	Suburban	Juvenile Offenses	Home

niques in addition to working with community agencies and arranging for concrete services.

Franklin County Children Services. This public agency program based in Grove City (Columbus area), Ohio, provided home-based services through MSW/BA teams to families in which a decision to place a child in out-of-home care had been made. Service was generally time-limited, lasting between six and nine months.

Supportive Child/Adult Network, Inc. (SCAN) of Philadelphia. SCAN is a private agency providing protective, home-based services under contract to the city of Philadelphia. Families were referred for child abuse or neglect and a large proportion were black. SCAN was one of the longer-term programs in this study and used a multidisciplinary approach combining social work, nursing, medical, and psychological services.

Family Treatment Programs

Oregon Children's Services Division. Oregon CSD's Intensive Family Services (IFS), the prototypical program representing the family treatment approach to family-based services, was time-limited (ninety days) and emphasized the use of family therapy techniques to effect change in family relationships. Services were often provided in an office setting. At the time of the study, IFS primarily served families of adolescents; more recently, and not reflected in this volume, there has been a growing proportion of families with younger children in the client population. Though described as one program, this site included the five county agencies directly providing IFS services.

Intensive Family Services, Multnomah County, Oregon. One of four projects originally piloted under contract to the state by the Oregon Children's Services Division, the Intensive Family Services program in Multnomah County maintained the same performance and caseload standards as the public agency programs. Most of the services, however, were provided in the families' homes.

Boulder County Department of Social Services, Colorado. Established as part of a statewide initiative to reduce residential placements by capping and diverting funds from placement to prevention and reunification, the Boulder County Intensive Family Treatment Program (IFT) served families with severe problems who were at risk of having a child placed in a residential facility. The program resembled the in-office family treatment model, though with a longer maximum service period (twelve months).

Iowa Department of Human Services. Originally part of a statewide effort to reduce placement and recidivism of juvenile offenders, the Iowa Department of Human Services established Family Therapy units in its district offices in the mid 1970s. In the Ottumwa district, which was the site for this study, family therapists generally saw families in the office over a three- to six-month period. A case manager from the local DHS office worked with the family in arranging for other needed services.

Dakota County Human Services Department, Minnesota. The Intensive Services program of the Dakota County Human Services Department provided intensive in-home family counseling in one- to two-hour sessions for an eight- to twelve-week time period, as well as information, education, and advocacy. Although data from this program are included in the statistical analyses, no case studies were drawn from this site.

Methodology

Data were collected in three stages: (1) semi-structured on-site interviews in each agency; (2) a survey of all social workers employed by the programs during the identified study period; and (3) coding of closed case records.

Stage 1

On-site interviews were conducted with agency and program administrators and family-based supervisors and workers. Written materials were also collected, including reports, regulations, and relevant program statistics. This information was used to create a social worker questionnaire, which was administered in Stage 2 of the project, and provides the basis for the program descriptions in the following chapters.

Stage 2

The Family Based Services Inventory, consisting of 105 items including both original questions and standardized scales, was sent to 134 social workers employed in the programs during the study period, generally 1983 to 1985. The questionnaire incorporated items from the Professional Satisfaction Inventory (Jayaratne & Chess, 1984); the Human Services Survey (Maslach & Jackson, 1981); Halper and Jones' treatment techniques scale measuring casework orientation (1981); scales measuring theoretical orientation to family therapy developed by Hamilton and Montayne (Montayne, 1986); and a fourteen-item scale measuring orientation to family-based services developed by Pecora, Delewski, Booth, Haapala, and Kinney (1985). The questionnaire also covered demographic information, educational and professional background, perceptions of the agency, information about the clients served, and definitions of success and failure in family-based services. A return rate of 89 percent was achieved for a total of 102 social worker responses from the eleven programs.

Stage 3

The case record review consisted of coding by trained personnel of 50 closed cases at each agency, approximately 25 in which a child was placed and 25 in which the family remained intact. The samples were drawn from the programs' lists of all families with a case goal of placement prevention seen during the study period. Using a table of random numbers, 25 nonplacement cases and 5 replacement cases were drawn from this list. If more than 30 cases ended with a child in placement, 30 were selected using the same procedure. In most agencies, however, all of the placement cases opened during the study period were used in the study. (See Table II–II for numbers of social workers, placement and non-placement cases at each site represented in this volume.)

Coders were hired at each site and trained in using the case review instru-
ment. Training was conducted over a two-day period by project staff from one of the two collaborating institutions, the National Resource Center on Family Based Services at The University of Iowa, or the Regional Research Institute at Portland State University. The case review instrument consisted of original items, The Schedule of Recent Experience (Holmes, 1981), and a combination of the Child Welfare League of America's Child Well-Being Scales (Magura & Moses, 1986) and Family Measurement Scales (Magura et al., 1987). Interrater reliability was checked by having two case readers at each site code two of the same cases independently (see Appendix B for interrater reliability of selected variables).

The original items included data measured at the time of intake, such as demographic characteristics, service and placement history, referral sources and problems, and case goals; measures of service provision, including specific services provided, number and location of contacts with the family-based worker, placements, and subsequent reports of abuse and neglect during the service period; and outcome measures, including achievement of case objectives, reason for termination of services, degree of involvement of family members with services, improvement in ten aspects of family functioning measured by the Family Systems Change Scale (a scale developed specifically for this study), and place-ment. Although recent debates have criticized the use of placement as a sole outcome measure, this study found a strong correlation between placement and other outcome measures, leading to the use of placement/nonplacement as the primary outcome measure in the following analyses. (For a further discussion of this issue, see Appendix A.)

Table II-II
NUMBER OF SOCIAL WORKERS AND CASES IN EACH AGENCY

State and Agency	Social Workers N = 92	Placement Cases N = 201	% Selected	Non-Placement Cases N = 246	% Selected
Iowa					
Iowa Department of Human Services	5	25	100	25	18
Iowa Children & Family Services	16	26	100	24	22
Minnesota					
Dakota County Human Services	9	25	64	25	16
Lutheran Social Services	16	17	100	33	47
Ohio					
Franklin County Children Services	3	15	100	33	100
Colorado					
Boulder County Department of Social Services	5	25	100	24	8
Pennsylvania					
SCAN	16	19	100	31	43
Oregon					
Children's Services Division	14	24	100	26	13
Intensive Family Services, Multnomah County	8	25	40	25	7

Note. % selected indicates the percentage of cases randomly selected from the list of cases opened during the study period, generally 1982–1985.

Definitions

Several key terms which will be used throughout the following chapters warrant definition at this time. A more extensive list of terms is included in Appendix C. Perhaps the most important term, as it serves as the basis for distinguishing successful and unsuccessful cases, is an outcome of "placement" or "nonplacement." Placement cases refer to those families who, at the termination of family-based services, had at least one child living out of the home, either in foster or residential care or in an informal living arrangement with friends or relatives, or for whom a clear intention to make such a placement was established in the case record. Nonplacement cases, conversely, were those in which none of the children involved in the current referral were in or headed toward out-of-home care at the time family-based services were terminated. Although there may have been temporary placements during the course of service, in nonplacement cases the family was intact at closure and intended to remain so. This definition reflects the clinical judgement of the family-based workers as documented in the case record. Since follow-up data were unavailable in most sites, it is not known if all of these placements actually occurred. Conversely, it is not known how many nonplacement cases experienced placement after the termination of family-based services.

Another key term requiring explanation is "imminence of risk." In this study, imminence of placement was assessed for each child in the family by the case reviewer based on written evidence in the case record. Each child was rated as being at low risk (no indication of possible placement in the case record); moderate risk (discussion of possible placement in the case record, but not imminent); high risk (placement seems imminent without family-based services, or just returned from a placement); or temporary placement (child is actually in a short-term placement of less than thirty days with a goal of reunification at the time services began). To make an assessment of high risk, coders were instructed that some action towards making a placement must have been recorded. Although the case readers had no direct interest in risk ratings (i.e., securing services for families) there was still considerable variability in their assessments of risk. At times the analyses will include the "number of children at imminent risk." This refers to the total number of children within a family who were assessed as being at high risk or were in temporary placements at intake.

Chapters Three through Nine refer to changes in family affect, behavior, structure, hierarchy, dynamics, perception of problems, use of available services, material resources, community's perception of the family, informal support networks, and/or degree of community involvement with the family. These items are derived from the Family Systems Change Scale, a scale developed by the National Resource Center on Family Based Services to detect systemic change not captured by individually-oriented measures. On each item, the case reader rated the family as having improved, made no change, or gotten worse between intake and case closure. The Family Systems Change Scale demonstrated a high degree of interrater ($r = .74$) and interitem (*alpha* = .94) reliability. (See Appendix D for a copy of this instrument.)

Data Analysis

Data from the social workers were linked to the cases that they carried. After a lengthy process of combining information through additive and factor-based scales, the data set was analyzed using frequency distributions, cross-tabulation, correlation, t-tests, analysis of variance, factor analysis, and discriminant analysis. Three different weighting systems were used: one which weighted social worker responses by the number of cases they carried in the sample so that larger programs would not overshadow small programs in the analyses of worker responses; one to equalize sample sizes when the same number of placement and nonplacement cases were not available in the site; and one to weight case data by the estimated incidence of placement in each agency. The latter method presents a more accurate picture of family and service characteristics than is provided by the unweighted sample, which included equal numbers of placement and nonplacement cases, since placement occurred in far fewer than 50 percent of the cases.

The following chapters present analyses of the National Resource Center's study with respect to both client populations (neglect, physical abuse, sexual abuse, and juvenile offense cases) and service delivery issues (rural and urban locales, in-home and in-office services, and public and private agencies). Following the research findings in each chapter are detailed case studies of one or two programs and two families served by these programs, one which experienced placement and one which remained intact.

The program(s) described in each chapter were selected because they served a large proportion of cases representing the client population discussed in the chapter or exemplified the service delivery issue under investigation. The families depicted were not selected randomly, but were chosen through purposive sampling techniques to illustrate the most important characteristics affecting placement identified in the multivariate analyses. In general, one family fitting the discriminant model for placement cases and one family with the characteristics associated with nonplacement were selected. The reader is cautioned against generalizing from these case studies to the larger population of clients and child welfare agencies.

Chapter Three

CHILD NEGLECT:
THE MOST COMMON CHILD WELFARE PROBLEM

One of the persistent problems hindering the development of research, policy, and practice in the field of child welfare is the lack of an adequate definition of child maltreatment (Giovannoni, 1989; Herzberger, 1990). The 1974 Federal Child Abuse Prevention and Treatment Act (P.L. 93-237) included neglect, sexual abuse, emotional abuse, and physical abuse under the general rubric of "child abuse." Similarly, many studies either fail to specify the population under consideration or combine two or more of the subtypes of child maltreatment. Yet there is growing evidence that physical abuse, sexual abuse, and neglect are distinct in etiology and treatment needs (Daro, 1988, p. 58). Thus, these problems are being examined in separate chapters with comparisons across types of maltreatment when appropriate.

Adding to and perhaps stemming from this lack of clear definition is the number of different theories which have been advanced concerning the causes of child maltreatment. In 1981, employing an ecological approach to reconcile these competing viewpoints, Belsky identified four causal factors: (1) ontogenic factors (rooted in the personal history of the abuser); (2) microsystem factors (related to family circumstances and dynamics); (3) exosystem factors (causes linked to the larger community); and (4) macrosystem factors (societal values and practices).

In a further refinement, Belsky provided a model of parenting behavior that includes interacting parent, child, and contextual factors (Belsky, 1984; Belsky & Vondra, 1989). He argues that the personal characteristics of some parents create a predisposition to child maltreatment that is either triggered or buffered by contextual stressors and resources, which are in turn partially determined by the characteristics and abilities of the parent. Although attributes of the child interact with other factors in producing maltreatment, Belsky views most of the child factors as resulting from poor parenting and subject to amelioration under conditions of improved parenting and resources (Belsky & Vondra, 1989).

Not all of the causal factors proposed by Belsky will be considered in the following review. Since the present study relied on case record data, the information available for analysis consisted primarily of caregiver and family characteristics, services provided, and short-term outcomes. For the most part historical and contextual data were not available.

OVERVIEW OF SELECTED LITERATURE

Child neglect is the most prevalent type of child maltreatment (National Center on Child Abuse and Neglect, 1988), and poverty is the most frequently documented characteristic of neglecting families (American Humane Association, 1988; Giovannoni & Billingsley, 1970; Nelson, Saunders, & Landsman, 1990; Wolock & Horowitz, 1979). Furthermore, contextual factors related to poverty such as unemployment, inadequate housing, and dangerous neighborhoods have been implicated at least as strongly in the etiology of child neglect as family problems or the personal characteristics of the caregiver (Gaines, Sandgrund, Green, & Power, 1978; Giovannoni & Billingsley, 1970; Nelson et al., 1990; Wolock & Horowitz, 1979; Zuravin & Greif, 1989). Among the latter, social isolation, depression, and substance abuse have been identified as contributing to neglect (Horowitz & Wolock, 1981; Polansky, Ammons, & Gaudin, 1985; Polansky, Chalmers, Williams, & Buttenweiser, 1981; Zuravin, 1988; Zuravin & Greif, 1989).

Although a recent study found psychological distress of caregivers to decrease in the months following a referral for neglect (Nelson et al., 1990), Polansky and his colleagues have provided evidence of an "apathy/futility" syndrome among neglecting caregivers and hypothesize that character defects and resulting social isolation are primary causes of neglectful behavior (e.g., Polansky, Ammons, & Gaudin, 1985; Polansky et al., 1981; Polansky, Gaudin, Ammons, & Davis, 1985).

With regard to family characteristics, single-parent families and families with large numbers of children are found more frequently among neglecting than among abusing or control families (American Humane Association, 1988; Giovannoni & Billingsley, 1970; Ory & Earp, 1980; Polansky, Gaudin, Ammons, & Davis, 1985; Wolock & Horowitz, 1979; Zuravin & Greif, 1989). One study of child maltreatment found nonreferred siblings of neglected children also to be at high risk of neglect (Jean-

Gilles & Crittenden, 1990). Poor parenting skills including lack of knowledge about child development, inappropriate expectations, and negative interactions are also associated with child neglect (Aragona & Eyberg, 1981; Bousha & Twentyman, 1984; Burgess & Conger, 1978; Herrenkohl, Herrenkohl, & Egolf, 1983; Jones & McNeely, 1980; Twentymen & Plotkin, 1982).

Although far from definitive, the existing research on child maltreatment does provide a context and basis for comparison with findings from the current study. While data are lacking on family and caregiver history and incomplete on extrafamilial stressors and support, many of the demographic characteristics and family problems cited in previous research have been included in the present analysis. In addition, information on services and their contribution to placement prevention provides the opportunity to link causal factors with treatment and preventive strategies.

STUDY SAMPLE

Most of the neglect cases came from three agencies, all providing home-based services (Table III–I). A third were from Supportive Child/Adult Network, Inc. (SCAN), a private agency that contracts with the Philadelphia County Children and Youth Agency to provide child protective and placement prevention services to an inner-city catchment area. This program and two of its cases are described later in this chapter. Another 28 percent of the neglect cases were from Franklin County Children Services, a public child welfare agency serving Columbus, Ohio, profiled in the next chapter on physical abuse. Iowa Children and Family Services, a private agency described in Chapter Eight, provided services to 10 percent of the neglect cases in the study. All three of these programs, which included 72 percent of the neglect cases, followed a home-based model. Overall, Franklin County (38) and SCAN (35) served the most child maltreatment cases.

Cases were classified according to the reason for referral. If more than one type of maltreatment was reported, the most important (the first one listed) was used to classify the case. Using this method, 67 neglect cases were identified from this group of agencies. Neglect was the primary reason for referral for 87 percent of these cases. Only 10 percent of the cases referred primarily for neglect were also referred for physical abuse (5 cases) or sexual abuse (2 cases).

Table III-I
NEGLECT SAMPLE BY SITE

Agency	Neglect n = 67	%	All Maltreatment n = 208	%
SCAN, Philadelphia, PA	22	32.8	35	16.8
Franklin County Children Services, OH	19	28.4	38	18.3
Iowa Children & Family Services	7	10.4	20	9.6
Oregon Children's Services Division	5	7.5	19	9.1
Intensive Family Services, Multnomah County, OR	3	4.5	20	9.6
Dakota County Human Services, MN	3	4.5	21	10.1
Lutheran Social Services, MN	3	4.5	15	7.2
Boulder County Social Services, CO	3	4.5	15	7.2
Iowa Department of Human Services	2	3.0	25	12.0

Note. Unweighted; *n*'s vary in subsequent tables due to weighting and missing data; percentages may not total 100 due to rounding.

STUDY FINDINGS

The Families

In many ways the problems of child neglect, physical abuse, and sexual abuse reflect different stages and phases during the family life cycle, compounded by disadvantages relating to race and social class. Regardless of family structure or geographic location, however, the majority of maltreating families were poor. Some were black and living in inner-city environments, others were headed by single mothers, and still others had unemployed caretakers.

Although different kinds of child maltreatment, particularly physical abuse and neglect, are often treated as a single entity, the only family characteristic consistent across all the maltreatment groups was average family size, four people, including 2.6 children. Beyond this, a different demographic pattern prevailed for each type of maltreatment, in part because of differences among study sites.

Families referred for child neglect were at an earlier stage of the family life cycle, with younger children, averaging 5 years, and younger mothers (28 years). In terms of family characteristics, this was the most distinctive group, since it included significantly more non-white families, single parents, unemployed adults, and poor families than the other two groups (Table III–II). Neglecting families also contained, on average, more than one child at high risk of placement (Table III–III). Over half (56%) of the children at highest risk of placement were girls. Neglecting families had multiple problems including lower-functioning, socially isolated caretakers; inadequate housing; and health, mental health, and family relationship problems (Table III–IV). Overall, 19 percent of the neglect cases were found to involve physical abuse and 11 percent involved sexual abuse (Table III–IV).

Table III-II
CHARACTERISTICS OF NEGLECTING FAMILIES: PERCENTAGES

| | Neglect | | All Maltreatment | |
Family Characteristics	n = 67	%	n = 219	%
Below Poverty Level	58	89.4*	161	72.6
Primary Caretaker				
Non-White	61	35.6*	207	20.4
Developmentally Disabled	65	23.0*	215	8.7
Married	63	21.2*	209	39.7
Employed	64	13.8*	209	32.6
Second Adult				
Employed	40	20.6*	147	48.0

* $p < .001$.

Despite the distinctiveness of neglecting families, some problems were reported consistently by families in all three maltreatment groups, including family-child relationship (80%) and child behavior (49%) problems. For 72 percent of the neglect cases family-child relationships were problematic and 40 percent were assessed as having children with behavior problems. Although reported more frequently in neglecting families (41%), discontinuities in parenting had occurred in nearly a third of *all* maltreating families in the year prior to services. In addition 46 percent of the neglecting families had children with health or mental health problems. Substance abuse was identified as a problem in a quarter of all the maltreatment cases and in 32 percent of the neglecting families.

Table III-III
CHARACTERISTICS OF NEGLECTING FAMILIES: AVERAGES

Family Characteristics	Neglect n = 67	m/sd	All Maltreatment n = 219	m/sd
Primary Caretaker				
Age	64	27.9** 8.1	208	31.6 7.9
CWBS—Parental Disposition Subscale	66	69.5† 13.7	217	72.9 13.4
Number of Children at High Risk[a]	67	1.2† 1.4	219	.9 1.1
Age of Child at Highest Risk[b]	65	6.1* 5.4	215	9.3 5.2
Total Number of Problems[c]	66	6.2** 2.7	219	5.0 3.0

[a]Range: 0–5. [b]Range: 0–17, 0–19. [c]Range: 0–14.
*$p < .01$. **$p < .001$.
†$p < .05$ with sexual abuse.

Services And Outcomes

Case objectives and services corresponded to families' needs and problems. With objectives focused on changing adult behavior, neglect cases received the most intensive and comprehensive services, including significantly more public assistance, protective services, information and referrals, parent education, paraprofessional services, and transportation, in addition to family and individual counseling (Table III–V). Nearly three-quarters of the neglecting families received AFDC, were referred for other services, or were simultaneously receiving child protective services. Role-modeling techniques were used to help change adult behavior. Neglect cases were open, on average, one month more and received substantially more services than physical or sexual abuse cases during the time they were open (Table III–VI).

In light of the differences in family characteristics and services, the different types of maltreatment cases were surprisingly similar in their outcomes. Overall, 22 percent of the families were re-reported for child maltreatment while their cases were still open (24% of neglecting families), substantially fewer than the 30 to 47 percent reported in other treatment

Table III-IV
PROBLEMS IN NEGLECTING FAMILIES

Problems[a]	Neglect n = 67	All Maltreatment n = 219
Marital Problems	43.8*	55.9
Family Relationships	68.5*	55.5
Economic Deprivation	64.2***	43.9
Health/Mental Health	54.4**	40.7
Housing Problems	40.0***	19.0
Social Isolation	36.3*	24.5
Parent-Child Conflict	25.0***	45.8
Physical Abuse	18.7***	43.8
Sexual Abuse	11.1***	26.5
Status Offense/Delinquency	10.0*	28.8

Note. Percentages.
[a]Coded: 1 = problem, 0 = no problem.
*$p < .05$.   **$p < .01$.   ***$p < .001$.

programs (Daro & Cohn, 1988). More than half of the neglecting families improved in behavior, family relations, emotional climate, perception of their problems, and use of services. Among maltreating families, only neglect cases improved significantly in material resources, a particularly important finding since these families were the most economically disadvantaged.

Placement rates, however, did differ among the three types of maltreatment cases, with 24 percent of the neglect cases terminating in placement, a rate nearly 10 percent higher than for physical or sexual abuse. This difference in placement outcome reflects (1) differences in starting points: neglecting families had more strikes against them to begin with, and (2) differential success in engaging families in treatment: less than two-thirds of the neglecting caretakers attended most or all the scheduled sessions compared to three-quarters of the caregivers in abuse cases (Table III–V).

Table III-V
OBJECTIVES AND SERVICES IN NEGLECT CASES

	Neglect n = 67	All Maltreatment n = 219
Case Objectives		
Adult Behavior Change	45.6**	30.8
Services		
AFDC	72.0***	48.6
Protective Services	71.7**	56.8
Information/Referral	69.6*	57.1
Parent Education	54.1**	38.8
Paraprofessional	44.7***	27.1
Role Modeling	42.3*	30.2
Money Management	40.1***	20.4
Accompanied to Appointment	38.1†	28.9
Transportation	37.9**	25.1
Marital Counseling	16.8**	32.8

Note. Percentages.
*$p < .05$. **$p < .01$. ***$p < .001$.
† $p < .05$ with physical abuse.

Factors Related to Placement

Several characteristics associated with placement were found across all three maltreatment types. Having at least one child at imminent risk of placement was consistently related to higher placement rates, as were lower functioning and less cooperative caretakers, poor family-child relationships, and failure of the primary caretaker to attend most or all of the sessions. Prior placements, lack of continuity in caretaking, the total number of problems, and the failure of the highest-risk child to attend most or all of the sessions also foreshadowed an outcome of placement in child neglect cases.

In order to determine the most important factors in avoiding placement in child maltreatment cases, a series of multivariate discriminant analyses was performed. Seven analyses covering different domains—family demographics and history, characteristics of second adults, resource

Table III-VI
INTENSITY OF SERVICE IN NEGLECT CASES

Intensity		Neglect n = 67	All Maltreatment n = 219
Total Number of Services[a]	m	15.8**	12.5
	sd	8.9	8.1
In-Home Contacts in First Month[b]	m	5.2†	4.1
	sd	4.8	4.2
In-Office Contacts in First Month[c]	m	.3†	.7
	sd	.8	1.3
Total Number of Contacts in First Three Months[d]	m	18.1†	14.8
	sd	13.4	11.3
Length of Service (months)[e]	m	7.6	6.6
	sd	6.1	5.0
Primary Caretaker Attended Most Sessions	%	60.3*	74.1

[a]Range: 1–40, 0–45. [b]Range: 0–20, 0–21. [c]Range: 0–20, 0–21. [d]Range: 3–67, 1–67.
[e]Range: 1.1–29.4.
*$p < .01$. **$p < .001$.
†$p < .05$ with sexual abuse.

problems, adult problems, child problems, interventions, and involvement in treatment—were performed separately for physical abuse, sexual abuse, and neglect cases. Overall, demographics and history explained the most difference between placement and nonplacement cases, and resource problems explained the least. Family characteristics were the best predictors, accurately identifying 30 percent of the placement cases. Lack of material resources predicted only 3 percent of the placements, probably because the majority of the families in the sample had very low incomes.

For neglect cases, the separate discriminant analyses revealed strong predictors in each domain. Only variables concerning a second adult had little predictive value, since so few families contained a second adult. A single discriminant model that combined significant predictors of placement in this study with those found in other studies identified the primary caretaker's attendance at most sessions and stability of caretaking as most predictive of placement prevention (see Appendix E for tables and an explanation of the analytic methods employed). Paraprofessional services also contributed to placement prevention in 49 percent of successful cases. The most important predictors of placement were the number of children at risk of imminent placement, prior placements (which had occurred in 40% of the placement cases), and the total number of problems in the family. Together the eight variables in the model correctly classified 95 percent of the nonplacement cases and 73 percent of the placement cases.

CASE STUDIES

In order to give a clearer picture of family-based services targeted to specific types of maltreatment, SCAN, the program serving the most neglect cases, will be examined in more detail along with two of its cases, one placement and one nonplacement. SCAN served 21 of the 67 neglect cases studied. Franklin County Children Services' Home-Based Family Centered Services program, which also served a large proportion of neglect cases, is profiled in the next chapter on physical abuse.

Supportive Child/Adult Network, Inc. (SCAN)

Agency Description

Based at the University of Pennsylvania's School of Nursing, SCAN provides home-based intensive services to severely disadvantaged families in the city of Philadelphia. The program began in 1973, with the establishment of a Child Abuse and Neglect Multidisciplinary Team based at Philadelphia General Hospital. The Philadelphia Child Guidance Clinic was also on the team. At that time SCAN employed paraprofessionals who resided in the area and were trained and supervised by a staff of nurses, social workers, and psychologists. Clients were referred to SCAN for preventive help by participating agencies.

In 1975, the SCAN group was awarded a two-year federally-funded Child Welfare Demonstration Grant and incorporated as a nonprofit organization. In 1977, SCAN entered into its first contract with the City of Philadelphia to provide protective services to children in their own homes and by 1985, the Philadelphia City Children and Youth Agency was the sole referral source and the primary funder of SCAN. Although it no longer accepts direct referrals from the hospitals, SCAN still maintains professional and administrative links with some of the founding organizations. SCAN is governed by an eleven-member board of directors, elected to two-year terms. The board assumes responsibility for policy, while the program director, who is appointed by the board, is responsible for SCAN's operations and activities. To date there has only been one program director in the program's history.

SCAN adheres to four central principles: (1) belief in the value of home-based services; (2) provision of comprehensive services to children and families that include treatment of medical, social, environmental, psychological, and educational problems; (3) commitment to filling gaps in service with new programming while strengthening already existing services through joint ventures and collaboration; and (4) dedication to high-quality service for a population of disadvantaged children and their parents.

SCAN offers a multidisciplinary approach to services that combines social work, nursing, psychological services, and medical consultation. Social work services offered by SCAN include protective casework, family counseling, and teaching daily living skills. Nursing services include home-based nursing care and teaching of nutrition, child care, and child development. Psychologists provide evaluations, referrals, and support for families in need of mental health services. Medical personnel offer health supervision and outpatient pediatric care at SCAN's weekly clinic.

Families referred to SCAN generally have an indicated abuse or neglect report or are at risk of abuse or neglect and will accept voluntary home-based services. SCAN serves about 500 families a year and receives about twenty-five referrals each month. The majority of families receive services for nine to fifteen months.

A comprehensive assessment at intake is seen as essential in order to make the most efficient use of services and to prepare families to use services most effectively. The initial home visit always includes the referring public social services worker and the SCAN intake worker, and sometimes other members of the multidisciplinary staff. Following this visit, the comprehensive intake assessment continues for ten to fifteen days and concludes with an intake study and family service description. From there, the case is assigned to a direct service worker.

Site-Specific Findings

Eighty-two percent of SCAN's client families were minority group members, a far higher proportion than in the other programs included in this research, in which minority group families made up 16 percent of the client population (see Appendix F for comparative tables). SCAN families were also more likely to be headed by single, unemployed caretakers and to contain younger children at less imminent risk of placement.

In keeping with the agency's origins and location, both children and adults in the families referred to SCAN more often had health and mental health problems, as well as problems involving poverty and housing. About a third of the cases were treated by teams of two, in most cases both professional workers, although paraprofessional services were used effectively to prevent placements. SCAN was much less likely than the other programs in the study to deal with adult relationship, child behavior, or delinquency problems and reported no instances of child substance abuse and few of status offenses or delinquency. Due to the nature of the families' problems, case objectives at SCAN involved increasing the families' use of concrete and supportive services and changing adult behavior.

SCAN was distinguished from the other sites in this study by its greater reliance on such services as role modeling, accompanying clients to appointments (especially in placement cases), outreach services, and information and referral services. More SCAN families received general assistance, subsidized housing, legal services, and special education than at any other site. They also received services over a longer time period, averaging eleven months, the longest in the study; however, there were a high number of failed contacts—an average of two per family in the first three months of service.

At SCAN primary caretakers were less likely to attend most or all of the family-based sessions, and only one-third of the cases were closed because case goals were achieved. However, more families than in most sites experienced improvement in material resources. Although more than three-quarters of the families improved in at least one area of functioning, a quarter got worse, and 22 percent of the cases ended with a placement, including a very high 37 percent of those referred for neglect. Over a third of the children were placed with relatives or friends. All of the physical abuse cases involving substance abuse terminated in placement.

Because of their location in large metropolitan areas and their target populations of young children and their families, SCAN and the Home-Based Family-Centered (HBFC) Program in Franklin County, Ohio, described in the following chapter, had a number of characteristics in common. These programs served populations similar to those of human service agencies in other large cities: young, unmarried, unemployed primary caretakers living in poverty and receiving AFDC.

Not surprisingly, given their situation and ages, the families seen by these programs were referred more often for neglect and family relationship problems and less often for parent-child conflict, delinquency, and status offenses. Family-based workers more often identified neglect and parenting skills as treatment issues and changing adult behavior as a case objective. They less often aimed at improving family communication and relationships. The families in these programs received many more counseling, supportive, and concrete services than did families at the other study sites, including public health or visiting nurse services, parent education, money management counseling, financial aid, emergency cash assistance, special education services, and medical care. These younger families in urban areas received nearly twice as many different kinds of service from the family-based programs and more than twice as many services from outside agencies.

Both SCAN and the HBFC program followed a home-based model with an average of one to two contacts a week over a seven- to eleven-month period. They also both made significant use of teaming: in the HBFC program, all families were seen by a MSW/BA team, while at SCAN about a third of the cases were treated by a team, most often comprising cotherapy by two professionals. Although placement rates were higher than the average for the study as a whole, placements were more often in the least-restrictive setting, with relatives or friends. In both programs, change was reported in material resources and the use of services more often than in other programs, and the overwhelming majority of case objectives were partially or completely achieved. Despite the number of services made available to families in these urban programs, fewer than 5 percent of the families were expected to function completely independently of social services after termination by the family-based program.

Case Examples

The Robinson Family

The Robinsons were a black family of five consisting of 19-year-old Manda, her girlfriend Anna, and Manda's three young daughters—2-year-old Latisha and twin infants. The Robinsons were referred to SCAN due to suspected child neglect. Neither Manda nor Anna had completed high school and neither was employed. The family resided in a low-income housing project and Manda supported the household on AFDC payments, SSI, and food stamps. The father of the three girls, Eddie, lived elsewhere in Philadelphia, and continued to have contact with the children, though conflict with Manda prevented the family from living together. All three children were assessed as being at high risk of placement at the time of intake to the family-based service program.

The family-based worker who served the Robinsons, Jewel, was a 48-year-old black woman, divorced with three children of her own. With a bachelors degree in social work and over eighteen years of experience in child welfare and family counseling, Jewel brought a considerable amount of experience to the program. She reported that she worked almost exclusively with low-income, single-parent families, most of them black, in which physical abuse or child neglect, poverty, substandard housing, and unemployment were prevalent problems. Her caseload ranged from about 15 to 25, and she generally worked with families in their own homes.

From their earliest meetings which centered around setting case goals, Manda appeared to have a very low level of motivation and limited capacity for child care or recognition of her own problems. Continuity in parenting was also noted as a serious problem and one which was to threaten the long-term welfare of the young girls. The Robinsons could be characterized as a "multi-problem" family, experiencing social isolation, maternal depression, poor family interaction, inadequate housing, unemployment, poverty, and homelessness. The case plan that Jewel and Manda developed focused on teaching about child care, infant stimulation, and nutrition; helping Manda keep medical appointments for the children; and assisting her to obtain mental health counseling. Motivation to participate in the service plan continued to compromise progress in this case.

The case was open for fifteen months, during which Jewel met with Manda twice or more each week for the first four months, and about weekly thereafter. Manda missed several of the sessions, an indication of her lack of engagement in services. Despite Jewel's assistance in scheduling appointments with the mental health center, Manda refused to go. She did follow through with medical appointments for the children, but only when Jewel actually accompanied her to the clinic. No significant progress was made in knowledge of proper child care techniques, due in part to Manda's mental health problems.

After about nine months, Manda moved without informing Jewel of her whereabouts. When Jewel finally caught up with the family, they had moved in temporarily with a new boyfriend and Manda's mental health appeared to be deteriorating further. The children were removed from the home due to substantiated neglect. Latisha was entrusted to her father's custody, while the twins were placed with a foster family.

Jewel considered about 80 percent of the families she worked with to have successful outcomes, evidenced by positive family interaction and improvement in coping and parenting skills. She characterized failure in placement prevention services as families becoming increasingly isolated and hostile towards kin, friends, and social service agencies. This seems to have been the case with the Robinson family.

The Davis Family

Sondra Davis, a 24-year-old black mother of two young children, Tony, a six-year-old mentally retarded boy, and two-year-old Maria, was referred to SCAN for suspected medical neglect of Tony. A local medical clinic had referred the family based on repeated failure to follow through on Tony's medical needs, including immunizations required for school enrollment. Sondra was unemployed, but enrolled in a vocational school and supporting the family through a variety of public assistance programs. At the time of intake, neither child was assessed as being at imminent risk of out-of-home placement and neither had ever been placed out of the home.

Assigned to work with the Davis family was Martin, a 31-year-old white, male MSW who, although relatively new to the agency, had six years of child welfare experience. He expressed a high degree of satisfaction with his job and planned to stay in his position for at least another year or two. Most of Martin's cases were black, low-income families with young children and without prior social services involvement. He saw the home as the most effective setting for working with families. Martin carried an average caseload of 14, and found that the predominant problems he encountered were poverty, multiple and multigenerational problems, poor housing, unemployment, child behavior and parent/child conflict, accompanied by physical and emotional abuse and child neglect. The situations with which he felt most effective were those involving child abuse and neglect.

When Martin first began meeting with the Davis family, a number of case goals were established, centering around attending to Tony's medical and special educational needs as well as providing guidance in child care to Sondra. He accompanied Sondra to the medical clinic, assisting her in requesting medical records and in scheduling appointments for immunizations. He also helped Sondra arrange for neurological and psychological examinations of Tony to get a clearer idea of his strengths and limitations, and enroll him in an appropriate special education class and recreational program. Martin supported Sondra in her search for safer housing, although this was not achieved during the service period.

Once the most pressing problems were dealt with, additional case goals were developed which focused on resolving Sondra's ambivalent feelings toward her developmentally disabled child as well as exploring her future employment possibilities and the logistical arrangements such as child care and transportation.

Martin worked with the Davises for 10 months, seeing them about once a week in the home or accompanying them to agencies in the community. Both Sondra and her children attended most of the sessions. A number of different services were provided directly—individual and family counseling, role modeling, teaching, accompanying to various places, advocacy, case management, money management, parent education, information and referral, and recreational activities—with other community agencies providing evaluation for mental retardation/developmental disability services, housing, employment assistance, and medical services.

In many ways this case had a favorable outcome. No placements occurred either during or at the termination of family-based services, and Sondra was evaluated as having increased motivation, recognition of the family's problems, and cooperation with services. She had also developed more appropriate expectations of her children, acceptance of Tony's limitations, and provided better supervision. The case was closed because services had been successfully completed; most of the case goals had been fully or at least partially achieved; and all family members had participated in the treatment plan.

Martin considered the achievement of case goals and elimination of risk to the children to be the most important indicators of a successful case outcome, while the continued presence of risk and lack of connection to other community services were characteristic of failure in family-based services. By these standards, the Davis family certainly meet the criteria for success in family-based services.

RELATION TO OTHER STUDIES

This analysis confirms the importance of poverty, large families, and multiple problems in child neglect. In one sense, placement in neglect cases is overdetermined (Daro, 1988, p. 34), with significant differences between placement and nonplacement cases in all areas except those relating to a second adult in the family. While preexisting characteristics such as instability in caretaking in the year prior to referral, previous placements, the number of children facing imminent placement, and multiple problems all contribute to placement, successfully engaging the caretaker in services is of the utmost importance in preventing placement.

Motivating neglecting caretakers is a most challenging task, but one which is more likely to succeed with families who receive comprehensive family-based services including parent education, transportation, counseling, and paraprofessional services (Ayoub & Jacewitz, 1982; Colon, 1980; Hartley, Showell, & White, 1989; Kagan & Schlosberg, 1989, ch. 3; Kaplan, 1986). Such a multisystemic approach has been found to be more effective with neglecting families than simply providing parent education (Brunk, Henggeler, & Whelan, 1987).

Other studies of family preservation services (Berry, 1990; Hartley et al., 1989; Yuan & Struckman-Johnson, 1991) have also found placement rates to be higher in neglect than in other types of child maltreatment. This may be due in part to the difficulty of treating chronically neglecting families. Their larger numbers of children and multiple problems tend to skew findings about neglect. Indeed, three of the predictors of placement in this study (number of children, prior placement, and multiple problems) have been found in a recent study by the authors to be characteristic of chronically neglecting families (Nelson et al., 1990).

It may be that chronically neglecting families require a longer period of service and that families with neglect of more recent onset may benefit more from short-term family-based services. While useful, traditional family therapy techniques need to be modified in working with more serious and chronic cases of neglect. Accepting the family's goals, working slowly to gain their trust, and only carefully challenging their perceptions and functioning may require working with subsystems, avoiding interventions that increase conflict and disequilibrium, and providing a strong model of positive parenting (Weitzman, 1985).

Whatever the treatment modality or the reason for referral, engaging the primary caretaker in the treatment process is critical (Dale & Davies, 1985; Green, Power, Steinbook, & Gaines, 1981; Orenchuk-Tomiuk, Matthey, & Pigler-Christensen, 1990; Weitzman, 1985). Motivation is a complex but important construct that has received little attention in social work research (Gold, 1990). Partly a predisposition of the client and partly a product of the success of the worker in engaging the family, motivation and cooperation are key to success in family-based services as well as in other types of therapy. Family-based techniques such as encouraging families to set their own goals, acknowledging their strengths, and instilling hope for positive change, are supported by psychological research on motivation (Gold, 1990; Gutierrez, 1990). Finding out how best to use information, recognition, and material assistance to motivate individual families is part of the larger task of identifying which of the wide range of interventions used in family-based services are most effective with families having different strengths and problems.

Chapter Four

PHYSICAL ABUSE:
THE MOST VARIED CHILD WELFARE PROBLEM

Two decades of "repetitive and fragmented" research on physical abuse, the first child maltreatment problem to become the object of widespread public concern, has failed to produce a body of validated knowledge with which to approach this problem (Herzberger, 1990). Although a comprehensive model of the causes of child maltreatment would include caregiver history, current family situation, and external support and stressors (Belsky, 1981), all of these elements could not be tested in this study due to a lack of data on historical and contextual factors. However, this analysis of physical abuse cases from nine family-based programs identifies both the family and case characteristics most important in predicting placement and services that made placement less likely.

OVERVIEW OF SELECTED LITERATURE

Despite the considerable amount of research on physical abuse, its causes, and its characteristics, a definitive causal model has not been identified (Pianta, Egeland, & Erickson, 1989). Family violence in childhood and spouse abuse have been linked to the physical abuse of children (Hartley, Showell, & White, 1989; Reid, Taplin, & Lorber, 1981; Straus, Gelles, & Steinmetz, 1980; Wolfe, 1985). Recent research, however, does not support the hypothesis that a pattern of physical maltreatment is handed down directly from parent to child. Rather, many parents who were themselves maltreated as children consciously reject their parents as role models and do not repeat their abusive behavior (Pianta et al., 1989; Rutter, 1989; Trickett & Susman, 1989).

Substance abuse and depression have also been associated with the physical abuse of children in clinical and officially-reported samples (Famularo, Barnum, & Stone, 1986; Famularo, Stone, & Barnum, 1986;

Susman, Trickett, Iannotti, Hollenbeck, & Zahn-Waxler, 1985; Webster-Stratton, 1985), but representative national surveys do not support these associations (Gelles & Cornell, 1990). Nor do they confirm evidence from clinical samples that stepfamilies may be at greater risk of physical abuse (Burgess, Anderson, Schellenbach, & Conger, 1981; Garbarino, 1989; Garbarino, Schellenbach, & Sebes, 1986, p. 24).

Most research and treatment in physical abuse now focus on family issues, particularly on unsatisfying marital relationships and conflict between parents (Gelles & Maynard, 1987; Panaccione & Wahler, 1986; Trickett & Susman, 1989; Wolfe, 1985). Although less severe than in neglecting families, contextual factors such as poverty, unemployment, health problems, and residential instability, in the absence of compensating factors, also contribute to high stress levels and physical abuse (American Humane Association, 1988; Belsky & Vondra, 1989; Conger, Burgess, & Barrett, 1979; Justice & Justice, 1990; Rodgers, 1987; Wolfe, 1985).

The role of child behavior and characteristics in eliciting abusive responses has also been studied. Although some abused children have been found to be irritable or aggressive, this behavior typically appears as part of an escalating cycle of negativity and aggression on the part of both parent and child (Belsky, 1981; Burgess & Youngblade, 1988; Engfer & Schneewind, 1982). This kind of parent-child conflict is especially characteristic in cases of adolescent abuse, which is almost as frequent as abuse of younger children (Garbarino, Sebes, & Schellenbach, 1984; Straus & Gelles, 1988).

The inconsistency of research on physical abuse may result from a failure to differentiate among subtypes of abuse. One study, for example, found different parenting styles and child behaviors in three subsamples of physically abusing caregivers who were labeled emotionally distant, intrusive, and hostile (Oldershaw, Walters, & Hall, 1989). In addition, Garbarino (1989) argues that "there can be little doubt that a distinctly *adolescent* maltreatment phenomenon exists" (p. 699). Families of abused adolescents are less likely to be poor, more likely to contain stepparents, and tend more toward the extremes of either authoritarian discipline or indulgence than families with younger children.

STUDY SAMPLE

Physical abuse cases were found across a wider range of agencies than sexual abuse or neglect cases. Of the programs with the most cases, the top three were in public agencies, and four out of five provided service in the families' homes (Table IV–I). The greatest number of physical abuse cases came from Franklin County Children Services, described later in this chapter. Second was the Dakota County (Minnesota) Human Services Department, a county-administered social service agency that also served a large proportion of status offenders, and the Iowa Department of Human Services, an office-based family treatment program described in Chapter Eight.

Table IV-I
PHYSICAL ABUSE SAMPLE BY SITE

Agency	Physical Abuse n = 91	%	All Maltreatment n = 208	%
Franklin County Children Services, OH	16	17.6	38	18.3
Dakota County Human Services, MN	14	15.4	21	10.1
Iowa Department of Human Services	14	15.4	25	12.0
Lutheran Social Services, MN	10	11.0	15	7.2
SCAN, Philadelphia, PA	10	11.0	35	16.8
Iowa Children & Family Services	10	11.0	20	9.6
Boulder County Social Services, CO	8	8.8	15	7.2
Intensive Family Services, Multnomah County, OR	5	5.5	20	9.6
Oregon Children's Services Division	4	4.4	19	9.1

Note. Unweighted; *n*'s vary in subsequent tables due to weighting and missing data. Percentages may not total 100 due to rounding.

Iowa Children and Family Services and SCAN, described in other chapters, both contributed 10 physical abuse cases as well as having large numbers of neglect cases. Lutheran Social Services, profiled in the chapter on rural services, also provided 10 physical abuse cases. Overall, Franklin County (38) and SCAN (35) had the most child maltreatment cases, over a third of the total. Classified according to the primary reason for referral, 91 physical abuse cases were identified in the child maltreatment sample. For 85 percent, physical abuse was the primary reason for their referral to family-based service. Neglect was also a consideration in 15 percent and sexual abuse in 4 percent of the physical abuse cases.

STUDY FINDINGS

The Families

Physical abuse cases included families in different life circumstances than those referred for sexual abuse or neglect. Primary caretakers were more often employed and more often married to an employed spouse than in the other groups (Table IV–II). Fewer lived below the poverty level. More than a quarter of the physically abusing families were remarried with at least one stepchild in the household. The children, averaging 8 years of age, were older than those in neglect cases, and usually only one child was at risk of imminent placement (Table IV–III). A little more than half the highest-risk children were female (54%).

Table IV-II
CHARACTERISTICS OF PHYSICALLY ABUSING FAMILIES: PERCENTAGES

| | *Physical Abuse* | | *All Maltreatment* | |
| | $n = 101$ | % | $n = 219$ | % |
Family Characteristics				
Below Poverty Level	75	60.7*	161	72.6
Married	95	55.4**	209	39.7
Primary Caretaker Employed	96	43.6*	209	32.6
Second Adult Employed	70	64.2**	147	48.0
At Least One Stepchild	86	28.6**	192	16.4

*$p < .01$. **$p < .001$.

Nearly two-thirds of the physically abusing families presented marital problems and almost 40 percent contained adults with health or mental health problems. Significantly fewer than in the neglecting group had problems with housing or social isolation (Table IV–IV). Nearly a quarter of the physical abuse cases were found to involve neglect as well, but only a few cases also involved sexual abuse or juvenile offenses. Some problems were reported consistently across all three maltreatment groups. As in the other maltreatment groups, 82 percent of the children in

Table IV-III
CHARACTERISTICS OF PHYSICALLY ABUSING FAMILIES: AVERAGES

Family Characteristics	Physical Abuse		All Maltreatment	
	n = 101	m/sd	n = 219	m/sd
Age of Primary Caretaker	94	32.2[†]	208	31.6
		7.4		7.9
Age of Child at Highest Risk[a]	97	9.7[†]	215	9.3
		4.4		5.2
Number at Imminent Risk of Placement[b]	101	.9	220	.9
		1.0		1.0

[a]Range: 0–17, 0–19. [b]Range: 0–5.
[†]$p < .05$ with neglect.

Table IV-IV
PROBLEMS IN PHYSICALLY ABUSING FAMILIES

Problems[a]	Physical Abuse n = 101	All Maltreatment n = 219
Family Relationships	44.7*	55.5
Neglect	22.0**	39.0
Social Isolation	15.1*	24.5
Status Offense/Delinquency	9.7**	18.8
Housing Problems	8.8**	19.0
Sexual Abuse	4.6**	26.5

Note. Percentages.
[a]Coded: 1 = problem, 0 = no problem.
*$p < .01$. **$p < .001$.

abusing families had problems with family relationships and 51 percent had behavior problems.

In physical abuse cases both objectives and services centered to a greater extent around marital problems than in the other types of maltreatment, although most families also received family and individual counseling, child protective services, and information and referral services. Significantly fewer had case objectives relating to the use of outside counseling, received AFDC, or were accompanied to appointments (Table IV–V). Only 20 percent of the families were referred again for abuse while their case was open. Placements occurred in 13 percent of the cases, the lowest rate among the three types of maltreatment. In addition, more than half the families showed positive change in behavior, family relations, emotional climate, perception of their problems, and use of services.

Table IV-V
OBJECTIVES AND SERVICES IN PHYSICAL ABUSE CASES

	Physical Abuse $n = 101$	All Maltreatment $n = 219$
Case Objectives		
Use Counseling	22.5***	38.1
Marital Relations	37.7*	28.9
Services		
AFDC	37.9**	48.6
Accompanied to Appointment	18.9**	28.9
Second Adult Attended Most Sessions[a]	51.9**	39.9

Note. Percentages.
[a]$n = 150$.
*$p < .05$. **$p < .01$. ***$p < .001$.

Some of the differences observed among families emanated from differences between specific programs. The programs for neglecting families were the most alike, with the exception that SCAN served most of the black families in the study. The greatest differences were observed in the treatment of physical abuse. At one extreme were the agencies that also saw a large number of neglect cases (Franklin County, SCAN, and ICFS). They served poorer families with younger children and more problems, especially with substance abuse. At the other extreme were programs located in public agencies (Iowa Department of Human Services, Boulder County and Dakota County) that served families with older children and more family relationship problems, but fewer problems overall. Because physical abuse cases were seen across the range of agencies, length of services, number of services and contacts, and participation rates were close to the averages for all maltreatment cases (Table IV–VI).

Table IV-VI
INTENSITY OF SERVICE IN PHYSICAL ABUSE CASES

Intensity		*Physical Abuse* *n = 101*	*All Maltreatment* *n = 219*
Total Number of Services[a]	*m*	11.4	12.5
	sd	7.6	8.1
In-Home Contacts in First Month[b]	*m*	4.0	4.1
	sd	4.0	4.2
In-Office Contacts in First Month[c]	*m*	.7	.7
	sd	1.3	1.3
Total Number of Contacts In First Three Months[d]	*m*	14.3	14.8
	sd	10.8	11.3
Length of Service (months)[e]	*m*	6.1	6.6
	sd	4.9	5.0
Primary Caretaker Attended Most Sessions	%	76.5	74.1

[a]Range: 0–45. [b]Range: 0–21. [c]Range: 0–5, 0–10. [d]Range: 1–56, 1–67. [e]Range: 0–24.3, 0–29.3.

Factors Related to Placement

Separate discriminant analyses for seven domains of variables were performed for physical abuse cases. The domains included demographics and history, characteristics of second adults, resource problems, adult problems, child problems, interventions, and involvement/empowerment. Placement in physical abuse cases was not dominated by any single domain. However, this may be the result of combining cases involving the abuse of adolescents with abuse of younger children. Since there were too few cases to enable separation of these two groups, predictors were combined in a single discriminant analysis (see Appendix E). The resulting statistical model revealed that the primary caretaker's score on the Child Well-Being Parental Disposition Subscale was the most important indicator of whether a child would be placed or not. This scale measured the caregiver's capacity for child care; acceptance, approval, and expectations of the children; recognition of problems, motivation, and cooperation; and family relationships. Placement prevention in physical abuse cases was significantly associated with several service characteristics, including marital counseling (41%), the caretaker's participation in most treatment sessions (80%), and the use of role modeling

(30%) in successful cases. Continued receipt of child protective services (69%) and additional reports of abuse in 36 percent of the unsuccessful cases led to placement. Several other variables including adult substance abuse (37% of placement and 19% of nonplacement cases) made less important contributions to predicting placement. Together the eleven variables in the model correctly classified 76 percent of the nonplacement cases, but only 48 percent of the placement cases.

When families were separated according to the age of the highest-risk child (0 to 11 and 12 to 18), caretaker functioning emerged as the most important factor in preventing placement of younger children and the involvement of child protective services in predicting placement of older children. Although the primary caretaker's participation in treatment was essential to placement prevention in both groups, role modeling was the most effective intervention for younger families, and marital counseling was most effective for families of older children.

In all the maltreatment groups, the predictive models were more accurate in identifying successful cases than in identifying placements. In cases of physical abuse, however, the problem of identifying families who did not remain together was even more acute. Even when the outcome was known in advance, the analysis did not produce an accurate model for predicting placement.

CASE STUDIES

Franklin County Children Services

Agency Description

Franklin County Children Services (FCCS) is typical of urban programs in this study in providing a great number of supportive services to families, but atypical in teaming all its cases. FCCS is a family-oriented public agency located in Grove City, Ohio. It is a unit of county government with statutory responsibility and authority for providing child welfare services. A policy-making Board of Directors, composed of eleven members appointed by the County Commissioner, governs FCCS.

The purpose of the Home-Based Family Centered (HBFC) program is to provide time-limited (6 to 9 months) in-home intensive services to families at a time when a decision has been made to place the child. The program is viewed as a last resort to prevent placement and is also used for reunification of families whose children are already in placement.

FCCS is one of four agencies delivering home-based services under an umbrella program. FCCS administers the program and purchases services from three private agencies, as well as providing two home-based teams directly through the HBFC unit. This program is considered unique in that public and private agencies combined efforts to write a grant proposal for start-up funds. As a result the Columbus Foundation awarded $40,000 to the project, with FCCS designated as the lead agency. A community mental health center, a settlement house, and a family service agency completed the consortium. The program began in 1983 as a two-year pilot project with an outside consultant evaluating the program. At the end of eighteen months, 90 percent of the families served by the pilot project remained intact, compared to 41 percent of those referred but not accepted for services. Positive behavioral change was also observed in families served by the program.

Currently the FCCS unit consists of two teams, each composed of an MSW social worker, a BA/BS-level family specialist, and a team supervisor. The social workers are responsible for psychosocial diagnoses and case plans; the family specialists provide concrete services and skills development. Intervention and assessment are based on a casework model that draws on cognitive and behavioral theory, learning theory, reality therapy, and family counseling. The team also does life-space work and advocacy. Much of the focus is on socialization and reparenting to develop trust and help the family find its own strengths and community support systems. Workers cite three unique aspects of the home-based program: their ability to spend more time with families due to reduced caseloads; their participation in family activities and recreation; and their ability to provide financial assistance, which is much more accessible than in a traditional service unit.

Site-Specific Findings

The children served by the HBFC program were slightly older than those seen by SCAN, and more of the highest-risk children in the families (27%) had been placed before. Nearly every family had a child at risk of imminent placement, and more families had multiple children at high risk than at any other site. Families were more often referred for adult relationship problems or court-ordered into service than at SCAN. Compared with other sites, the HBFC program had a higher proportion of referrals for physical abuse and adult substance abuse (see Appendix F).

Since each family in the HBFC program was seen by a team including an MSW and a BA-level worker, families received many more supportive services than in other programs, including family planning, transportation, homemakers, and housekeeping services. Families also received more crisis intervention, recreational services, and psychiatric and psychological services of all kinds. With two workers on each case, families in the HBFC program had twice as many contacts in the first three months of family-based services as those at SCAN, more than in any other site.

HBFC families experienced a much higher rate of worker turnover than in other programs, and only 64 percent of the primary caretakers attended most or all of the sessions. This did not prevent the families, however, from achieving high rates of change in behavior, material resources, use of services, and family's perception of the problem. Cases were more likely to be closed because case goals had been achieved in this program than in any of the others. HBFC workers were especially effective in using parent education to prevent placement in neglect cases. All the families changed for the better in at least one area of functioning, and only 7 percent got worse, the lowest proportion in the study. Although 25 percent of the cases ended in placement at the termination of services, the highest overall placement rate in the study, children in the HBFC program were most likely to be placed with a friend or relative. Finally, a long-range plan was recorded for at least one child in nearly two-thirds of the placement cases.

Case Examples

The Anderson Family

The Anderson family consisted of Bob and Jane, both aged 23, and two children, six-year-old Jill and one-year-old Jimmy. The family was referred by the child protective services unit for founded physical abuse against Jill. Jill was Jane's biological child and Bob's stepchild; Jimmy was the biological child of both parents. Bob, with a tenth-grade education, was employed as a custodian at a local factory, while Jane was a full-time homemaker. Their income was quite low and this created continual financial strain in the household. Although neither child had ever been placed out of the home previously, both were assessed as being at high risk at the time of intake. The child protective service worker noted that in addition to the physical abuse, inadequate housing and acting out by the six year old were problems in need of attention.

The social worker assigned to this case was Mary, a 35-year-old black woman with a master's degree in social work and about seven years of experience in child welfare services. Mary's caseload averaged ten families, most of whom were low-income, many experiencing problems with neglect, physical and emotional abuse, family conflict, inadequate housing, chemical dependence, marital problems, child behavior difficulties, and depression. At the time she was surveyed, Mary personally felt very satisfied with her job, though she characterized turnover and morale in the agency as moderate. She believed that the largest contributing factor to turnover was stress related to the demands of family-based services.

Case goals established between Mary and the Andersons focused on preventing further physical abuse and neglect and reducing Jill's disruptive behaviors. Both Bob and Jane's scores on the Child Well-Being Scales revealed a high level of parental functioning, in terms of motivation, cooperation, capacity for child care and providing stable caretaking. Areas that needed some work included acceptance and expectations of the children, recognition of their own role in the problems the family was having, and learning to express approval toward the children. The team provided a number of services to the Anderson family. As the professional social worker, Mary provided marital counseling to address the strained relationship between Bob and Jane. In addition, Mary was responsible for individual and family counseling, advocacy, and arranging for psychological testing of Jill and community mental health services. The family specialist, Mae, worked with the parents in role modeling of more effective disciplinary techniques, important in preventing the recurrence of physical abuse, helping to build their self-esteem through teaching, assisting the family in planning recreational activities, and providing transportation when needed.

The Anderson family was seen for eleven months, mostly in their home, although at times meetings occurred at other community agencies which were involved. Jane and the children attended most of the sessions, demonstrating a high degree of engagement in the service plan. While not as involved as the rest of the family, Bob still attended more than half of the meetings with the family-based workers. Contacts with the family-based team occurred once a week or more in the first three months of service, and then tapered off to twice a month by the end of the service period. Although there was one founded report of child neglect filed during this eleven-month period, no subsequent reports of abuse and no placements had occurred. By termination the family was assessed as having made substantial changes in behavior, affect, structure, dynamics, use of services, and material resources.

In Mary's opinion, the most important indicators of success in family-based services are the family becoming stabilized, remaining together, achieving case objectives, and making positive changes in interaction, behavior, and communication. By these standards, she considered about 95 percent of the families she worked with in the family-based program to have had successful outcomes. The Anderson family was among those successes.

The Kelley Family

The Kelley family was referred by a child protective services worker following a substantiated report of physical abuse by Susan, a 35-year-old divorcee, against her three teenaged daughters: 17-year-old Allana, 14-year-old Jenna, and 12-year-old Lara. The referring worker also noted emotional abuse and neglect in the family. All three daughters had previously experienced multiple out-of-home placements in foster care and informally with relatives, and Jenna and Lara had also been in residential treatment before. At the time of intake to family-based services, all were considered to be at high risk of placement.

Susan, with less than an eighth grade education and no employment history, was supporting her daughters with Aid to Families with Dependent Children. Her ratings on the Child Well-Being Scales placed her at a fairly low level of parental functioning. In particular, the stability of her parenting, her excessive use of physical discipline and poor supervision, and acceptance and approval of her children were highly problematic. She showed little recognition of her own role in contributing to the family's difficulties and did not appear to be highly motivated to avert placement or to work with the family-based service team.

The team assigned to this case included a paraprofessional homemaker and Mary, a 35-year-old black woman with a master's degree in social work, who also served the Anderson family described above. The case objectives established between the family-based team and the Kelleys focused on improving the daughters' self-esteem, reducing their uncontrollable behavior at home, and preventing the recurrence of abuse and neglect in the family. The team directly provided numerous interventions including individual, family, and group counseling; teaching and homework assignments; advocacy; case management; information and referral; transportation; arranging for emergency cash and housing; money management counseling; and recreational activities. The Kelleys also received psychiatric evaluations, outpatient counseling, and day treatment services from the community mental health center. In addition, Child Protective Services remained involved with the Kelleys throughout the service period, as another report of abuse was filed during this time.

Despite more than ten months of service consisting of several weekly contacts in the home or elsewhere in the community, the team was unable to prevent the eventual placement of the two younger children with a relative. Allana moved out on her own at the age of eighteen. Susan had attended very few of the counseling sessions, while the daughters had attended nearly all of them. Although there had been some positive changes in the girls' behavior and some improvement in the family's use of available services, Susan's level of understanding and motivation had not changed. The service period was also marked by considerable chaos, with Susan changing residences a number of times and an additional founded incident of abuse. An alternative to keeping the Kelley family intact was chosen as being in the best interests of all family members.

In Mary's opinion, the timing of services and the family's capacity and motivation to change were more important contributing factors to failure than inaccurate case assessment, intensity of services, or lack of needed supportive services. She believed that the most important indicators of failure in family-based services were no positive change or stabilization in the family, failure to achieve case objectives, and out-of-home placement of a child. By these standards she considered only about 5 percent of the families she worked with as failures. The Kelley family met these criteria.

RELATION TO OTHER STUDIES

Although they included more employed and married caretakers, families referred for physical abuse of children were also more likely to contain stepparents and to have marital problems, both risk factors identified in previous research (Garbarino, 1989; Garbarino et al., 1986; Hartley et al., 1989). Health problems appeared to create additional stress in these families (Conger et al., 1979). While placement is less predictable in cases involving physical abuse (Cicchetti & Carlson, 1989, p. 140 ff), it is also less determined by historical factors and more amenable to preventive interventions, especially marital counseling and role modeling. These interventions relate directly to the marital conflict and lack of parenting skills that have been associated with physical abuse in prior studies (Gelles & Maynard, 1987; Hartley et al., 1989; Reid et al., 1981). The level of parental functioning and the degree to which caretakers are engaged in services, however, remain important determinants of case outcome (Justice & Justice, 1982, 1990; Ory & Earp, 1980).

The specifics of interventions within a family systems model have been less fully developed for cases involving neglect and physical abuse than for sexual abuse. Observing that research and demonstrations involving prevention and early intervention have replaced earlier efforts to identify effective interventions in cases of physical abuse, Kaufman and Rudy (1991) identify four promising treatment approaches—social learning, ecobehavioral, family-centered home-based, and multisystemic—which merit more research and development. The programs in this study were eclectic, integrating aspects of each of the above approaches.

Multisystemic therapy has been found to be more effective than parent education groups in improving parenting (Brunk, Henggeler, & Whelan, 1987). Role modeling to teach parenting skills and marital counseling within a systemic context have also been helpful in preserving physically abusive families (Dale & Davies, 1985). In one of the few studies of family-based services to examine the different types of child maltreatment separately, researchers in Oregon found the family treatment model to be most effective with physical abuse. Specifically, the use of multiple impact therapy was rated as very effective in physical abuse cases. Physically abusing families also expressed more satisfaction with services than other families (Hartley et al., 1989).

Despite their differences, several of the predictors of placement or nonplacement cut across different programs. Risk to the child, the functioning and cooperation of the primary caretaker, and a history of prior placements have all been found to correlate with placement in past studies of child protective (Meddin, 1984) and family preservation services (Fraser, Pecora, & Haapala, 1989; Yuan & Struckman-Johnson, 1991). This consistency, however, should not lead to the conclusion that some " 'hard core' parents . . . are virtually untreatable" (Green, Power,

Steinbook, & Gaines, 1981), since placement remains a rare and hard-to-predict event.

Instead, the continuing inconsistency in research results regarding physical abuse should be taken as evidence of the need for further differentiation among subtypes of abusing families. Whether disaggregated by age (Garbarino, 1989) or parenting style (Oldershaw et al., 1989), this approach may help to detect more consistent predictive factors and to identify interventions effective within specific subgroups.

Chapter Five

SEXUAL ABUSE:
THE MOST CONTROVERSIAL CHILD WELFARE
PROBLEM

Both the wisdom of preserving families in which sexual abuse is a problem and of treating perpetrators in the context of the family have been questioned. Indeed, many family-based programs refuse treatment to families if the perpetrator of sexual abuse is living in the home and denying responsibility for the abuse. However, many also accept and successfully treat families in which sexual abuse is the primary problem. More commonly affecting older children than other forms of child maltreatment, sexual abuse is complicated since it can occur outside the immediate family (Daro, 1988, p. 38). Therefore, family-based services take a variety of forms and focal points.

OVERVIEW OF SELECTED LITERATURE

Because of the intimate nature of sexual abuse and the secrecy that typically surrounds it, it is difficult to detect and describe in a reliable way (Daro, 1988, p. 105). Sexual abuse appears in all socioeconomic strata and seems to result much less directly from environmental stress than do physical abuse or neglect (Daro, 1988, p. 65; Finkelhor, 1984; Tzeng & Schwarzin, 1990). Indeed, one of the few studies using a sample representative of the general population found incest to be more common in higher-income families (Russell, 1986).

Central to most studies of incest or intrahousehold abuse has been the relationship between the perpetrator and the victim's mother (Glaser & Frosh, 1988, pp. 42–47; Gomes-Schwartz, Horowitz, & Cardarelli, 1990, pp. 115–127). Poor marital relationships have often been implicated in the etiology of sexual abuse, and marital breakup may precede as well as follow sexual abuse (Gomes-Schwartz et al., 1990, pp. 118, 143–145; Sirles & Lofberg, 1990).

A distant or conflictual relationship between the child and the mother has also been thought to contribute to sexual abuse. Although most mothers take active steps to protect their children once sexual abuse has been discovered, in a minority of cases mothers ally with the abuser rather than the child (Everson, Hunter, Runyon, Edelsohn, & Coulter, 1989; Glaser & Frosh, 1988, p. 45; Gomes-Schwartz et al., 1990, p. 118; Sirles & Lofberg, 1990). Denial of the abuse has been identified both as a treatment problem (Hoke, Sykes, & Winn, 1989; Orenchuk-Tomiuk, Matthey, & Pigler-Christensen, 1990) and as a reason for placement (Everson et al., 1989; Pellegrin & Wagner, 1990). In particular, the mother's denial and lack of support has been identified as the best predictor of both placement and psychopathology in the child (Everson et al., 1989; Hunter, Coulter, Runyan, & Everson, 1990).

Finally, significant child behavior problems accompany sexual abuse: school problems, problems with peers, juvenile offenses, inappropriate sexual behavior, and substance abuse have all been associated with this form of abuse (Finkelhor, 1990; Gomes-Schwartz et al., 1990; Singer, Petchers, & Hussey, 1989).

Spurred by an influx of research funds in the mid-1980s, more attention has been given to the treatment of sexual abuse than to physical abuse or neglect (Kaufman & Rudy, 1991). A recent survey of program characteristics found that two-thirds of sexual abuse treatment programs treated the family and the victim together, excluding only perpetrators who denied responsibility for the abuse (Keller, Cicchinelli, & Gardner, 1989).

There is considerable controversy about when and if specific family members should be included in conjoint treatment. Coleman and Collins (1990) define the three general approaches to treatment in sexual abuse cases as child advocacy, family systems, and reconstructive. The first approach emphasizes the separation of either the perpetrator or the child from the family; the second stresses preserving the family unit including the perpetrator; the third approach offers a middle position including aspects of both of the other two.

Defenders of a family therapy approach have argued that removal of the perpetrator is not inconsistent with a family systems approach and can help not only to protect the child, but to ally the mother with the child and empower her as a parent (Fish & Faynik, 1989). Family therapy can also be coordinated with legal interventions by protective services and the courts in families where this is necessary to ensure the child's safety and appropriate treatment (Cornille, 1989). Removal of the child, however, continues to be the most frequent response to intrafamilial sexual abuse (Hunter et al., 1990).

STUDY SAMPLE

Cases from the nine programs included in the child maltreatment sample were classified according to the reason for their referral. If more than one type of maltreatment was reported, the most important (the first one listed) was used to classify the case. Using this method, 50 sexual abuse cases were identified in this sample of nine agencies. Of these, 86 percent were referred primarily for sexual abuse. Five (10%) of the cases referred primarily for sexual abuse also involved physical abuse and three (6%) also involved neglect.

Almost half of the sexual abuse cases came from the Children's Services Division of the Oregon Department of Human Services. Within Oregon, the majority of sexual abuse cases were seen in Multnomah County Intensive Family Services, a private agency offering in-home family treatment services in the Portland area (Table V–I). The others were from five publicly-administered IFS programs that offered both in-office and in-home services using a family treatment model of service. Although these programs are profiled in the following chapter, since at the time of this study their services were focused primarily on juvenile offenders, the Multnomah IFS program and two of its sexual abuse cases are described in this chapter. It is notable that 78 percent of the sexual abuse cases were seen in programs following a family treatment model and that out of 50 cases, only two or three in each home-based program involved sexual abuse.

STUDY FINDINGS

Sexual abuse cases differed in several respects from cases involving neglect or physical abuse (Tables V–II and V–III). They contained the oldest caretakers and children and the vast majority were white. Nearly two-thirds of the highest risk children in sexual abuse cases were female. Fewer children were at risk of imminent placement, primarily because the perpetrator was not in the home; however, more of the highest risk children had been placed before. Nearly a third of the sexually abusing families had experienced a divorce within the last year. The family was

Table V-I
SEXUAL ABUSE SAMPLE BY SITE

	Sexual Abuse		All Maltreatment	
Agency	n = 50	%	n = 208	%
Intensive Family Services, Multnomah County, OR	12	24.0	20	9.6
Oregon Children's Services Division	10	20.0	19	9.1
Iowa Department of Human Services	9	18.0	25	12.0
Dakota County Human Services, MN	4	8.0	21	10.1
Boulder County Social Services, CO	4	8.0	15	7.2
Iowa Children & Family Services	3	6.0	20	9.6
SCAN, Philadelphia, PA	3	6.0	35	16.8
Franklin County Children Services, OH	3	6.0	38	18.3
Lutheran Social Services, MN	2	4.0	15	7.2

Note. Unweighted; *n*'s vary in subsequent tables due to weighting and missing data; percentages may not total 100 due to rounding.

significantly less likely to contain two adults if the perpetrator of the sexual abuse was a parent or an adult acquaintance of the parent.

Table V-II
CHARACTERISTICS OF SEXUAL ABUSE CASES: PERCENTAGES

	Sexual Abuse		All Maltreatment	
Family Characteristics	n = 52	%	n = 219	%
Non-White	50	9.0*	207	20.4
Divorced	52	32.1	219	23.1
Prior Placement	50	34.5*	207	21.6

*$p < .05$.

With the exception of marital and family relationship problems, most of the issues presented by these families had to do with the children: parent-child conflict, problems with peers or school, or juvenile offenses (Table V–IV). Physical abuse was also found to be a problem in 16 percent of the cases, but neglect was a problem in only 7 percent of the sexual abuse cases. Although family-child relationship (82%) and child behavior (57%) problems were found more often in sexual abuse cases

Table V-III
CHARACTERISTICS OF SEXUAL ABUSE CASES: AVERAGES

Family Characteristics	Sexual Abuse $n = 52$	*m/sd*	All Maltreatment $n = 219$	*m/sd*
Primary Caretaker				
Age	49	35.4†	208	31.6
CWBS – Parental		6.4		7.9
Disposition Subscale	52	75.7†	217	72.9
		11.5		13.4
Number of Children at High Risk[a]	52	.6†	219	.9
		.7		1.1
Age of Highest-Risk Child[b]	52	12.6*	215	9.3
		4.1		5.2

[a]Range: 0–3, 0–5. [b]Range: 0–19.
*$p < .01$.
†$p < .05$ with neglect.

than in other types of maltreatment, these differences were not statistically significant.

Table V-IV
PROBLEMS IN SEXUAL ABUSE CASES

Problems[a]	Sexual Abuse $n = 52$	All Maltreatment $n = 219$
Peer/School	53.5*	39.0
Status Offense/Delinquency	47.9**	18.8
Health/Mental Health	25.2*	40.7
Physical Abuse	15.8**	43.8
Neglect	6.7**	39.0

Note. Percentages.
[a]Coded: 1 = problem, 0 = no problem.
*$p < .05$. **$p < .001$.

Services were primarily oriented toward helping the families use other longer-term sources of counseling (Table V–V). Sexual abuse cases were distinctive in receiving more volunteer services and in participating more in self-help groups and activities. They were the least likely to receive paraprofessional, parent education, and child protective services concurrently with other family-based services. Additional reports of child maltreatment were recorded for 24 percent of the families. Services were generally less intensive in sexual abuse than in neglect cases (Table V–VI).

Table V–V
OBJECTIVES AND SERVICES IN SEXUAL ABUSE CASES

	Sexual Abuse n = 52	All Maltreatment n = 219
Case Objectives		
Use Counseling	60.7***	38.1
Adult Behavior	9.7***	30.8
Services		
Protective Services	43.2*	56.8
Self Help/Volunteer	41.1**	25.5
Parent Education	25.7*	38.8
Role Modeling	19.6†	30.2
Transportation	14.9†	25.1
Paraprofessional	13.5*	27.1

Note. Percentages.
[a]Range: 0–12, 0–21. [b]Range: 0–10.
*$p < .05$. **$p < .01$. ***$p < .001$.
†$p < .05$ with neglect.

Overall only 15 percent of the sexual abuse cases ended in placement and 70 percent or more made positive changes in family relationships, behavior, and emotional climate of the family. Sexual abuse cases changed most in family structure and hierarchy, and least in material resources when compared to physical abuse and neglect cases. These successful outcomes were accomplished with a high rate of participation in services by the primary caretaker, but a very low rate of participation by second adults (Table V–VI).

Factors Related to Placement

In order to determine the most important factors in avoiding placement in sexual abuse cases, a series of seven discriminant analyses covering different domains (family demographics and history, characteristics of second adults, resource problems, adult problems, child problems, interventions, and involvement in treatment) were performed. Although sexual abuse cases shared some predictors of placement such as initial

Table V-VI
INTENSITY OF SERVICE IN SEXUAL ABUSE CASES

Intensity		*Sexual Abuse* $n = 52$	*All Maltreatment* $n = 219$
Total Number of Services[a]	m	10.3	12.5
	sd	6.6	8.1
In-Home Contacts in First Month[b]	m	2.6†	4.1
	sd	3.2	4.2
In-Office Contacts in First Month[c]	m	1.2†	.7
	sd	1.7	1.3
Total Number of Contacts in First Three Months[d]	m	11.5†	14.8
	sd	7.9	11.3
Length of Service (months)[e]	m	6.5	6.6
	sd	3.5	5.0
Attended Most Sessions			
Primary Caretaker	%	87.4*	74.1
Second Adult[f]	%	22.6*	39.9

[a]Range: 1–28, 0–45. [b]Range: 0–12, 0–21. [c]Range: 0–10. [d]Range: 1–42, 1–67. [e]Range: 0–15.2, 0–29.4.
[f]$n = 150$.
*$p < .05$.
†$p < .05$ with neglect.

risk of placement, lower functioning of caretakers, and poor family-child relationships with physical abuse and neglect cases, the discriminant analysis of the seven different domains revealed several unique relationships.

As in physical abuse, the presence of a second adult in sexual abuse cases was important, but in predicting an outcome of placement rather than nonplacement. Although the primary caretakers in sexual abuse cases were the most motivated and compliant at the outset of services, assisting them to support their children and to obtain further services was essential for placement prevention. Simply referring the families for further services was not an effective preventive measure. Employed mothers with employed spouses who were involved in treatment were the most likely to have children placed. The specific problems presented by the adults or the children had little impact on outcome.

Combining these characteristics into a single predictive model for sexual abuse cases, cases ending in placement more often included a child at imminent risk of placement (84%), a less compliant primary caretaker, a second adult at most or all of the sessions (41%), and an employed primary caretaker (62%) (see Appendix E). Placement prevention, on the other hand, was associated with a case objective of increasing the family's use of outside counseling services, which occurred in two-thirds of the successful cases. Together the eleven characteristics included in the sexual abuse model correctly classified all the nonplacement cases and 75 percent of the placement cases.

CASE STUDIES

Intensive Family Services

Agency Description

In contrast to the programs described in the previous two chapters, the IFS program in Multnomah County, Oregon, served families with older children, including a large number of sexual abuse and juvenile offense cases, many of whom had prior placements. The program followed a family treatment model with brief, focused services. Since the Multnomah IFS program is described in more detail in the following chapter on family-based services in juvenile justice cases, only those features most relevant to treating sexual abuse cases will be presented here.

The IFS program in Multnomah County was one of four pilot projects begun in 1980 through a legislative initiative in Oregon (see Chapter Six for more details). This program serves families in the most populated and urban county in Oregon, including part of the Portland metropolitan area. At about the same time the IFS program was begun, a separate sexual abuse treatment program was established to provide individual and group treatment to child victims and nonoffending parents. Until a coordinated protocol was established in 1987, there was some tension between the family systems approach in IFS and the child advocacy perspective of the CSD sexual abuse treatment program.

During the study period, the IFS program operated out of the public Children's Services Division branch office. Cases are referred by a CSD social service worker who retains case management responsibilities. Services are provided to families for a maximum of three months initially, but can be extended on a case-by-case basis. Each worker serves a minimum of nine families at a time, and service is delivered primarily in families' homes.

In keeping with the program's family treatment orientation, service begins with an in-depth family assessment in which the therapist develops an hypothesis for understanding the whole family system; this forms the basis for strategies and interventions. Treatment focuses on restructuring the way family members respond to the abused child and on creating new ways for them to understand their behavior. The majority of cases receive cotherapy, often with one therapist directing and the other observing the session.

Site-Specific Findings

In most respects, the IFS program in Multnomah County was very like the rest of the CSD projects, with a somewhat different client population. Serving the Portland metropolitan area, Multnomah IFS saw more minority families and more unemployed caretakers than the other CSD sites (see Appendix F for comparative tables). Over two-thirds of the highest-risk children had prior placements and 79 percent were judged to be at risk of imminent placement. Only a little more than half (54%) of the sexual abuse cases, however, contained a child at risk of imminent placement.

Multnomah IFS families had the lowest-functioning children and the second lowest-functioning caretakers in the study. There were no intact two-parent families among the sexual abuse cases and half had experienced a divorce in the previous year. Fewer primary caretakers were employed than in other study sites, and families were referred more often for sexual abuse and child substance abuse. Referral rates for delinquency, status offenses, adult substance abuse, family relationship problems, and parent-child conflict were also higher than average. The sexual abuse cases had an average of six different problems, two more than other types of cases. Associated problems included a mentally impaired child, an income below poverty level, and moving in the past year.

The Multnomah County program most often delivered services in the families' homes, with an average of six contacts in the first three months of service. The median length of service was 3.5 months. Self-help services, parent education, accompanying family members to appointments, and advocacy services were provided much more often to sexual abuse cases than to other types of cases served by IFS. On average, sexual abuse cases received six different kinds of service, nearly twice as many as other types of families.

Primary caretakers in sexual abuse cases were more compliant with treatment than those in other cases, and attended most or all of the sessions. The rate of participation of the child at highest risk was double for sexual abuse (82%) compared to other kinds of cases (44%), while the participation of second adults was nearly nonexistent (3%).

In Multnomah IFS 15 percent of the families experienced placement at the end of service, most of them in foster homes, group homes, or institutions. Over 80 percent of the sexual abuse cases showed positive changes in behavior, generational boundaries, relationships, emotional climate, and perception of their problems. A fifth of the families became worse in at least one area, and two-thirds required continuing services after placement.

All the children in sexual abuse cases who ended up in placement had been placed before and only 25 percent of those who had to be placed had attended most or all of the treatment sessions. In contrast, only half of the nonplacement cases had prior placements, and 87 percent of the highest-risk children regularly participated in IFS services. All the second adults involved in the placement cases were employed and none were coresidential spouses. None of the cases that identified increasing the family's use of outside counseling services as an objective ended in placement.

Case Examples

The Jones Family

The Jones family, Susan and Robert, a married couple who had recently separated after a founded incident of sexual abuse by Robert against two of his sons, was referred to family-based services by the Children's Services Division. The Jones children, 13-year-old Bob Jr., 11-year-old Jane, 9-year-old Jim, and 6-year-old Ralph, were all living with their mother, who did not work outside of the home. Robert Sr. had moved into a separate residence. None of the children had ever been in out-of-home placement previously, and at the time of intake none of the children were considered to be at imminent risk of placement. The two sexual abuse victims were Bob Jr. and Jim.

In addition to the presenting problem, the referring worker noted that Robert Sr. had a history of mental health problems, that the parents had been experiencing severe marital conflict, and that the childrens' behavior was out of their mother's control.

The family-based services worker assigned to the case, Alice, was a 35-year-old married woman with a masters' degree in social work and about five years of experience in family counseling at the agency. Carrying an average caseload of twelve families, Alice worked with families either in the home or in the office, depending on the case. Among the types of families she worked best with were those experiencing sexual or physical abuse, delinquency or status offenses, child behavior problems, parent-child conflict, marital conflict, and unresolved divorce issues.

Upon assessment, Alice noted that all of the children had been caught up in the severe conflict that had characterized their parents' relationship. Susan was having a difficult time managing her four children, all but one of whom were displaying problems at home, with school attendance, and with peers. In her favor, from the beginning Susan was cooperative with services and motivated, if somewhat lacking in self-confidence. The case goals established mutually between Alice and the Joneses included setting up ongoing sources of counseling for the children and mental health care for Robert Sr., involving the children in the Big Brothers/Big Sisters program, and working with Susan in increasing her assertiveness as a parent. Family-based services proceeded without any further involvement by child protective services.

During a three-month service period, Alice went to the Jones's home, almost weekly at first, then every other week until the case goals had been largely achieved. Susan and the children had attended all of the treatment sessions, while Robert Sr. had been involved to a lesser extent. Susan's skills in managing her children had improved substantially, and Robert Sr. had followed through with mental health counseling. The childrens' behavior had improved considerably both at home and in the community.

Alice defined success in family-based services as the family being empowered to make their own decisions, children's needs being appropriately met, and the family being together at the time of case closure. She regarded family-based services as being unsuccessful when a family failed to make changes or to become stabilized. The Joneses were successful by Alice's definition, with Susan functioning more effectively as a parent and Robert Sr. engaged in a program of ongoing counseling to meet his more extensive needs.

The Morrison Family

The Morrisons, a family consisting of a divorced mother, Deborah, aged 34, and three children: 13-year-old Susan, 10-year-old Mark, and 7-year-old Larry, were referred to Multnomah IFS by the Children's Services Division due to sexual abuse of Susan and her subsequent acting out behaviors. Deborah seemed to be of limited intellectual functioning and had been through a stressful year of divorce with a reduced standard of living due to loss of both her partner and her job. At the time of intake to family-based services, she was once again employed full-time in a local factory. The perpetrator of the abuse, a boyfriend of Deborah's, was no longer on the scene at the time of referral to family-based services, and Susan was living in an emergency shelter. This was not Susan's first experience in out-of-home care; she had spent some time in a residential treatment center and in shelter care previously due to behavioral problems and physical abuse.

The family-based worker assigned to the case was Maria, a 35-year-old married woman with two children and a master's degree in counseling. Maria had been working with Multnomah County's family-based services program for about five years at the time she was surveyed, and worked mostly with white, middle-income two-parent and step families. Maria saw almost all of her client families in their own homes, and generally carried a caseload of eight or nine families.

When Maria first met with the Morrisons, Deborah did not appear to be very motivated. In addition to the presenting problems, physical abuse, delinquency, and severe conflict between Deborah and Susan, Susan was also having difficulties in school, with teachers as well as peers. Case objectives established early in the service period included improving communication and stress management skills, and dealing with the effects of the perpetrator's alcohol abuse on the family, as well as Susan's sexually acting out behaviors in the community. During the course of service, it was discovered that Susan had sexually abused her brother, Mark; additional case goals were established to involve both mother and children in support groups for coping with sexual abuse and alcoholic family members.

The Morrisons were seen in their home every other week for eleven months. All family members, including the children's father, participated actively in treatment. Maria provided family therapy, case management, and referrals to a number of other community agencies including the community mental health center, a psychiatric treatment center, a substance abuse counseling center, and school social work services. During the service period, Susan was hospitalized briefly for psychiatric assessment and, subsequently, was placed in a foster home. The reason specified for terminating services was that the time limit had been reached.

There were many positive outcomes in this case: a number of case goals had been achieved, including attendance at support groups, progress towards dealing with the sexual abuse incidents, increased understanding of the role of alcoholism in the family, and improved stress management and communication skills. The family was assessed as having improved in many areas of functioning, including dynamics, affect, perception of the problem, and structure. However, progress was still not sufficient to avert out-of-home placement.

Maria believed that referring families to other counseling services beyond those offered by IFS, maintaining a philosophy of keeping children in their own homes, and promoting self-determination are important aspects of preventive services. She recommended placement in only about 2 percent of the families she served, usually because a child was at risk of serious harm due to his/her own behavior or parenting was inappropriate to the needs of the child. The Morrison case is an example of a family that, despite being referred to and participating in a number of different counseling programs, was not successful in avoiding out of home placement. Susan's sexual abuse and psychiatric problems, as well as her mother's limited abilities, were important factors contributing to the outcome of this case.

RELATIONSHIP TO OTHER STUDIES

Families experiencing sexual abuse presented a strikingly different profile from other maltreating families, with high rates of divorce and prior placements, perhaps related to the abuse itself (Gomes-Schwartz et al., 1990, pp. 52, 143, 118; Hunter et al., 1990; Sever & Janzen, 1982; Sirles & Lofberg, 1990). Although due to the absence of the perpetrator from the home most of the children were not at risk of imminent placement, they did have a considerable number of behavioral problems. Most caretakers were very motivated and cooperative with services, and successful cases were directed toward engaging families in long-term treatment (Daro, 1988, pp. 105–108; Gomes-Schwartz et al., 1990, pp. 163–65; Keller et al., 1989; Pellegrin & Wagner, 1990). A distinctive subset of characteristics was identified which made placement more likely. As in other studies, this research found that caretakers seen conjointly with spouses or significant others tended to be less compliant, increasing the likelihood of placement, particularly when both adults were employed (Daro, 1988, p. 38; Garbarino, 1989, p. 699; Glaser & Frosh, 1988, pp. 140–153; Green, 1988). In these cases, inappropriate inclusion of a perpetrator may have placed the child at risk and contributed to an outcome of placement (Daro, 1988, p. 121; Giaretto, 1982; Glaser & Frosh, 1988, pp. 140–153).

Our findings support the pivotal role of the mother in the outcome of sexual abuse cases. If she sides with the perpetrator who is also included in treatment, the child is likely to end up in placement (Hunter et al., 1990). Taking the child's side, however, often entails divorcing or separating from the perpetrator and a large decline in family income (Sirles & Lofberg, 1990; Weiss, 1984). That employed mothers with employed spouses were less likely to take this risk suggest that economic considerations are important even among higher-income families.

Chapter Six

FAMILY-BASED SERVICES
FOR JUVENILE OFFENDERS[1]

Even though it has been nearly forty years since the Gluecks established a link between juvenile delinquency and family structure and functioning (Glueck & Glueck, 1950), family treatment of youthful offenses is relatively new and still not widely practiced (Ulrici, 1983). Instead, most programs focus services on the individual offender and do not involve families in treatment (Geismar & Wood, 1986, pp. 35–36). Indeed, Geismar and Wood (1986) characterize the family as "the most underutilized resource in the corrections field, despite the fact that it has the greatest investment in the well-being of its young" (p. 215).

Ironically, many of the earliest family-based placement prevention and reunification programs, such as those in Iowa and Colorado, were begun in response to the juvenile justice reform movement of the late 1960s and early 1970s. In 1967 the President's Commission on Law Enforcement and the Administration of Justice recommended the adoption of community-based alternatives to incarceration, especially for status offenders, and this mandate was a contributing factor in the development of a growing number of family-oriented programs (Blomberg, 1983; Roberts, 1989; Sarri, 1983). The Juvenile Justice and Delinquency Prevention Act of 1974 also encouraged alternatives to incarceration and the formal processing of youthful offenders through the juvenile justice system (Roberts, 1989; Schwartz, 1989) and has led to funding for family-based programs to prevent out-of-home placement and to reunify children who have been placed.

The Adoption Assistance and Child Welfare Act of 1980 (P.L. 96-272) gave this trend further impetus. P.L.96-272 established a broad mandate for the development of preventive and reunification services for placement or potential placement cases in public social service systems. Recent research has made it clear that youthful offenders and their families are one of the key populations receiving these services (AuClaire & Schwartz,

87

1986; Haapala & Kinney, 1988; Nelson, 1990; Nugent, 1991; Showell, Hartley, & Allen, 1988; Stroul, 1988).

Juvenile crime is once more a national issue. More than two decades after the first wave of reform, proposals to change the way the criminal justice system deals with juveniles are resurfacing, reflecting many of the same problems that the first wave of reform attempted to solve. These proposals in their more popular form call for a return to a "tougher" stance toward juvenile criminals (Roberts, 1989; Schwartz, 1989). Yet the evidence from family- and community-based alternatives over the past decade, as well as data from the current study, suggests strongly that a family-based approach is effective and, indeed, essential to the successful treatment of juvenile offenders.

OVERVIEW OF SELECTED LITERATURE

Research on juvenile justice problems has consistently documented the importance of family issues. (See Tolan, Cromwell & Brasswell, 1986, and Ulrici, 1983, for reviews of the literature.) Youthful crime has been found to be related to a number of structural features of families such as single-parent households, large families, and working mothers; to the existence of multiple problems in the family, including mental retardation, mental illness, substance abuse, criminal behavior, and physical abuse; and to economic deprivation (Geismar & Wood, 1986, pp. 14–19, 26–29; Roberts, 1989, pp. 220–223). A recent meta-analysis of past studies, however, indicates that the association between single-parenthood and delinquency is largely due to sampling error (Wells & Rankin, 1991).

Of particular interest to family-based programs is the relationship of juvenile offenses to inadequate parenting and dysfunctional family relationships including lack of acceptance, affection, supervision and discipline of the child, and marital and parent-child conflict (Geismar & Wood, 1986, pp. 20–26, 43–50; Norland, Shover, Thornton, & James, 1979; Olweus, 1980; Roberts, 1989, p. 223; Simcha-Fagan, 1979; Simons, Robertson, & Downs, 1989; Tolan et al., 1986). In fact, family relationship problems, especially parental rejection, play a greater role than any external or structural factor in producing delinquency, especially in higher-income families who are less affected by environmental problems (Johnstone, 1978; Olweus, 1980; Simons et al., 1989).

Indeed there is strong evidence that the oppositional behavior often displayed by juvenile offenders is learned within families characterized by negativity and conflict, which may lead to the separation or divorce of the adults (Dadds, 1987) or the placement of the child (Spaid & Fraser, 1991). Severe economic deprivation and parental mental health problems also indirectly affect oppositional behavior through parental relationships. Regardless of income level, however, external stressors or supports may increase or soften the impact of family conflict on child behavior (Dadds, 1987).

Research on family interventions in juvenile justice cases has supported the effectiveness of a systemic family therapy approach, combined with behavioral interventions or skill training, in comparison with other interventions (Barton, Alexander, Waldron, Turner, & Warburton, 1985; Geismar & Wood, 1986, p. 145; Gordon, Arbuthnot, Gustafson, & McGreen, 1988; Mann, Borduin, Henggeler, & Blaske, 1990). Functional family therapy, the primary model for this type of intervention, grew out of research conducted by Alexander and Parsons (1973, 1982; Friedman, Tomko, & Utada, 1991; Lantz, 1985; Parsons & Alexander, 1973). One study demonstrated that, even when effective in reducing child behavior problems, parent training had to be supplemented by marital counseling to deal with conflict between the parents (Dadds, 1987). Conjoint family therapy and structural family therapy have also been used effectively with families of youthful offenders (Tavantzis, Tavantzis, Brown, & Rohrbaugh, 1985; Tolan et al., 1986; Ulrici, 1983).

STUDY SAMPLE

In the current study, data collected on families referred for status offenses or delinquency are examined to further assess the usefulness of a family-based approach with juvenile justice problems. This analysis includes all cases in which delinquency or status offense was a reason for referral, even if it was not the primary reason. In recording referral reasons from the case records, *delinquency* was coded if the child had committed an offense which would be a crime if committed by an adult. *Status offenses* included those offenses which would not be crimes if committed by adults, e.g., runaway, truant, ungovernable. Up to four reasons for referral were coded for each case in order of importance. In the 19 percent of families in which both status offenses and delinquent acts were given as reasons for referral, the one listed first was used to categorize the case.

Only eight programs are included in this chapter since one program

(SCAN) had no referrals for juvenile offenses. The analysis includes case record data on 159 families. Three-quarters of the cases came from five of the sites: the public and private Intensive Family Service programs in Oregon, Dakota County and Lutheran Social Services in Minnesota, and the Intensive Family Therapy program in Boulder, Colorado (Table VI–I). The Oregon program, a prototype of the family treatment model, will be described in a full case study in this chapter. The Intensive Family Treatment program in the Dakota County Human Services Department also follows a family treatment model and serves a large number of physical abuse cases. The Intensive In-Home Treatment Program of Lutheran Social Services, which serves 29 counties in west-central Minnesota, delivers home-based services in a largely rural area and is used as an example in Chapter Seven. Finally, the Intensive Family Therapy program operates out of three branch offices of the county-administered Department of Social Services in Boulder County, Colorado, and employs an office-based family treatment model of service delivery, integrating intensive family therapy into regular DSS service teams. It is discussed more fully in Chapter Nine.

Table VI-I
JUVENILE OFFENDERS SAMPLE BY SITE

Agency	n	Total $n = 159$ %	Status Offense $n = 88$ %	Delinquency $n = 71$ %
Dakota County Human Services, MN	32	20.1	38.0	5.7
Intensive Family Services, Multnomah County, OR	32	20.1	26.8	14.8
Lutheran Social Services, MN	24	15.1	7.0	21.6
Boulder County Social Services, CO	22	13.8	12.7	14.8
Oregon Children's Services Division	21	13.2	4.2	20.5
Iowa Department of Human Services	15	9.4	5.6	12.5
Iowa Children & Family Services	9	5.7	4.2	6.8
Franklin County Children Services, OH	4	2.5	1.4	3.4
SCAN, Philadelphia, PA	0	0	0	0

Note. Unweighted; n's vary in subsequent tables due to weighting and missing data. Percentages may not total 100 due to rounding.

STUDY FINDINGS

The Families

In families containing status offenders or delinquent children, an unusually high 20 percent of the primary caretakers were male, mostly single parents, unemployed men with working wives, or, in stepfamilies, the biological fathers of the children at risk of placement. With an average age of 39, the primary caretakers were older than those in the child protective services (CPS) cases discussed in the previous chapters. More than 90 percent were white, reflecting the fact that most of the cases were from rural or suburban areas in the Midwest or Northwest. These families were more affluent as a group than the CPS families, and two-thirds of the primary caretakers were employed full- or part-time. However, almost a third of the families had incomes below poverty level and almost half were headed by single parents. In delinquency cases primary caretakers were more likely to be separated or divorced, while those in status offense cases were more likely to be married (Table VI–II).

Table VI-II
FAMILY CHARACTERISTICS AND PROBLEMS IN JUVENILE OFFENSE CASES

	n	*Status Offense* *n* = 68	*Delinquency* *n* = 72
Family Characteristics			
Single Parent-Family	135	37.4	56.5*
Highest-Risk Child Male	140	39.6	62.8**
At Least One Step or Adopted Child	119	37.8**	13.4
Problems			
Parent-Child Conflict	140	63.1	80.8*
Child Behavior	140	62.4	79.4*
Child Peer Relations	140	46.0	67.2*
Court Referred	140	23.7	64.6***

Note. Percentages.
*$p < .05$. **$p < .01$. ***$p < .001$.

In families with a second adult, 43 percent of the children at highest risk of placement were the stepchildren or adopted children of the second adult. Significantly more status offenders came from stepfamilies. In keeping with their status as youthful offenders, the children at highest risk of placement were older than those in CPS cases, averaging 14 years of age. Overall, males and females were equally represented, although there were more male delinquents and more female status offenders (Table VI–II). At the beginning of family-based services, 79 percent were judged to be at risk of imminent placement.

Many of the families had been experiencing problems for some time; nearly a quarter had previously received services for six months or longer and 36 percent of the highest-risk children had one or more prior placements. Most of the families had problems with parent-child conflict and child behavior. Highest-risk children in delinquency cases were even more likely than status offenders to have problems with parent-child conflict, child behavior, and child peer relations (Table VI–II). Almost half the families were identified as having family relationship problems and 45 percent had marital problems. A third or fewer had problems with substance abuse (34%), sexual abuse (17%), or physical abuse (9%). Overall, the families with youthful offenders had fewer problems recorded than CPS families, an average of two compared to five. Referrals most frequently came from law enforcement personnel and 24 percent of the families were under a court order to receive services.

Services and Outcomes

In addition to family counseling, families most often received individual therapy (53%), case management (46%), and information and referral services (43%). One-third or fewer received school social work services (30%), marital counseling (28%), and child protective services (22%) (the majority from another unit in the agency). Status offense cases received significantly more marital counseling, information and referral services, case management services, child protective services, and services from a treatment team than delinquency cases (Table VI–III).

On average, families received services for five months, including about one face-to-face contact a week in the first month of service (Table VI–IV). Delinquency cases received an average of one more contact in the first month and nearly two more months of service than status offense cases. For 42 percent of cases involving juvenile offenses, the majority of contacts were in the office, and caseloads averaged 11. Families received, on average, seven different services.

Participation rates for individuals in the families demonstrate that the

Table VI-III
SERVICES IN JUVENILE OFFENSE CASES

Services	Status Offense $n = 68$	Delinquency $n = 72$
Case Management	56.4*	36.7
Information/Referral	54.1*	32.4
Marital Counseling	38.8*	18.8
Child Protective Services (within agency)	24.1*	9.0
Team Approach	60.2**	26.7

Note. Percentages.
*$p < .05$. **$p < .001$.

Table VI-IV
INTENSITY OF SERVICE IN JUVENILE OFFENSE CASES

Intensity		Status Offense $n = 68$	Delinquency $n = 72$
Total Number of Services[a]	*m*	7.3	6.8
	sd	4.9	4.6
Contacts in First Month[b]	*m*	3.8	5.0*
	sd	1.9	3.5
Total Number of Contacts in First Three Months[c]	*m*	10.1	12.1†
	sd	5.1	8.7
Length of Service (months)[d]	*m*	3.9	5.6*
	sd	2.2	5.3
Primary Caretaker Attended Most Sessions	%	75.3	79.4

[a]Range: 1–23, 1–28. [b]Range: 1–9, 1–15. [c]Range: 1–25, 2–36. [d]Range: 0–13.6, .5–33.9.
†$p = .11$. *$p < .05$.

services were truly family-based. Primary caretakers attended most or all of the family-based sessions in three-quarters of the cases. The highest-risk children and second adults (if they were living in the household) attended regularly in about half of the cases. The majority of families improved in half of the areas of functioning measured by the Family Systems Change Scale, including improvement in behavior, generational boundaries, relationships, emotional climate, and perception of the problem. For most, there was no change in material resources, use of available services, informal support network, level of community involvement in the family, or perception of the family within the community. At the termination of services, placement had occurred or was planned in only 20 percent of the status offense cases and 29 percent of the delinquency cases.

Factors Related to Placement

Since many of the characteristics that differ between placement and nonplacement cases overlap, discriminant analysis was used to identify those that were most important in predicting placement. Critics of the research on juvenile offenders have cited the need to distinguish between different types of offenses (Blomberg, 1983; Tolan et al., 1986), so separate analyses were conducted for delinquency and status offense cases (see Appendix E).

In *delinquency* cases, families experiencing placement were more likely to contain a child or adult with substance abuse problems (58%), to have a child at risk of imminent placement at intake (96%), and to be under high stress. Families that remained intact had higher-functioning caretakers (as measured by the Child Well-Being Scales). In successful cases over half (59%) the children at highest risk attended most or all the sessions and 89 percent were in a regular class in school. In *status offense* cases, families experiencing placement more often had a history of prior placements (36%) and services were more often focused on improving parenting (65%). Again, in families that remained intact, 70 percent of the highest-risk children attended most of the sessions. These and other less significant characteristics included in the statistical models were slightly more accurate in classifying nonplacement cases than placement cases, yet over 70 percent of the placements were predicted by the models.

In general, family and child characteristics were more important in predicting placement in delinquency cases (including school status, one of the characteristics of placement in status offenses cases as well), while service characteristics were more important in averting placement in status offense cases. Involvement of the highest-risk child in services was critical to family preservation in both types of cases, but half of the successful status offense cases received interventions that involved teaching skills in parenting, budgeting, coping, or social relations. Nearly two-thirds (62%) also had more than one worker on their case, either as cotherapists or a single worker receiving regular consultation from others on the team.

Nearly three-quarters of the status offense cases with objectives focused on parenting terminated in placement, compared to half of those who had parenting problems but no objectives specifically addressing them. Among status offense cases, objectives related to changing either parenting or family relationships seemed to be ineffective. The only case objective associated with lower placement rates was changing marital relationships. In delinquency cases, on the other hand, objectives relating to parenting, marital relationships, parent-child conflict, and child behavior were found more frequently among nonplacement cases. Delinquency cases with family relationship change objectives, however, had higher placement rates than those without such objectives.

These differences illustrate the importance of careful attention to goal setting in family-based services. Especially in adolescent cases, focusing on parenting or child behavior problems may reinforce the tendency to blame individuals rather than enabling the family to see their situation differently. On the other hand, setting objectives in the therapist's terms, for example, focusing directly on family relationships, may fail to engage families by denying them the opportunity to define service in their own terms. Directing attention to adult relationships reinforces parental responsibility without blaming any individual family member (Gordon et al., 1988).

In general, family-based services were more successful with status offenders than with delinquents, and there was less variation among programs in success rates (67% to 100% for status offense cases and 50% to 92% for delinquency cases). Only home-based programs geared primarily to families with younger children and problems of abuse and neglect had low success rates with status offenders.

CASE STUDIES

Children's Services Division

Agency Description

The application of a family-based approach to cases involving adolescents can be best illustrated by a detailed examination of the Children's Services Division (CSD) of the Oregon Department of Human Resources.

CSD was established in 1971 to provide child welfare services, juvenile corrections programs, and mental health services to families with out-of-control or delinquent children. CSD is state administered and operates out of four regions with branch offices in thirty-six counties.

In 1980, the first four Intensive Family Services (IFS) projects were implemented, based on a proposal approved by the 1979 legislature to divert money from the foster care budget. Although the original proposal had been to train CSD staff to provide family treatment, the legislature instead required the program to contract with private providers of family therapy.

Each of the four pilot projects was located in a different sociocultural area selected for a relatively high number of children in placement. Based on the pilot projects' success, the program was expanded in late 1981 and 1982 to sixteen projects. During this expansion, qualified private providers were not available in five of the counties. At these sites, new CSD employees were hired to provide Intensive Family Services. These five counties constituted the public CSD sites in this study. Project standards and regulations are the same for the in-house (public) projects as for the contracted programs. Two family treatment specialists operating out of the central Family-Based Services Program Office provide leadership, clinical consultation, training and program monitoring.

Intensive Family Services are characterized by small caseloads (maximum of 11) and a service period limited to ninety days, although this may be extended. The program operates from a family treatment model based on family systems theory. The behavior of one family member is seen as affecting the behavior of other family members: a "problem child" is viewed as an indication of a problem family with the child as the symptom bearer. Family treatment is directed toward relationships between parents, as well as between children and their parents. About a third of the work with families is accomplished through cotherapy.

Initially, most family treatment was in the home. After collecting outcome data for five years, however, it appeared that similar outcomes were obtained whether services were delivered in the home or in the office (Showell & White, 1990). Currently, some programs remain home-based, while others have moved toward providing services in the office. There is also a trend toward using a one-way mirror and video equipment in office-based work with families. Office-based services and multiple impact therapy have been found to be especially effective in treating delinquency (Hartley, Showell, & White, 1989). (See Balmer, Kogan,

Voorhees, Levin-Shaw, & Shapiro, 1979, for another example of in-office treatment of status offenders and their families).

Intensive Family Services in Multnomah County was one of the four pilot projects begun in 1980. Originally contracted to Catholic Family Services, the program incorporated in 1987. During the study period, the program operated out of the CSD branch office in Multnomah County, the most populated and urban county in Oregon and one of three counties comprising the Portland metropolitan area. Cases are referred by a CSD social service worker who retains case management responsibilities. Services are provided to families for a maximum of three months initially. Each worker serves at least nine families at a time, and service is based primarily in the family's home.

A majority of families served have an adolescent child who is seen as a high placement risk. Often these children are victims of physical or sexual abuse or have experienced serious neglect. In addition they may be delinquent, truant, suicidal, and/or chemically dependent. Because of the program's family therapy orientation, these problems are seen as systemic in nature.

Service begins with an in-depth family assessment in which the therapist develops an hypothesis for understanding the whole family system; this forms the basis for strategies or interventions. Families typically come to the attention of CSD when they are in crisis, a factor that is thought to increase the potential for change. Treatment focuses on restructuring the way in which family members respond to the "problem child," particularly the symptomatic behavior, and on creating new ways for them to understand this behavior. Originally, the program used Multiple Impact Therapy (Balmer et al., 1979) as its primary mode of treatment; currently MIT sessions lasting from four to six hours are used with only half of the families at some time during the course of treatment. The model used now draws heavily on both structural and strategic family therapy.

Site-Specific Findings

Study data reflect the program targets and standards set for IFS by the state. The highest-risk children in the CSD sites were older than the study average, and the primary caretakers were more likely to be divorced (Appendix F). Fewer families received public assistance or Medicaid. Serving the Portland metropolitan area, the private Multnomah County program had more minority group families and fewer employed caretakers than the other sites serving juvenile justice cases. The Multnomah County families had the lowest-functioning children and the second-lowest-functioning caretakers of all the study sites. Sexual abuse and child substance abuse were also more frequent than in the other sites. In averaging nine different problems, Multnomah County families were comparable to other urban families in the study.

Treatment in the IFS program was focused more on family dysfunction and less on parenting skill than in the other programs in the study. Case objectives more frequently included increasing the use of counseling services, a consistently important feature of successful cases in Oregon. Since an average of only three or four case objectives was established for each family, they covered a narrower range of problems than in other sites. A third to half of the families were seen primarily by two workers in cotherapy. Workers in the private agency program in Multnomah County used teaching and case management less often than those in the CSD branch offices. Otherwise, the services were very similar, although more often delivered in the families' homes.

On average, IFS families received fewer direct contacts (two to three a month) and fewer services than families in other programs. The majority of the contacts in the public CSD projects were in the office, although home visits were also frequent. Services continued for an average of four months in the public programs and five months (median of 3.5 months) in the private agency.

The Oregon sites had among the lowest placement rates in the study, 11 percent in the public CSD sites and 15 percent in Multnomah County. In the five office-based CSD projects an unusually high 79 percent of the children at highest risk of placement and 92 percent of the primary caretakers participated in most or all the sessions. Despite this high level of success, more than a third of the cases were closed due to the time limit rather than because either social workers or families felt satisfied that service goals had been accomplished.

Case Examples

To further illustrate the differences between families with presenting problems of status offenses and delinquency, two case scenarios will be presented. The Culver family terminated the program without a placement episode; the Moore family did experience child placement at the end of the service period. Both families were clients of the Multnomah

County IFS program. In the following case descriptions, some of the facts have been altered to protect clients' and workers' confidentiality.

The Culver Family

Elizabeth Culver, a divorced mother with three children, 13-year-old Tracey, 11-year-old Mark, and 8-year-old Karen, was referred to family-based services after discussing her situation with a caseworker at the Children's Services Division. Mark had frequently been truant at school, and both of the younger children were exhibiting behavioral problems at school. Mark was the child identified as being at high risk of placement. In addition to the school problems, the referring CSD worker noted physical abuse and child relationship problems as issues for this family.

The social worker assigned to the case was Bob, a 38-year-old M.S.W. who was married with three children at home. He had been working in family-based services with the IFS program for about four years and had previous child welfare and family counseling experience. Bob was accustomed to dealing with status offenses, delinquency, child behavioral problems, parent-child and marital conflict in his work with families, and believed families experiencing adolescent rebellion, families in crisis, and those voluntarily seeking services to be among the most promising candidates for family-based services. Bob believed that techniques such as outreach and accompanying family members to meetings for purposes of support, encouragement, and teaching negotiation skills were important in achieving case objectives. The case goals that Bob and the Culvers established involved improving communication between the family and the school and working on the childrens' problematic behaviors at school, teaching Elizabeth more effective ways of dealing with her childrens' behavior at home, and increasing the family's extended support network.

Bob and Ellen, another social worker at IFS who joined as cotherapist with this family, met with the Culvers in their home for seven months. Elizabeth and the children were active participants in the sessions. In addition to individual and family therapy, the cotherapists used homework assignments and teaching as interventions, and accompanied the family to meetings with the school to discuss the childrens' problems. A school social worker became involved with the family as well, which was important in resolving the truancy and school behavior problems. The case was closed because services were considered to have been successfully completed.

A number of improvements were noted in the family from the time of intake to termination. For the children these included positive change in the childrens' behavior both at home and at school and elimination of the school truancy. Elizabeth had increased her level of motivation and had become more aware of her own role in contributing to the family's difficulties. Her use of physical discipline was replaced with more effective means of changing her childrens' behavior.

According to Bob's philosophy of success in family-based services, it is important for adults to feel more competent in their roles, the family to be stabilized, childrens' needs to be appropriately met, and the family to feel better about themselves. The Culvers' progress in resolving problems with the school and at home would certainly characterize them as a successful case.

The Moore Family

Shirley Moore, a 31-year-old divorced, unemployed mother, and her daughter Cheryl, a 15-year-old high school dropout, were referred to Multnomah County IFS by CSD for Cheryl's delinquent activities, sexual abuse by her mother's boyfriend, substance abuse, and severe parent-child conflict, all of which were placing her at high risk of being removed from her home. Shirley was unable to enforce her rules or adequately supervise Cheryl, did not take responsibility for the family's problems, and preferred to have Cheryl placed. She blamed Cheryl's problems on her former boyfriend, but had failed to adequately protect Cheryl from being abused. Cheryl agreed that placement was the best solution to her conflictual relationship with her mother.

Cheryl had had several placement episodes prior to this referral: in a psychiatric hospital for emotional problems, in emergency shelter care for sexual abuse, and informal placement with a relative for status offenses. The Moores had received services from several agencies prior to this case opening, although this was their first referral to family-based services.

Sandy, a 35-year-old woman with a master's degree in counseling, was assigned as the worker on this case. Sandy had had about four years of experience in individual and family counseling, all within this private agency's family-based service program. Unlike Bob, the worker described in the previous case example, Sandy characterized her agency as having low to average morale and high turnover, and fair to good relationships with other community agencies. She intended to stay at her job for another year or two.

Sandy believed that families who have had children placed previously and who have extensive service histories are less likely to benefit from family-based services than are families new to the service system, voluntary clients, families in crisis, and families experiencing problems with substance abuse. Three-quarters or more of the families she saw had problems with emotional abuse, parent-child conflict, child behavior, marital relationships, dysfunctional family relationships, and/or multiple problems.

According to this worker, it is very important that service providers adhere to the philosophy that children are better off in their own homes, that families be encouraged toward self-determination, and that families be referred to other counseling services. She did not view concrete services, night/weekend and 24-hour coverage, or brief and intensive services as important in delivering effective preventive services. Sandy saw most of her families in their own homes, and carried an average of from eight to nine cases.

Upon assessment, Sandy learned that Shirley had had a troubled relationship with her own family of origin, including having grown up as the daughter of an alcoholic. One of the case objectives was to refer her to a support group for adult children of alcoholics. The other objectives were to refer Cheryl to a therapy group for sexually abused teenagers as well as a support group, to improve the mother/daughter relationship, and to develop Shirley's own parenting skills through cotherapy with a community mental health worker.

In a four-month service period, the family was seen in the home six times. They had also missed at least one visit during each month, resulting in having missed nearly one half of the total appointments. At termination, Cheryl was placed in a group home. Neither mother nor daughter had cooperated with services, and Shirley had taken no responsibility for the problems the two were having. Placement was her preferred solution.

RELATION TO OTHER STUDIES

The high incidence of parent-child conflict, marital conflict, and relationship problems in these families reinforces findings reported by other studies (Garbarino, Schellenbach, Sebes, & Associates, 1986; Geismar

& Wood, 1986, pp. 20–26; Mann et al., 1990; Showell et al., 1988; Wodarski, 1981). Indeed, family problems overshadowed other problems commonly associated with juvenile offenses such as substance abuse, physical abuse, mental illness, and mental retardation, although the presence of such additional problems made placement more likely.

In both delinquency and status offense cases the programs were less successful with children who were not in school or who were in a special class and, in status offense cases, with those who had at least one prior placement. In identifying substance abuse as the most important reason for placement in delinquency cases, this study concurs with others that underline the importance of substance abuse treatment in family preservation (Landsman, 1985; Kagan, Reid, Roberts, & Silverman-Pollow, 1987) and support the effectiveness of family therapy in reducing adolescent substance abuse (Friedman et al., 1991).

Within a context of systems-oriented family therapy, teaching skills and teaming seemed to contribute to placement prevention in status offense cases. These findings are consistent with other studies of the effectiveness of different types of interventions with juvenile offenders and their families (Alexander & Parsons, 1973; Dadds, 1987; Geismar & Wood, 1986; Gordon et al., 1988; Mann et al., 1990). This analysis also supports previous findings that low parental and child functioning, prior placement, larger families and higher risk of placement at intake contribute to a greater likelihood of placement (Landsman, Leung, & Hutchinson, 1987; Leeds, 1984; Showell et al., 1988; Spaid & Fraser, 1991).

The findings support the importance of a family-based approach in treating juvenile offenses. Overall, 71 percent of the families referred for delinquency and 80 percent of those referred for status offenses remained intact. Family motivation and cooperation, especially involving the highest-risk children in treatment sessions, have been found to be important to successful outcomes (Friedman et al., 1991). Families who showed systemic change (in behavior, structure, relationships, emotional climate, and perception of the problem) were also more likely to remain together.

The findings of this study and of previous research indicate that a systemically focused family-based and community-based approach both meets well-established public policy goals and preserves for children the continuing support and care of their families which is so important as they move toward adulthood and independence.

Endnote

1. Portions of this chapter are reprinted with special permission from *Children and Youth Services Review, 12,* 183–212, 1990.

Chapter Seven

FAMILY-BASED SERVICES
IN URBAN, SUBURBAN AND RURAL AREAS

One of the concerns in replicating family-based services across the country has been about their transferability from the rural states of the Midwest and Northwest, where they were first developed, to more urban areas. Critics cite the intractability of urban problems and the difficulty of systemic change in complex urban environments as factors that make the replication of successful service models difficult (Kamerman & Kahn, 1990). This chapter identifies program, worker, and family characteristics that differentiate rural family-based programs from those in urban and suburban areas and discusses the special features of intensive and comprehensive services in a rural environment. One program with a nontraditional approach to service delivery adapted to rural needs is profiled, along with families illustrating the most important features of successful and unsuccessful cases in the rural agencies studied. Programs exemplifying family-based practice in urban and suburban environments are profiled in Chapters Three, Four, and Nine.

OVERVIEW OF SELECTED LITERATURE

The professional literature on human services in rural areas has been based on several assumptions about differences between practice in urban and rural areas. Most authors assume that rural residents are more isolated, more traditional, and more likely to rely on informal networks for help and support than urban residents (York, Denton, & Moran, 1989). However, York and his colleagues (1989) found, contrary to these expectations, that rural families received less help from informal networks than urban families. Glenn and Hill (1977) noted as well, in their extensive review of the sociological literature, that the differences between rural and urban attitudes and behaviors are "modest" and there is a tendency to "overinterpret" small differences.

104

In the last decade, some of the assumptions about differences in social work and community mental health practice between urban and rural settings have been tested. Researchers have found either no or very few differences in stressors, roles, or practice behaviors (Perlman, Hartman, & Bosak, 1984; Whitaker, 1986; York et al., 1989).

Although it seems that social work practice is similar across various localities, important differences between urban and rural areas do affect the delivery of human services. The most consistent differences are in the areas of financial, service, and staff resources. Both rural community mental health and social services agencies are poorly funded (Wagenfeld & Buffum, 1983), exist in communities with fewer services (Coward, 1983), and have fewer professional staff (Heyman, 1986) than urban agencies.

In the early 1980s Perlman et al. (1984) found that rural mental health agencies had significantly lower salaries and budgets than nonrural agencies. Since then the continuing crisis in the farm economy and its effects on other businesses in rural areas have deepened the economic problems of human service agencies and the populations they serve (Jurich & Russell, 1987). The economic problems of rural areas are also reflected in a shortage of educational, health, and social services, particularly for special populations such as the elderly, preschool children, and the developmentally disabled (Coward & Smith, 1983).

The shortage of funds and resultant lack of professional staff and clinical supervision necessitate broader practice roles and special efforts to provide staff support. Jerrell (1983), for example, found that team support and clinical supervision were almost as important in determining job satisfaction as salary level in a rural area of Pennsylvania. Although individual therapy is the most prevalent mental health service in rural as well as urban agencies (Pulakos & Dengerink, 1983), a survey of rural Wyoming mental health practitioners found that they also provided consultation, linked clients to services outside the community, developed new services, and performed administrative duties. To support their effectiveness in these multiple roles, in the face of minimal training opportunities, practitioners relied on peer consultation "even though this might involve traveling as far as 50 miles" (Elkin & Boyer, 1987).

Finally, economic factors have also been found to decrease utilization of mental health services in rural areas. In a telephone survey in rural Ohio, Stefl and Prosperi (1985) found cost the most frequently cited barrier to seeking needed mental health services, distantly followed by lack of knowledge of available services, lack of transportation, and social stigma.

Thus, while social work practice has been found to differ little between rural and nonrural areas, a lack of funding, community services, and professional staff creates problems in service delivery. These problems are particularly severe in family-based services given their comprehensive, intensive nature. To examine these issues, families in the nine programs in this study were classified according to whether they lived in urban, rural, or suburban areas and both case record and social worker data were examined for differences based on geographic location.

STUDY SAMPLE

Previous researchers have used varying definitions of "rural." Most reject a dichotomous approach, and some have developed rankings based on population, density, and proximity to urban areas (Whitaker, 1986; York et al., 1989). For the purpose of this analysis, and in order to divide the sample into roughly equal segments, rural families were defined as those who lived in towns of less than 20,000, suburban families as those in cities and towns of 20,000 to 90,000, and urban families as those in cities of more than 90,000.

All the urban families came from three study sites in Standard Metropolitan Statistical Areas (SMSAs): Portland, Oregon (1980 population, 366,383); Columbus, Ohio (1980 population, 564,871); and Philadelphia, Pennsylvania (1980 population, 1,688,210). Nearly three-quarters of the suburban cases also came from three locations: Dakota County, Minnesota; Boulder County, Colorado; and the five publicly-administered IFS programs in Oregon. The first of these locations is adjacent to a large metropolitan SMSA (Minneapolis), while the other two include small cities of 76,685 (Boulder) and 89,233 (Salem). Similarly, nearly three-fourths of the rural families came from two Iowa agencies covering ten rural counties in southeastern Iowa and from the Lutheran Social Services program, serving eleven counties in rural west-central Minnesota (Table VII–I).

In addition to differences in population size, rural, suburban, and urban programs tended to vary systematically in auspices, service populations, and location of service delivery (Table VII–II). Programs in suburban areas were most likely to be delivered by public agencies

Table VII-I
LOCATION OF PROGRAMS BY FAMILY'S PLACE OF RESIDENCE

Agency	Total $n = 452$ n	Rural $n = 151$ %	Suburban $n = 150$ %	Urban $n = 149$ %
Lutheran Social Services, MN	51	32.8	.5	0
Iowa Department of Human Services	50	20.8	12.3	0
Iowa Children & Family Services	49	18.7	13.5	0
Oregon Children's Services Division	50	13.5	19.6	0
Dakota County Human Services, MN	50	11.9	21.2	0
Boulder County Social Services, CO	48	0	32.0	0
Franklin County Children Services, OH	50	2.3	.8	30.2
Intensive Family Services, Multnomah County, OR	50	0	0	33.6
SCAN, Philadelphia, PA	54	0	0	36.3

Note. Weighted to approximate incidence in the population; n's vary in subsequent tables due to weighting and missing data. Percentages may not total 100 due to rounding.

and those in urban and rural locations by private agencies. Urban programs were much more likely to serve neglect cases and to provide services in the families' homes. Rural families were equally likely to be served by a public as a private agency, were more often referred because of juvenile offenses, and were more likely to be seen in their homes than in an office.

Because of the overlap and interaction between these program features, four-way analysis of variance, controlling for the level of functioning of the primary caretaker, was used to identify those characteristics that differed primarily because the families lived in rural locations. Since geographic location is a given in program planning, it was entered first, followed by the auspices, target population, and location of service delivery. The tables present program, worker, and family characteristics (weighted to correct for the imbalance in placement and nonplacement cases) as they were reported. Only relationships that remained significant after controlling for the severity of caretaker problems and significant interactions with auspices, type of case, and location of service delivery are reported.

Table VII–II

PROGRAM CHARACTERISTICS BY LOCATION OF CLIENT POPULATION

Program Characteristics	Rural $n = 151$	Suburban $n = 150$	Urban $n = 149$
Auspices[a]			
Public	48.5	86.0	30.2
Private	51.5	14.0	69.8
Primary Reason for Referral[a]			
Neglect	5.5	3.2	20.7
Physical Abuse	7.1	7.6	8.2
Sexual Abuse	2.4	2.7	1.8
Status Offense	15.2	14.4	11.3
Delinquency	16.9	18.2	5.6
Non-Statutory	52.9	53.9	52.4
Location of Service[b]			
Home	64.2	40.6	96.5
Office	35.8	59.4	3.5

Note. Percentages.

[a]$p < .001.$ [b]$p < .01.$

STUDY FINDINGS

The Workers' Perspective

Reflecting the decline in rural economies during the study period (1982 to 1985), nearly all of the rural workers reported that their agencies had experienced a decrease in funding (Table VII–III). These financial difficulties may account for the higher rate of worker turnover in rural agencies, the lack of funds for developmental activities, and the lower rates of workshop attendance. They may also explain why programs serving rural families were less likely to employ a team approach. Only a quarter of rural families received teamed services, compared to over a third of suburban families and nearly two-thirds of urban families. Despite similarities in the percentage of workers' time spent in face-to-face contacts, because of the distances involved, workers in rural programs spent more time traveling than workers in other programs (Table VII–IV). This left them with less time for informal discussion of cases

Table VII-III
AGENCY RESOURCES BY GEOGRAPHIC LOCATION

		Rural $n = 28$	Suburban $n = 28$	Urban[a] $n = 19$
Agency Resources				
Decreasing Financial Resources	%	90.6**	64.9	21.3
Low Turnover	%	29.9*	59.4	58.0
Funds Generally Available For				
Conferences	%	39.6	12.6	100.0**
Education	%	10.7	19.2	76.9**
Books	%	12.7	21.3	56.3*
Consultants	%	12.3	64.0**	24.0
Number of Workshops Attended[b]	m	2.1	3.3*	2.6
	sd	1.1	2.3	1.1
Teamed Services[c]	%	24.6	34.5	61.9*

Note. Worker report, weighted by number of cases in sample.
[a]Franklin County excluded due to insufficient responses. [b]Range: 0–5, 0–10, 0–4. [c]n = 451 families.
*$p < .05$. **$p < .001$.

Table VII-IV
WORK ALLOCATION AND RELATIONS BY GEOGRAPHIC LOCATION

		Rural $n = 28$	Suburban $n = 28$	Urban[a] $n = 19$
Allocation of Time				
In person contact	%	44.1	40.4	47.0
Travel	%	17.1*	10.6	12.5
Hours per Month of Informal Case Discussion[b]	m	3.8	6.6	9.3***
	sd	3.6	4.8	5.6
Co-worker Relations Score[c]	m	5.6*	4.9	4.2
	sd	1.9	1.7	1.2

Note. Worker report, weighted by number of cases in sample.
[a]Franklin County excluded due to insufficient response. [b]Range: 1–16, 1–16, 1–20. [c]From Jayaratne & Chess (1984), Professional Satisfaction Inventory; higher score is negative.
*$p < .05$. **$p < .01$. ***$p < .001$.

and may have contributed to their more distant relationships with coworkers as well as to turnover.

Rural workers differed somewhat from workers in other locations in their approach to family-based services. They saw night and weekend appointments, concrete services, and intensive services as more important and referral to other counseling services as less important than other workers (Table VII–V). These emphases reflect their need to provide comprehensive services in areas where referral to other services may not be an option.

Table VII–V
FAMILY-BASED SERVICES PHILOSOPHY BY GEOGRAPHIC LOCATION

	Rural n = 28	Suburban n = 28	Urban[a] n = 19
Most Important[b]			
Night and Weekend Appointments	54.7**	17.5	23.5
Concrete Services	48.4	17.2*	43.0
Intensive Services	62.9*	30.4	30.1
Least Important[c]			
Referral to Other Counseling	52.6	45.3	27.0*

Note. Worker report, weighted by number of cases in sample. Percentages. Scales from Pecora et al., 1985. [a]Franklin County excluded due to insufficient response. [b]Moderately to extremely important. [c]Not to slightly important.
*$p < .05$. **$p < .01$.

The Families

Examining differences in treatment populations, practice, and outcomes that are more typical of rural than suburban and urban areas, a number of interesting characteristics emerge. Selection of rural sites in the Midwest (Iowa and Minnesota) meant that only 8 percent of the rural families were nonwhite. Many of the other differences in demographics are due to the contrast in conditions between urban and rural environments (Table VII–VI). Primary caretakers in rural families were more likely to be married or remarried than those in urban areas. Although many more of the urban families lived in poverty, more than half of the rural families did as well, and a quarter of all the rural families contained second adults who were unemployed. Many fewer neglect cases were referred for family-based services in rural areas, but rural families had both more and older children, so there were as many children at risk of imminent placement in rural as in urban families.

Rural families received services for a shorter period of time, three months less than families in urban areas, and fewer received paraprofessional services (Table VII–VII). Although these services were more

Table VII-VI
FAMILY CHARACTERISTICS BY LOCATION OF CLIENT POPULATION

Family Characteristics		Rural n = 151	Suburban n = 150	Urban n = 149
Married	%	55.6	54.8	30.0**
Stepfamilies[a]	%	28.1	20.9	12.7*
Below Poverty Level[b]	%	52.8	31.4	85.5**
Second Adult in Home Unemployed[c]	%	38.2	23.3	66.2**
Child Characteristics				
Number	m	2.9*	2.6	2.5
	sd	1.4	1.2	1.4
Age	m	11.0	11.0	7.5*
	sd	4.3	4.1	5.6
Number at High Risk[d]	m	.9	.6*	1.0
	sd	.7	.8	1.2

[a]n = 385. [b]n = 314. [c]n = 304. [d]Range: 0–5, 0–4, 0–5.
*$p < .05$. **$p < .001$.

often provided to families with children younger than those typically served in rural programs, they were also less available in rural areas, especially parent education services. Second adults in the rural families were much more likely than those in urban or suburban families to participate in most or all of the treatment sessions, and primary caretakers were more motivated and cooperative with services than those in urban areas.

In terms of outcome, rural families exhibited less change in family functioning than those in more populous areas, and only 19 percent were expected to be independent of social services once their case was closed to family-based services (Table VII–VII). Given the paucity of resources, it is perhaps not surprising that placement rates were nearly as high as in urban programs.

Factors Related to Placement

Combining service and family characteristics that differed significantly between placement and nonplacement cases with those that characterized family-based services in rural areas, fifteen factors that contributed to family preservation or placement in rural areas were identified in a

Table VII–VII

SERVICES AND OUTCOMES BY LOCATION OF CLIENT POPULATION

		Rural n = 151	Suburban n = 150	Urban n = 149
Services				
Length (months)[a]	m	5.2	6.4	8.1***
	sd	3.3	5.9	5.8
Paraprofessional Service	%	11.7	4.8	37.7***
Second Adult Attended Most Sessions[b]	%	51.5***	39.7	28.6
Caretaker Compliance Score	m	75.7	76.6	70.5*
	sd	15.5	16.4	16.7
Outcomes				
Number of Areas of Positive Change[c]	m	3.5	3.0	4.7*
	sd	2.3	2.1	3.1
No Additional Services	%	19.5	34.2**	14.3

[a]Range: 0–19.1, .2–28.9, 0–29.4. [b]n = 403. [c]Range: 0–10, 0–8, 0–10.
*$p < .05$. **$p < .01$. ***$p < .001$.

discriminant analysis (see Appendix E). Most important was the number of children at high risk of placement. Families experiencing placement had 1.2 children at risk, compared to .8 in nonplacement families. The characteristics of the children at highest risk also predicted placement. Older children (average age of 13) with prior placements (52%) and juvenile offenses (49%) were more likely to be placed than younger children (average age of 12) with no prior placements (67%) and no juvenile offenses (73%). Other family problems contributing to placement included substance abuse (38%), divorce (24%), and family dysfunction (51%). Families with marital problems (40%) and more compliant caretakers were less likely to experience placement.

Some services also contributed to an outcome of placement or nonplacement. Most importantly, case management services were given to 57 percent of placement cases versus 37 percent of nonplacement cases, probably in preparation for removal. Similarly, 38 percent of placement cases received psychiatric evaluation or treatment, compared to 26 percent of nonplacement cases. Families who remained together, on the other hand, were more likely to receive marriage counseling (40% versus 25%). All together these characteristics correctly classified two-thirds of the cases. The statistical model was much more successful in identifying nonplacement (92%) than placement cases (43%). The five most important predictors were also significant in the individual analyses of the five programs that served rural families (Nelson, Landsman, Emlen, & Hutchinson, 1988).

CASE STUDIES

Lutheran Social Services of Minnesota

In order to further clarify the central characteristics and highlight the unique service delivery approach of programs operating in rural areas, one agency and two of its cases are described below.

Agency Description

Lutheran Social Services of Minnesota (LSS) provides an Intensive In-Home Treatment Program employing a home-based model, patterned after FAMILIES, INC., with families who have at least one child at risk of placement. At the initiation of the study, the program covered sixteen rural counties in western Minnesota, with a central office in Fergus Falls. The family-based program is part of the statewide LSS organization governed by a board of directors and an executive committee. Personnel policies, management procedures, and ethical guidelines are included in a statewide policy manual. The director of the Intensive In-Home Treatment Program is accountable to the regional director.

The Intensive In-Home Treatment Program began in 1981, one of the first four established in the state. Funding was initially provided by two counties and covered two staff positions. Four workers were added between 1983 and 1984. Trained in strategic and structural family therapy, they influenced the program in that direction. In 1984, LSS reorganized into a system of six regions. In 1986, the original Intensive In-Home Treatment Program was split along new district lines into two programs, one based in Fergus Falls and one in Willmar. The Fergus Falls program is included in this study.

Program philosophy and treatment approaches are based on family systems theory, and in-home treatment is provided for the whole family. Work with the family unit is viewed as the most viable option for resolving problems, even when only one child is identified as having difficulties. The program subscribes to the idea that children are often placed out of the home, not because families cannot change, but because community resources do not allow the intensity of staff time or a treatment orientation that would help children remain in their own homes. While the program provides family therapy, it also emphasizes working with the community and providing whatever concrete services are needed (transportation, cleaning, networking). Parent education, health services, and support groups are also used when they are available.

All services are delivered in the families' homes, unless there is a specific reason to meet elsewhere, such as a need for live supervision, danger to the worker, or a need to meet outside the home for therapeutic purposes. The family-based workers live in the counties they serve and work out of their own homes, coming together once a week for case discussion, supervision, and training. Clients are referred from contracting departments of social service and community corrections offices. The program works closely with county departments of social services, schools, and other human service professionals and resources to enhance total family functioning.

Site-Specific Findings

Located in a rural state, the LSS program had several characteristics in common with the Iowa programs described in the next chapter (see Appendix F for comparative tables). LSS served older families, over half headed by a married couple. There were more male primary caretakers (32%) than in any other site, and all the primary caretakers were white. More were employed (nearly 70%), and fewer families were living in poverty, with only 18 percent receiving AFDC. The children at highest risk of placement were older than the study average and over a third had been placed before. Eighty percent were considered to be at risk of imminent placement, one of the highest rates among the study sites. Nearly 20 percent were court-ordered into family-based services.

About a third of the families were referred to LSS for abuse or neglect, a third for delinquency, and nearly two-thirds for parent-child conflict (up to four referral problems could be coded). Except for neglect, these proportions were higher than was typical for the study population as a whole. Substantial numbers of problems were reported in all areas, including substance abuse by a child but excluding sexual abuse and child neglect. Family relationships, parenting skills, and child behavior were targeted more often as treatment problems, with case objectives focusing particularly on individual change and adult and family relationships. In keeping with these problems and objectives, LSS workers more often used individual counseling as an intervention, but less often provided case management services or accompanied families to appointments.

Family-based workers provided an average of five different types of interventions to each family, mainly family therapy, individual counseling, homework assignments, and marital counseling. Families received an average of six contacts a month, mostly in their homes, over a five-month period. Only two agencies serving younger child abuse and neglect cases, Franklin County Children Services and Iowa Children and Family Services, provided more total contact in the first months of service than Lutheran Social Services. While families seen by LSS received a greater variety of interventions from the family-based program itself, they received fewer direct services, including concrete and supportive services, from all sources combined. Further, LSS provided services for a shorter period of time than most other sites.

More than 20 percent of the highest-risk children in the rural families served by LSS were placed by the end of service, over half in foster homes, group homes, or institutions. Even though primary caretakers (82%) and second adults (66%) attended sessions more often than in most other sites, only 32 percent of the highest-risk children participated this regularly, perhaps because of the strong focus on marital counseling or the high level of parent-child conflict. At the termination of services, two-thirds of the families had improved in at least one area of functioning, but more than a third grew worse. Families changed least in the area of material resources. Only 14 percent were receiving no additional services after closure with LSS.

The results of the discriminant analysis of factors distinguishing placement from nonplacement cases in LSS were very similar to those from the analysis of all rural cases. Juvenile offenses and substance abuse problems were the most important factors leading to placement. Having children at high risk also made a substantial contribution. Perhaps because they served a combined population of juvenile offense and child maltreatment cases, the discriminant model for LSS was one of the weakest in the study, correctly identifying only 23 percent of the placement cases.

Case Examples

The Burns Family

The Burns family consisted of Barbara and John, both in their early 40s, and two children, 18-year-old Matthew (who no longer lived at home) and 15-year-old Julie. The Burnses were referred to Lutheran Social Services by the Department of Social Services following Julie's attempted suicide. Both parents were high school graduates; John was employed full-time as a salesperson for a local business and Barbara worked part-time as a waitress in the town coffee shop. The town in which they resided had a population of less than 2,000; thus job opportunities were limited.

At the time of referral, Julie had just returned home after being hospitalized for an overdose of an over-the-counter medicine. The referring social worker described severe conflict between Julie and her parents as well as Julie's behavioral and emotional problems as contributing to this high-risk family situation. This was, however, the first experience that the Burns family had had with social or mental health services.

The caseworker assigned to work with the Burns family was 30-year-old Ron, who had a masters degree in social work and about four years of employment experience in child welfare. Ron described morale in the agency as high and was quite satisfied with his work, though he planned on leaving the agency within a couple of years. He saw families in their own homes and usually carried a caseload of six families.

Residing in small towns and rural areas, Ron's clients were almost all white and about half were two-parent families. Many of the families he saw were experiencing child behavioral problems, marital problems, multigenerational problems, parent-child conflict, substance abuse, and unemployment. The Department of Social Services was the main referral source for the program, and cases were assigned largely on the basis of geographic location, openings in the worker's caseload, and the referring worker's preference.

When Ron met with the Burnses to establish case objectives, the plan focused on strengthening the marital subsystem: helping the parents work together to establish rules and methods of discipline, to plan times for the couple to spend alone together, and to give John a more supportive role in the family with both Barbara and Julie.

In three months of service, Ron met twice a week in the home with Julie and her parents. Matthew attended the few sessions to which he was invited; the others attended all of the sessions. Family and couple therapy were the primary treatment methods employed. Services were terminated because the family felt that sufficient progress had been made and that they no longer needed intensive in-home services, although they continued to receive services from the community mental health center. At the time of case closure, the family was assessed as having made considerable improvement in communication and behavior.

The Yoder Family

Frank and Lucille Yoder and their three children, eighteen-year-old Mark, sixteen-year-old Fred, and thirteen-year-old Nancy, were referred to Lutheran Social Services directly by the court due to an incident of Fred breaking and entering a liquor store. Lucille was employed part-time as a clerical worker, and Frank worked full-time as an electrician. Mark, who did not complete high school, lived in another town and worked in an unskilled factory position. Fred and Nancy were still attending high school, though Fred had had problems with truancy.

The referring worker considered both children at home to be at risk of placement, though Fred, with two previous placement experiences, was at a higher level of risk. In addition to the delinquency which was the presenting problem, Fred's alcohol use and the strained relationships between the parents and the children were noted in the referral report.

Thirty-five-year-old Bill was assigned to work with the Yoder family. Married with one child of his own, Bill held a master's degree in family counseling and had about seven years of experience in counseling individuals and families. At the time he was surveyed about his experiences with the family-based program, Bill was no longer working in that field. He reported having a steady caseload of six families and working almost exclusively in the home, resulting in spending about 40 percent of his time in travel.

When Bill met with the Yoders to develop a service plan, the primary problems addressed included conflict between parents and Fred, dealing with anger and disappointment around the law violations, and handling emotional difficulties that both of the children at home were experiencing. Later on in the treatment process, goals related to Fred's chemical dependency and increasingly disruptive school behavior were added.

To achieve the agreed-upon goals and avert out-of-home placement, family therapy, individual counseling, substance abuse counseling, and advocacy with the school were tried. While Lucille and Nancy consistently participated in the family sessions, Frank was not involved in the process and Fred refused to participate more often than not. After three months of intensive services, involving two to three contacts each week, Fred was placed in a group home following another incident of delinquency. Although some of the case goals had been partially met, progress had not been sufficient to forestall a placement.

RELATION TO OTHER STUDIES

Despite being similar in many respects to urban families (Tremblay, Walker, & Dillman, 1983), rural families receiving family-based services more often were headed by two parents, contained stepparents, and had more and older children. Their problems centered on juvenile offenses and family conflict. Many of the highest-risk children had been placed before and were again at high risk of placement. Services were brief, delivered primarily by a single worker, and focused on counseling, although they included a comprehensive array of supportive and concrete services when needed and available. Both primary caretakers and second adults were more cooperative with services than in urban and suburban programs.

Placement was related to factors found in other studies. Older children with prior placements and juvenile offenses have consistently been found to be at higher risk of placement than younger victims of child abuse and neglect (AuClaire & Schwartz, 1986; Fraser, Pecora, & Haapala, 1989; Nelson et al., 1988). Addressing the relationship problems between adults in the family was the single most important service in averting placement. Other researchers have also identified family and marital counseling as important in work with rural families (Coward & Smith, 1983; Craig & Hurry, 1981), especially those with status-offending children (Gross, 1990; Jurich & Russell, 1987).

This examination of data both from rural families in several programs and from one rural program strongly supports findings from previous research. As in the inner cities, economic deprivation creates family stress (Hurn, 1990; Weeks & Drencacz, 1983) and problems in service delivery (Wagenfeld & Buffum, 1983). Poverty, unemployment, and lack of material resources are compounded for families facing removal of a child by a lack of community services, a scarcity of professional helpers, and declining funding for family-based services. These findings mirror those reported by Coward and Smith (1983), Jurich and Russell (1987),

Perlman et al. (1984), and Wagenfeld and Buffum (1983), for other human service programs.

Although creative methods of service delivery such as the outposting model used in FAMILIES, INC. and the LSS program, as well as others adapted to rural conditions (Buffum, 1984), can help family-based programs reach troubled families, the lack of funding and supportive services will continue to limit their effectiveness. As in inner cities, family-based services cannot compensate for poverty and its effects on families, or for a lack of other counseling, supportive, and concrete services. Since the vast majority of rural families require further support after completing a brief family-based program, the lack of such services will ultimately compromise the effectiveness of family-based interventions and lead to unnecessary placements.

Given their target populations and context, short-term, intensive, and comprehensive family-based services are particularly appropriate in rural areas. The lack of other services, the focus on older children and their families, and the shortage of financial resources mean that family-based workers must be prepared to offer a variety of services, to focus services, and to limit the length of their involvement in order to see as many families as possible. The difficulty of the cases, the distances involved, the lack of resources, and isolation from peer support make this work difficult, as reflected in higher turnover rates and more distant relations with coworkers.

While suburban programs serve similar types of cases, they have more internal and external resources and serve more affluent families making a family treatment approach most appropriate. Urban agencies serve families with the most complex array of problems, but have more resources available to the family-based workers. Services are more often delivered by a team of workers over a longer period of time, indicating that the home-based model may be particularly suited to urban agencies serving low-income, single-parent families with younger children and a wider array of problems.

Rural programs also tend to follow a home-based model, although with a shorter time frame. Since specialization is not frequently an option, the home-based model appropriately offers the most flexibility in services and their delivery, enabling family-based programs to meet the needs of a larger variety of cases, ranging from maltreatment of younger children to cases involving older status offenders and delinquents. Optimally both family treatment and home-based services would be available, coordinating services to efficiently meet the needs of more families than either could individually. An example of such coordination in a rural area in Iowa is offered in the next chapter.

Chapter Eight

THE PUBLIC-PRIVATE CONNECTION

The appropriate role of the public and private sectors is a controversial subject among advocates and providers of family preservation services. Those who favor private agency provision question whether public social services can accommodate the low caseloads, flexible work hours, and 24-hour availability characteristic of family preservation services. Supporters of direct public provision stress the public agency's responsibility to ensure that reasonable efforts are made to prevent placement and to reunify families, and point to models of service that have been successfully implemented in public agencies.

Aided by the examples of states such as Iowa, Oregon, and Colorado, which had implemented family-centered services in advance of the mandates of P.L. 96-272, the National Resource Center on Family Based Services developed a model for the direct provision of family-based services by public child welfare agencies (Hutchinson & Nelson, 1985). Many states, however, still debate whether to provide intensive family services directly or to contract them out to private agencies.

OVERVIEW OF SELECTED LITERATURE

Historically, the private sector has always played a large part in developing and delivering child welfare services (Gronbjerg, 1987; Hall, 1987; Hart, 1988). In the typical pattern, voluntary organizations identify needs and initiate programs to meet them. The public sector then steps in to provide the legislation and stable funding necessary to institutionalize the program (Smith, 1989). Family-based services are no exception. Intensive in-home services to prevent the out-of-home placement of children were initiated in the early 1970s by private agencies with state or federal funding for deinstitutionalization or from Title XX of the Social Security Act (Kramer, 1985). The passage of the Adoption Assistance and Child Welfare Act of 1980 (P.L. 96-272), however, greatly accelerated the national trend toward public provision of preventive services.

At the same time that the federal government was requiring public child welfare agencies to provide preventive services, however, the new Reagan Administration was drastically cutting federal funds available for human services. When combined with ever-increasing numbers of child abuse and neglect reports, this exacerbated chronic problems of high caseloads and high turnover in child welfare programs. As in other human services (Hall, 1987; Reagen & Musser, 1984), the response to this dilemma in many public agencies was to purchase family-based preventive and reunification services from existing private agencies rather than develop the new service themselves (Smith, 1989).

Turning to private agencies seemed doubly appropriate under these circumstances, first because the Reagan Administration was committed to reducing the scope of the federal government and to strengthening the private sector, and second because the apparent strengths of private agencies matched the need to provide flexible services to a diverse population while containing costs (Kramer & Grossman, 1987; Pecora, Kinney, Mitchell, & Tolley, 1990; Salamon, 1987). Private agencies are presumed to offer greater flexibility in establishing and abolishing services, less bureaucracy, less governmental intrusion, and a reduction in costs to taxpayers (Kramer, 1985; Kramer & Grossman, 1987; Pecora et al., 1990; Salamon, 1987; Terrell & Kramer, 1984).

Some of the potential problems with private provision include lack of performance standards and accountability, negative impacts of cost cutting on the quality and professionalism of services, and increasing dependency for program direction and funding on government sources (Hart, 1988; Hurl, 1986; Salamon, 1987). However, these considerations were not as salient as the need to deploy family-based services quickly under impoverished circumstances. Nor was the impact of budget cuts on the private sector foreseen. In the early 1980s, private agencies experienced a great deal of turbulence in their major funding sources, especially in federal funding, with agencies serving the poor taking the biggest cuts (Gronbjerg, 1990).

There has been considerable debate about the relative merits of public and private provision of services, but little research has been done to substantiate the various contentions (Pecora et al., 1990). This chapter highlights the differences in the way family-centered services are implemented in public and private agencies and underlines some of the strengths and problems of public/private partnerships in this field of practice. Of the nine programs included in this analysis, five are based in public agencies and four in private agencies located in Oregon, Colorado, Iowa, Minnesota, Ohio, and Pennsylvania. Originally a public and a private agency were selected for each state in the study. However, two programs left the study before data collection commenced and the private agency in Colorado, a day treatment program for adolescents, has been dropped from this analysis because it is based on a different treatment model than the other placement prevention programs in the study. Although located in different states, the programs in Philadelphia and Ohio provide examples of private and public programs that serve low-income urban families.

PROGRAM DESCRIPTIONS

The agencies in the study illustrate a variety of approaches to direct provision of services by public agencies and to the purchase of service from private agencies. Four of the five public programs work in concert with private agencies to provide a range of family-based and placement prevention services. All four private agencies receive a large proportion of their referrals and funds through purchase-of-service agreements with public social service agencies. Although there was not a significant difference in the type of referrals received by public and private agencies, there were significant differences between them according to whether they were located in urban or rural areas and whether services were delivered in the home or in the office. Suburban programs were more often located in public agencies and the private agencies delivered almost all their services in families' homes (Table VIII–I).

Public Programs

In Oregon the public Children's Services Division (CSD) of the Department of Human Resources works cooperatively with private agencies providing the same services in different catchment areas. The Intensive Family Services (IFS) program began in 1980 through purchase-of-service agreements with private agencies, but later expanded to include direct public provision of services in five counties where no private provider was available. Both public and private providers work under the same program guidelines which mandate that they maintain, on average, a

Table VIII-I
PROGRAM CHARACTERISTICS IN PUBLIC AND PRIVATE AGENCIES

		Public Cases $n = 249$	Private Cases $n = 207$
Program Characteristics	*n*	%	%
Geographic Location$_a$			
Rural	152	29.7	38.4
Suburban	150	52.1	10.4
Urban	149	18.1	51.2
Primary Reason for Referral			
Physical Abuse	36	7.6	8.1
Sexual Abuse	10	2.4	2.1
Neglect	44	5.7	14.4
Delinquency	61	14.2	12.6
Status Offenses	62	15.2	11.4
Non Statutory	243	54.8	51.4
Location of Service$_a$			
Home	306	45.9	93.3
Office	147	54.1	6.7

Note. Weighted to approximate incidence in the population; *n*'s vary in subsequent tables due to weighting and missing data. Percentages may not total 100 due to rounding.
$_a p = .01$.

ninety-day service period, caseloads of eleven, and a 75 percent success rate in preventing placement during the treatment period. The IFS program emphasizes therapeutic interventions, while complementary services such as homemakers and parent education are coordinated by a CSD case manager. The Oregon IFS program was one of the first to develop a family treatment model of services.

The four remaining public programs provide specialized intensive services as part of more inclusive placement prevention packages. Three follow a family treatment model and one a home-based model. The Intensive Family Therapy program in the Boulder County (Colorado) Department of Social Services was established as part of a comprehensive plan to reduce placement, initiated statewide in 1980 by Senate Bill 26 (Alternative to Out-of-Home Placement Act). The primary focus of the Intensive Family Therapy program, which follows a family treatment model, is to prevent institutional placement and to reunify families in which children have already been placed. However, the county-based Placement Alternatives Commission also funds less-restrictive alternatives to residential placement such as day treatment and therapeutic foster care.

The Family Therapy Unit of the Ottumwa District Office of the Iowa Department of Human Services was initiated with grant funding in the early 1970s to reunify adolescents in residential placement with their families. Family therapy teams were established in district offices to serve the surrounding county human services offices. The units in each district office operated somewhat independently until 1985, when a uniform statewide policy for family-based services was adopted (Iowa Department of Human Services, 1985). In the Ottumwa District Office, a complementary division of labor has evolved between public and private agencies. In this partnership, the public Family Therapy Unit conducts assessments and provides office-based treatment to families who can be appropriately served through weekly appointments within a family treatment model and purchases intensive home-based services from private providers for other families. This cooperative effort will be examined in a detailed case study later in this chapter.

The Intensive Services Program of the Dakota County (Minnesota) Human Services Department is part of a Placement Alternatives Program initiated in 1980. The goals of this program are (1) to reduce the number of out-of-home placements by providing family treatment and homemaker services, (2) to provide less restrictive placement alternatives, and (3) to reduce placement costs by seeking parental and third-party payments. All services are provided through the county Human Services Department. The Intensive Services program follows a family treatment model of services.

The remaining public program examined in this analysis is Franklin County Children Services (FCSS), one of four agencies delivering home-based services under an umbrella program in the greater Columbus, Ohio, area. FCSS administers the program and purchases services from three private agencies, as well as providing two home-based teams directly through the Home-Based Family-Centered unit. Services are delivered by a MSW/BA team to families for whom a decision to place a child in a FCSS-paid placement has already been made. This study included only the public agency teams.

Private Programs

The four family-based programs in private agencies in this study receive the bulk of their referrals and funding through purchase-of-service agreements with public social service agencies. Three of the four offer home-based programs and the fourth follows a family treatment model. The In-Home Family Counseling Program of Iowa Children and Family Services (ICFS) was initiated in response to a request for proposals from the Iowa Department of Human Services to provide home-based family counseling. ICFS accepts referrals from local courts as well as from the Department, although all families must meet Department of Human Services eligibility requirements.

The Intensive In-home Treatment Program of Lutheran Social Services in Fergus Falls, Minnesota, was begun in 1981 through contracts with two counties to provide home-based placement prevention and reunification services. The program has expanded to serve twenty-nine counties in west central Minnesota. All referrals come from county social service or corrections departments.

The Supportive Child/Adult Network, Inc. (SCAN) contracts with the city to provide protective services to children and families in an inner-city area of Philadelphia. After an initial assessment visit with the referring public worker, services are provided by a multidisciplinary team to families at risk of child maltreatment or placement.

Intensive Family Services of Multnomah County, Oregon, was one of the original programs contracted to private agencies by the Children's Services Division of the Oregon Department of Human Resources. Initially part of Catholic Family Services, the program incorporated independently in 1987 but still operates in conjunction with CSD branch offices in Multnomah County. Under CSD guidelines, the program provides in-home services following a family treatment model to families referred by county social service workers who retain case management responsibilities.

STUDY FINDINGS

A wide variety of variables was examined to determine whether there were systematic differences between family-based programs operating under public and private auspices. Four way analyses of variance controlling hierarchically for caretaker functioning and rural, suburban, or urban location of the programs enabled identification of characteristics primarily associated with the auspices of the program. Program and social worker characteristics, which were much more diverse, will be discussed first, followed by those case characteristics (family characteristics, services, and outcomes) which showed significant variation between public and private agencies after other factors were controlled.

Program Characteristics

The private agency programs did seem to offer more accessibility and flexibility in providing family-based services (Table VIII–II). Private agency workers were much more likely than public workers to see families in their homes and on weekends. Private agency workers also spent more time in in-person contacts with families and more time traveling to families' homes. In part due to their higher caseloads, public agency workers reported spending a greater percentage of their time on administration and paperwork. They also spent more time on the phone and consulting with other workers.

Table VIII–II
WORK ALLOCATION IN PUBLIC AND PRIVATE AGENCIES

	Public[a] n = 37	Private n = 38
Work Allocation		
Appointments on Weekends	17.0	52.0**
Allocation of Time		
In-Person Contact	40.4	46.5†
Travel	10.6	16.3**
Administration	16.3**	10.2
Phone	8.3*	5.9
Peer Consultation	4.6*	2.8
Coordination with Referring Worker		
Quarterly Case Plan	40.0	75.0**
Weekly Phone Contact	5.1	42.8***
Case Goals		
Set by Referring Worker	27.2	64.0**
Contribute to Failure	20.2	46.2*

Note. Worker report, weighted by number of cases in sample. Percentages.
[a]Franklin County excluded due to insufficient response.
†$p < .10$. *$p = .05$. **$p < .01$. ***$p < .001$.

This analysis supports the view that private programs are more accessible and flexible than their public counterparts, but the data raise questions about their autonomy. Nearly three quarters of the private agency workers reported receiving most or all of their referrals from public agencies. In turn, private agency workers were held to much stricter reporting requirements, including, most frequently, weekly phone contacts with the referring worker and quarterly case plans (Table VIII–II). Workers in private agencies also expressed a sense of having less influence in setting case goals, reporting that the referring public agency workers wielded considerable control in this regard. This influence was not altogether benign, since private agency workers believed that their cases failed more frequently because of inappropriate case goals.

Social Worker Characteristics

Information gleaned from the social workers in these public and private agencies provides some interesting and powerful insights into the differences between public and private provision of family-based services. Despite similarities in years of education and gender, workers in public agencies were significantly older and more experienced than those in private agencies (Table VIII–III). They had also been employed by the agency longer and earned 27 percent more than workers in private agencies. These differences contributed to higher turnover rates and declining morale in private agencies.

Over half the workers in private agencies believed that their salaries were lower than those in public agencies and a third thought they earned less than workers in other private agencies. In contrast, more than a third of the public agency workers thought that their salaries were higher than average for public agencies. The private agency workers said that it was difficult to attract workers who would accept these salaries and attributed turnover directly to greater opportunity elsewhere.

As if in compensation for their lack of experience, a third of the private agency workers noted that funds for training had increased during the study period (Table VIII–III). This is in marked contrast to public agencies, in which nearly three-quarters of the workers reported a decrease in training funds, universally viewed as having a negative impact on the program. The only area in which funds were more available to public than private workers was for external consultation; conse-

Table VIII–III
SOCIAL WORKER CHARACTERISTICS AND TRAINING RESOURCES
IN PUBLIC AND PRIVATE AGENCIES

		Public[a] $n = 37$	*Private* $n = 38$
Worker Characteristics			
Age	*m*	37.3***	34.1
	sd	6.5	6.5
Years of Experience[b]	*m*	10.0***	6.5
	sd	4.4	4.5
Years in Agency[c]	*m*	5.8***	2.6
	sd	4.0	2.2
Salary[d]	*m*	23,271***	18,303
	sd	3,158	3,653
Agency			
High Turnover	%	11.1	28.4*
Declining Morale	%	29.3	49.2**
Training Resources			
Increased	%	19.5	32.7*
Decreased	%	71.9***	19.5
Hours of External Consultation Per Month[e]	*m*	2.2**	.6
	sd	2.0	2.6

Note. Worker report, weighted by number of cases in sample.
[a]Franklin County excluded due to insufficient response. [b]Range: 2–18, 0–27. [c]Range: 1–19, 0–10. [d]$n = 72$.
[e]Range: 0–8, 0–25.
*$p < .05$. **$p < .01$. ***$p < .001$.

quently external consultants were used by the public programs for an average of two hours a month.

What impact did the differences in worker experience, agency resources, program flexibility, and worker autonomy have on professional practice? Although over three-quarters of workers in both types of agencies accepted the basic tenets of family-based practice—the importance of empowering families and keeping children in their own homes—there were significant differences in emphasis between them. Public agency workers placed much more importance on goal-oriented treatment plans (Table VIII–IV), whereas private agency workers stressed accessibility through providing intensive services in the home. Private workers also placed more importance on scheduling appointments at clients' convenience, and on 24-hour availability, although these were generally viewed by all workers as less important to effective preventive services than other factors.

Table VIII–IV
FAMILY-BASED SERVICES PHILOSOPHY IN PUBLIC AND PRIVATE AGENCIES

		Public[a] n = 37	Private n = 38
	n	*%*	*%*
Philosophy			
Most Important[b]			
Clients Set Goals[c]	75	57.1***	12.6
Goal-Oriented Case Plans	73	88.7**	57.0
Two to Three Contacts Per Week	74	13.9	39.0*
Services in Home	75	14.3	44.1***
Least Important[d]			
24-hour Availability	75	73.1**	40.1
Appointments at Clients' Convenience	75	66.8***	23.2

Note. Worker report, weighted by number of cases in sample. Scales from Pecora et al., 1985.
[a]Franklin County excluded due to insufficient response. [b]Quite and extremely important on a 5-point scale. [c]Extremely important only. [d]Not at all or slightly important.
*$p < .05$.   **$p < .01$.   ***$p < .001$.

Case Characteristics

Family Characteristics

The public and private programs served quite different types of families (Table VIII–V). Private agencies tended to serve younger, poorer families who had, on average, more problems than those seen in public agencies. Out of 39 possible referral problems, private agency clients had an average of 8, two more than public agency clients. Families served by private agencies were more likely to have problems related to poverty and family relationships.

In general, the services provided by public and private agencies did not differ significantly. In addition to family counseling, more than two thirds of the families received individual therapy, and half, information and referral services. Supportive services such as parent education groups, homemakers and parent aides were provided to less than a quarter of all families. However, families served by public agencies received significantly more skill teaching and families in private programs received more outreach and advocacy services (Table VIII–VI). Case management, a requirement in many public programs, was a more frequently recorded activity in public agencies. However, in four of the five public agencies,

Table VIII-V
FAMILY CHARACTERISTICS IN PUBLIC AND PRIVATE AGENCIES

Family Characteristics		*n*	*Public* *n = 249*	*Private* *n = 207*
Primary Caretaker				
Age	*m*	416	36.2**	32.8
	sd		7.2	9.7
Non-white	%	429	7.2	28.0**
Below Poverty Level	%	319	47.6	67.9**
Age of Highest Risk Child	*m*	448	11.9**	10.1
	sd		4.4	5.2
Problems				
Economic Deprivation	,%	456	20.7	48.3**
Family Relations	%	456	43.8	65.7**
Total Number[a]	*m*	454	5.4	7.7**
	sd		3.7	3.2

[a]Range: 0–14.
*$p < .01$.   **$p < .001$.

case management services were provided by a worker outside the family-based service unit. Other services provided directly by public agencies such as child protective and paraprofessional services were also recorded more often for these families.

Table VIII-VI
SERVICES IN PUBLIC AND PRIVATE AGENCIES

Services	*Public* *n = 249*	*Private* *n = 207*
Case Management	61.6**	42.3
Teaching	51.2*	40.2
Protective Services	45.1**	30.1
Paraprofessional Services	26.4**	11.1
Advocacy	21.5	39.3**
Outreach	4.6	16.3**

Note. Percentages.
*$p < .05$.   **$p < .001$.

Differences in the intensity of services provided to families in public and private programs paralleled the differences between the types of families served in each setting (Table VIII–VII). Public workers had more families in their caseloads, but also teamed cases and saw families in the office more often. Private agency workers, on the other hand, saw families for an average of two months longer.

Table VIII-VII
INTENSITY OF SERVICE IN PUBLIC AND PRIVATE AGENCIES

Intensity		n	Public $n = 249$	Private $n = 207$
Average Caseload[a]	m	71	14.4*	9.0
	sd		8.9	3.9
Teamed Cases	%	454	53.5**	23.2
In-Office Contacts in First Three Months[b]	m	452	4.0**	.2
	sd		4.9	.7
Length of Service[c] (months)	m	406	5.3	7.2**
	sd		4.3	5.1

[a]As reported by workers. Range: 1–35, 3–18. [b]Range: 0–29, 0–5. [c]Range: 0–28.9, 0–29.4.
*$p < .05$. **$p < .001$.

Outcomes

As noted in Chapter Two, the most common outcome measure in studies of placement prevention services is whether the child at risk remained at home or was placed at the time services were terminated. In this study, out-of-home placement as an outcome was more common among families served by the private agencies (20% versus 16%). This difference was not statistically significant. In terms of functioning, families served by public agencies were found to have improved more often in behavior, family structure and hierarchy, in emotional climate, and in understanding of their problems. Clients served by private agencies were more likely to have shown improvement in their relationships within the community.

These factors, taken together, point to differential targeting of services by public and private programs. Private agencies tended to serve poorer, younger, "multiproblem" families. To respond to this population, the private agencies provided services in the families' homes and coordinated the services of other providers themselves. The success of this approach is reflected in the fact that private agency families showed the most improvement in use of community resources and that the communities developed greater understanding and tolerance of the families.

In contrast, public agency clients tended to be older, had higher incomes and fewer problems, and were referred primarily for family relationship problems. Public workers more often saw families in the office, and the office setting enabled more teamwork on cases. The public programs focused on providing therapy, relying on case managers in other units to coordinate services. In keeping with this focus, families in public programs evidenced more clinical change (family structure, affect, and understanding of the problem).

CASE STUDIES

The case studies provide an in-depth look at how a public and private agency complement each other's efforts to provide family-based services. The two programs are the Family Therapy Unit of the Ottumwa District of the Iowa Department of Human Services (IDHS), a family treatment program, and the In-Home Family Counseling Program of Iowa Children and Family Services (ICFS), a home-based program, also in Ottumwa. Established in response to an IDHS call for proposals to provide in-home services to multiproblem families, ICFS complements the services offered by the public Family Therapy Unit, and together they provide a comprehensive array of services to families in a largely rural area. Brief descriptions of the two programs and case examples from each agency will be presented. The case studies further illustrate the practical effect of the differences between public and private programs described previously.

Agency Descriptions

Iowa Department of Human Services

The Iowa Department of Human Services' family therapy program originated in 1969 with the goal of reducing placements and recidivism at the Iowa Training School for Boys by providing in-home family therapy using a cotherapy approach. This federally-funded effort was followed by Law Enforcement Assistance Administration (LEAA) grants to most of the sixteen district offices. Iowa DHS continued to fund family therapists when these grants were discontinued in the early 1980s, but contained costs by increasing caseloads and abandoning cotherapy. Statewide implementation of administrative rules for family-centered services established a uniform policy for IDHS family therapists and all IDHS social workers (IDHS, 1985).

The philosophy of the family therapy program is based on the belief that children's needs are best met by their own families in their own homes. The family is regarded as the service recipient, and the program goal is to preserve the family, either by preventing placement or by achieving reunification. In compliance with the "reasonable efforts" standard of P.L. 96-272, all families are offered family therapy before a placement is made. Families with children already in placement are selectively offered therapy. Therapists use a systems approach involving short-term, brief therapy with a limited, problem-solving focus.

In the Ottumwa district, family therapists see clients primarily in their offices, although in-home work is done at times, often for assessment. Families are usually seen over a three- to six-month period, weekly at first and then every two weeks as service draws to a close. IDHS family therapists provide only therapy; a case manager from the family's county office is responsible for arranging other supportive and concrete services.

Families in need of service are referred to their county office; from there a referral to the district for family therapy may be initiated. Criteria for entry into the program include the presence of child abuse or neglect, risk of placement, predelinquency or delinquency, or a court mandate. Referrals may come directly from probation officers, from area education associations (school social workers), or under court order. If a case manager or protective services worker receives the case first, he or she does the initial assessment. Throughout the time the IDHS Family Therapy Unit has the case, the family therapist keeps the referring worker informed of case progress. If family therapy is unsuccessful, the case reverts back to the case manager. Families needing more than weekly contact, cases involving chronic neglect, and those needing parent education are generally referred to one of two purchase-of-service providers (ICFS being one) for home-based services.

Iowa Children and Family Services

Iowa Children and Family Services (ICFS), now Children and Families of Iowa, is a nongovernmental, nonsectarian, statewide human service agency with programs in several cities throughout Iowa. One of the agency's programs, In-Home Family Counseling, arose during a period of general interest in family-based services in the state. It began in Des Moines in 1977, with Comprehensive Education and Training Act (CETA) and United Way funds. IDHS made referrals to the program and over the next eight years prompted the replication of the program in six additional locations.

In-Home Family Counseling is a coordinated family intervention service originally designed to allow youth to remain in their own homes by offering a range of family-strengthening services. In-Home Family Counseling is used as an alternative to institutional, residential, and/or foster care placement, or as a preventive service for families who may otherwise be potentially abusive, neglectful, or headed toward family breakdown. The program's philosophical commitment is to keep families together. Additional goals include advocating for the family, intervening to change the community's response to the family, and in situations where preserving the family is not possible, protecting children by placing them.

In-home family counselors spend the first one or two weeks observing the family in its home and community. Visits at prearranged times with the family allow the in-home counselor to complete a family assessment that details family relationships, conflict resolution abilities, socioeconomic functioning, family communication patterns, children's interrelationships, and parental functioning in the context of the presenting problem. Based on this assessment, the in-home family counselor develops a family treatment plan in conjunction with the entire staff and the referring worker. Direct service and family treatment usually begin two to three weeks after the start of the observation period.

The in-home family counselor, carrying a caseload of four to six families, provides intensive and ongoing service to the family. The counselor is responsible for the development and execution of the family's treatment plan, which may involve such varied activities as individual and family counseling, teaching, role-modeling, and advocating for the family. Since Ottumwa is in rural Iowa and ICFS is the only service provider in certain localities, workers may also perform paraprofessional tasks. Families are seen two to four hours a week for six to nine months, more intensively during assessment and less frequently toward the end of the service period to test maintenance of gains prior to closure.

Eligibility for service is determined by the Iowa Department of Human Services, although self-referrals are also accepted. The increasing number of court-referred cases take priority and go to the top of the waiting list. Clients have generally been through a period of service before they are referred to this program, and many families, particularly those who have had multiple IDHS workers, are discouraged, hopeless and resistant by the time they reach ICFS.

Site-Specific Findings

Both Iowa programs saw mostly white families, half of whom were married couples. Half of the families received AFDC and food stamps and only one-third of the primary caretakers were employed, reflecting poverty comparable to that found in the urban sites in the study (see Appendix F for comparative tables). About 20 percent of the highest-risk children had a prior placement, and half were considered to be at imminent risk of placement. This rate is lower than in most sites, since ICFS served families at risk of child maltreatment as well as placement and IDHS served less dysfunctional families in weekly office appointments. In both agencies a high proportion of families were court ordered into service (20% at ICFS; 42% at IDHS). About half the families were referred for physical abuse, sexual abuse, or neglect, and a quarter or more were referred for marital problems, family relationship problems, or parent-child conflict. Families had significantly fewer problems than those in most of the other study sites.

Treatment goals focused on improving parenting skills and less often involved increasing the families' use of outside counseling services, perhaps because few counseling services were available to families in this rural area. Budgetary considerations also eliminated the use of cotherapy. As a result, Iowa families did not receive as many different kinds of service as those in more urban areas.

Treatment sessions were well attended, with at least 80 percent of the primary caregivers and 50 percent of the second adults who resided in the home attending most or all of the sessions. More than half the primary caregivers cooperated fully with services. Iowa families changed the most in behavior and family relationships, but demonstrated little change in material resources, emotional climate, or perception of their problems. Of the children who were placed by the end of service, one-third to one-half had long-range case plans toward permanency that were documented in the case record.

Due to its target population, the ICFS program had more in common with urban programs serving child protective cases than with its neighbor,

IDHS. The highest-risk children averaged only nine years of age, scored higher on the Child Well-Being Scales, and were more often the biological children of both parents in the family. At 31 years, the primary caregivers were younger than in all but the urban programs and, because they were primarily divorced females receiving AFDC, more frequently lived in poverty.

ICFS families were more often referred and treated for neglect, family relationship problems. and parenting problems than IDHS families. Although they received fewer counseling services, they received more services from other agencies and had more home visits than families in all but one of the other programs, averaging five home visits a month over a seven-and-one-half-month service period. Workers were also more likely to accompany clients to appointments and provide transportation than in most other programs.

Despite the fact that case objectives were often achieved and 86 percent of the families demonstrated positive changes, 19 percent of the cases ended in placement, and 87 percent of the families required continuing services after being closed by ICFS. Older children and those initially at high risk of placement were most likely to be placed.

The IDHS Family Therapy program was more like other programs in the study than ICFS, serving families with older children (average age 13) referred for delinquency, adult relationship problems, and parent-child conflict. Since the family-based program focused on providing therapy, IDHS families received more services from other units in the agency and fewer directly from family-based workers. In-office contacts averaged two in the first month of service and seven over a median service period of three months.

Although only 12 percent of the cases terminated with a placement, 40 percent of the families failed to achieve their service objectives. Despite this, 76 percent showed positive changes and 37 percent required no further services after termination.

Case Examples

Case examples from each of these two agencies provide a picture of the differences between public and private family-based service programs in our study. Two cases which illustrate differences between public and private agency cases across the variety of programs in our sample are described here. Services to the White family, seen by Iowa Children and

Family Services, ended with a placement, while the Larsen family, served by the Iowa Department of Human Services, successfully avoided out-of-home placement.

The White Family

Jenny White and her boyfriend, Jim Jones, lived in a small Iowa town with Jenny's three children: Susan, age 6; Sally, age 4; and Jeff, not quite 1. Jenny, 24 years old, had never been married, dropped out of school in her late teens, and had no employment history. Jim, 26 years old, also had never married and was unemployed although available for work. His occupational history consisted entirely of low paid, unskilled jobs. The family was supported by public assistance programs.

At the time of intake to the family-based service program, the three children were all considered to be at high risk of out-of-home placement due to parental neglect. Susan was attending school; Sally was enrolled in Head Start and considered developmentally at risk. Susan's teacher reported the family to child protective services after frequent unexplained absences. Upon investigation, Susan was found at home caring for her two younger siblings and Jenny was in her bedroom, distraught over a quarrel with Jim. The Iowa Department of Human Services referred the White family to Iowa Children and Family Services, and the family was under court order to participate in services.

The social worker assigned to work with the White family, Beth, was 24 years old, single and without children. She held an associate degree in general studies and had been employed at the agency for nearly two years, earning less than $13,000 annually. Beth characterized worker turnover in the agency as high and morale as low during the time of the study, and expected to leave the agency within a couple of years.

Beth believed in the philosophy that children are better off in their own homes, that families should be encouraged to assume greater responsibility and self-determination in their own lives, and that families should be involved in identifying and prioritizing their treatment goals. In her own practice, Beth considered outreach to resistant families, accompanying families to appointments, educating families through information and role modeling, and promoting or discouraging certain behaviors by suggestion or advice to be extremely important. She believed it was less important to encourage clients to examine their current behavior and its effects on self and others, explore feelings, and delve into the clients' developmental history. Beth felt that she worked best with cases of physical and emotional abuse, child behavior problems, and unemployment. The cases she found most difficult were those involving sexual abuse, chronic neglect, chronic mental illness, and marital problems.

The primary problems identified during the assessment included Jenny's low self-esteem, poor communication with her boyfriend, and the poor parenting skills of both adults. Case objectives focused on working with Jenny to identify her own needs, develop personal interests, and become more involved in the community; to build a more trusting and open relationship with Jim; and to learn about child development, home management, establishing family responsibilities and rules, and setting consequences for breaking those rules.

Beth met with the family intensively in their home for nearly a year, providing family counseling and parent education, as well as accompanying the family to various appointments and meetings. A paraprofessional was employed to work with the family on household management, model appropriate behavior, and provide transportation. Despite these efforts, another report of neglect was made during the service period. Family-based services were terminated and all three children were placed in foster care. While gains had been made in home management skills, in expectations of the children, and in Jenny's recognition of the family's problems and motivation to resolve them, family relationships actually worsened during the year of service, culminating in the separation of Jenny and Jim.

The Larsen Family

Anna and Lars Larsen, aged 51 and 48 respectively, were a married couple living in a small town of fewer than 2,000 people. Both were high school graduates. Anna worked occasionally in unskilled positions, while Lars was employed full-time as an assistant manager of a small business. The family lived on a relatively low income, but did not qualify for any public assistance programs. Nell, aged 15 and in the 11th grade, was Anna's daughter and Lars' adopted daughter. Involved with DHS for the first time when Nell ran away from home, the family was referred by an ongoing service unit of DHS for family therapy. The referring worker noted, in addition to the runaway incident, a high degree of parent-child conflict and other "acting out" behaviors.

The family therapist assigned to this family was 31-year-old Monica, of Asian descent. Married with two children of her own, Monica held a bachelor's degree in counseling and had completed some work toward a master's degree in education. Monica had been employed in the DHS system for six years, half of them in the Family Therapy Unit itself, and earned an annual salary of $20,000. With an average caseload of 35 families, Monica characterized morale as low, work demands as excessive, and turnover as moderate, with staff leaving due to stresses related to the demands of the job and agency policies rather than for greater opportunities elsewhere. At the time we queried her about her experiences, Monica had no plans to leave her position.

Monica felt that the cases she worked best with were those involving physical and sexual abuse, delinquency, parent-child conflict and dysfunctional family relationships; those she found most difficult involved chronic neglect, status offenses, and substance abuse.

In practice philosophy, Monica felt that some of the more important techniques were sympathetic listening, encouragement of clients, outreach to resistant families, educating clients, role modeling, setting mutually-agreed-upon goals, encouraging examination of behaviors and their effects on others, and examining patterns of behavior and feelings.

During the assessment, Nell's runaway behavior and extreme conflict between Nell and her mother were identified as major problems to be addressed by improving communication between Nell and Anna and by helping the family establish and enforce rules. Monica met with Anna and Nell in the office for nearly three months. Mother and child both attended most of the sessions, while Lars was involved in a few sessions. The primary interventions employed were family therapy, education in parenting skills, and homework assignments between sessions. Services were terminated when the family failed to keep several appointments.

At the time the case was closed, Monica noted an improvement in Nell's behavior and in the family's emotional climate. The parents had developed more realistic expectations of Nell and had become more cooperative with the therapeutic process, although they still appeared to have some difficulties enforcing rules at home. Nell, on the other hand, had started to miss school occasionally and had become less actively involved in service. Nevertheless, she had not had any further runaway incidents.

These case examples illustrate some of the typical characteristics of families and social workers served by public and private agencies: the younger, poorer, multiproblem White family was served intensively in the home for an extended period of time by the private agency; the Larsen family, older, better educated and more economically stable, with a more focused problem area, was briefly served through weekly office sessions by the public agency. The case outcome, placement of the White children, and nonplacement for the Larsen family, is understandable given the differences in their circumstances.

The social worker serving the White family was relatively young and inexperienced, holding an associate degree in an unrelated field, yet adhering to the principles of family empowerment. The family therapist in the Larsen case had considerably more professional experience and education, and was a parent herself. While both workers characterized turnover as high during the period of our study, Beth was planning to leave the private agency within a year or two, while Monica expected to remain with the public agency.

The service delivery features of each program matched the needs of its clientele: low caseloads and longer in-home services in the private agency enable workers to spend more time with the families whose needs are greatest. Brief services delivered in the office to higher-functioning families with more limited problems enable the public workers to serve more families (although in this case, the caseloads of IDHS were certainly too high). Where this system falls short is in the salary discrepancies between the public and private agencies, which make recruitment and retention of experienced staff difficult in the private agencies.

RELATION TO OTHER STUDIES

What do these findings suggest about public and private provision of family-based services? In some ways, the data fail to support a number of commonly held beliefs about public social services. First, in contrast to the general experience of service providers in public agencies (Pecora et al., 1990), the public agency workers in this study had a lower turnover rate, better morale, and higher salaries than those in private agencies. In Iowa, which was experiencing critical economic difficulties during the study period, public agency morale and turnover were more problematic than in other states. Even so, IDHS still fared better than its private counterpart, ICFS. Cost savings in private agencies appear to derive from lower salaries, which in turn contribute to higher turnover and the employment of less experienced personnel.

Second, public agencies control intake and screening in family-based services and in this study, served families with older children and fewer problems, while referring low-income, multiproblem families to private agencies. Although this is contrary to the image of public agencies as the primary service providers for the poor, it may be a quite rational response to maintaining services in the face of budget cuts and high caseloads. Furthermore, such a division of labor may in fact result in low-income families receiving more comprehensive services than public agencies can normally provide (Gibelman, 1981). This advantage, however, may be offset by the difficulty private agencies face in attracting and retaining experienced personnel.

The data support the perception that private agencies provide more accessible and flexible services than public agencies, and that they have more success in working with the community. To meet contract requirements, however, private workers must in general countenance greater involvement by the referring public agency workers in goal setting on their cases and report with greater frequency on their progress. Although coordination and accountability may require frequent reporting, restricting the ability of private agency workers and their clients to set case goals mutually appears to be counterproductive, since private agency workers were more likely to report case failures due to inappropriate goals. Controlled by government contracts, private agencies may be in danger of losing their historic differences and of becoming simply an arm of the public bureaucracy (Smith, 1989).

How, then, do we resolve the controversy over private versus public provision of family-based services? In practice, the question is addressed in the mechanisms that the agencies themselves have established. The public agency is responsible for implementing the requirements of P.L. 96-272 and may do this either by providing service directly or by purchasing services from private providers and monitoring those services. The data indicate that when providing the service directly, public agencies keep the clients that can be served with less intensive services, and refer families with multiple needs to private agencies which can provide more frequent and accessible service. While this is not without its own set of problems, it represents an ecological approach to rationing the community's social service resources in financially troubled times, assures that the families at greatest risk receive services, and provides the necessary public funding to extend private agency services to the poor (Gronbjerg, 1990; Smith, 1989).

The existing system for delivering family-based services reflects its diverse developmental history. The growing numbers of programs are provided by both public and private agencies. In fact, as Salamon (1987) has noted, the real question facing service planners and administrators is not whether services should be provided by the public or by the private sector, but how public and private agencies can best cooperate in a coordinated service delivery system. In practice, the most successful community-based service delivery systems combine public and private efforts, effectively and efficiently melding existing resources with new initiatives.

Chapter Nine

PROVIDING FAMILY-BASED SERVICES IN AN OFFICE

Since many of the oldest and best-known placement prevention programs provide in-home services (e.g. Homebuilders in Washington State and FAMILIES, INC. of West Branch, Iowa) it has become almost axiomatic that services to prevent out-of-home placement of children should be delivered in families' homes. Initially, "home-based" referred to the location of the child rather than the location of services. However, in one of the earliest publications of the National Resource Center on Family Based Services (then the National Clearinghouse on Home Based Services), Bryce (1979) offered the following definition:

1. Home-based care is provided primarily in the home.
2. The parents remain in charge, and are counted on to participate.
3. The family system and natural habitat are utilized and the family is related to as a unit.
4. The program will help, or arrange for help, with any problem area presented by the family or observed to be a problem by the service providers.
5. The program makes a commitment of contractual substance to the family. . . .
6. Extensive use is made of the natural resources of extended family, neighborhood, and community (p. 20).

Programs with differing theoretical orientations, such as Homebuilders and FAMILIES, INC., provide services in the home in order to improve outreach and accessibility, assess problems more accurately, model behavior in a realistic setting, and realize maximum self-determination for families (Kinney, Haapala, Booth, & Leavitt, 1988; Leverington & Wulff, 1988). Other placement prevention programs, especially those whose original goal was deinstitutionalizing youth, have developed in-office services. Oregon's Children's Services Division has experimented with both in-home and in-office delivery of their Intensive Family Services program and has found few differences in outcome that are attributable to the location of services (Showell & White, 1990).

ADVANTAGES OF IN-HOME SERVICES

Long identified with social work practice, in-home interventions became disassociated from therapy when a Freudian-based medical model became predominant in psychotherapy (Leverington & Wulff, 1988). Although a psychiatric model of social work practice still prevails in mental health agencies and private practice, its limitations in treating poor multiproblem families, social work's traditional clients, have become apparent.

Starting with the St. Paul Family Project in Minneapolis, family-based programs worked to overcome the barriers to service erected by office-based practice and to reach out to families in their own homes (Horejsi, 1981). More recently, complex treatment models building on the advantages of in-home interventions have been developed for chronically dysfunctional families (Kagan & Schlosberg, 1989; Kaplan, 1986; Rabin, Rosenbaum, & Sens, 1982). These treatment approaches recognize that poor families with few material and emotional resources are unlikely to see the relevance of office-based therapy, lack reliable transportation and child care, and therefore often fail to keep office appointments. At the same time, as a result of previous negative experiences with social service workers and other helpers, they are likely to be suspicious and distrustful of professionals (Rabin et al., 1982).

In-home services overcome these barriers by meeting families on their own turf where they are in control and by demonstrating their concern for the family in coming to them. Providing services in the home also tacitly acknowledges that, although families may be propelled involuntarily into services, actually changing the situation is ultimately up to them (Kagan & Schlosberg, 1989).

In-home services provide increased access to information for assessment purposes. In addition to observing the physical environment of the home, workers can directly observe family interactions, the presence or absence of friends and extended family, and symbolic cues to the family's problems. Home visits reveal the family's strengths as well as their deficiencies and enable the worker to comment on what the family is doing well in addition to assessing their problems (Kagan & Schlosberg, 1989; Leverington & Wulff, 1988).

In the home, talking therapy can be supplemented by concrete services and direct teaching of skills. The provision of services such as financial assistance, transportation, child care, and food or furniture, not only meets basic needs often found in poor families, but offers tangible evidence of the worker's concern and helpfulness (Rabin et al., 1982). Thus, these services often create the trust and relationship necessary for therapeutic effectiveness. Direct teaching of skills and behaviors through role modeling, role playing, and task assignments also helps to engage families in change. Assisting the family to negotiate community services simultaneously teaches skills and secures services to meet needs (Leverington & Wulff, 1988).

ADVANTAGES OF IN-OFFICE SERVICES

Although in-home services are a necessary alternative for some families, others with more material and emotional resources or with more anxiety and motivation may benefit from office-based services. Both Compher (1983) and Hutchinson and Nelson (1985) offer typologies that recognize different levels of family need that may require different timing, intensity, length, and location of services. Families with adequate parenting skills who need assistance securing concrete and other services may require brief service from a case manager, while families with behavioral problems and adequate resources may primarily need counseling. In these cases of limited, situational problems office-based services may suffice, whereas families needing multiple concrete and therapeutic services may require in-home services.

Even when services are delivered in the office, home visits may be used for assessment of the physical and social environment. As researchers employing direct observation have long noted, infrequent or intimate behavior may be difficult to observe even in its natural setting. Experiments have demonstrated that structuring a task for families to accomplish reveals problem behaviors more quickly than naturalistic observation in home or office settings and accelerates assessment (Webster-Stratton, 1985).

When services center more on therapy than on meeting material needs or teaching skills, an office setting may offer advantages such as increased control of disruptive behavior, a focus on the therapeutic task, assessment of motivation to change, and special facilities such as videotaping and one-way mirrors. Especially in cases involving delinquency or sexual abuse where family hierarchy and boundaries are most at issue, the additional structure of an office interview may facilitate change.

Finally, office-based interventions offer a certain degree of protection for workers in terms of both physical safety and emotional distance. Therapists warn against the emotional overidentification that can occur when workers become involved in family processes in the home (Reynolds-Mejia & Levitan, 1990). Teams involving two professional workers or a combination of therapists, case managers, and paraprofessionals can also provide both physical and emotional safeguards (Compher, 1983; Rabin et al., 1982), but are often not used due to the expense involved in sending more than one worker to a family's home.

Despite a rich clinical literature on the advantages of both in-home and in-office services, there has been no research comparing the use or benefits of each setting. Location of service has been a constant in most studies of family-based services. A notable exception is the family treatment program of the Children's Services Division in Oregon. Comparing outcomes for families served in home and office settings, CSD researchers found neglect cases to have better outcomes when seen at home, delinquency cases to be better served in office settings, and both settings to be effective for physical and sexual abuse cases (Hartley, Showell, & White, 1989). Although rigorously testing the effectiveness of in-home services compared to in-office services requires an experimental study with random assignment to different treatment locations, the present study offers an opportunity to examine the different conditions under which families are seen in office or home settings and, with statistical controls, to identify features that differentiate in-office from in-home services.

STUDY SAMPLE

The nine programs in this study included three in-office programs and six in-home programs. All three of the office-based programs were administered by public agencies, as were two of the in-home programs. The other four in-home programs were provided by private agencies. Workers who saw families in the office most often used office interviews for assessment, to provide more structure or control, to test a family's motivation for service, or to save travel time.

Although in-home workers strongly believed in the necessity of delivering services in the family's home, not all workers thought the location of service delivery was critical to the success of family-based services. More than half the workers (62%) believed that the most effective location of service delivery depended on the individual case. Therefore, rather than characterizing an entire program as in-office or in-home, classification for this analysis was done on a case-by-case basis according to where the majority of contacts took place (Table IX–I). There was still a strong tendency for programs to deliver services to families in one location or the other; no program used in-home and in-office services equally.

Table IX-I
PERCENTAGE OF FAMILIES WITH MAJORITY OF CONTACTS
IN HOME AND OFFICE BY SITE

	n	*Home* *n* = 306	*Office* *n* = 147
In-Office Programs			
Boulder County Social Services, CO	46	12.4	87.6
Oregon Children's Services Division	48	12.4	87.6
Iowa Department of Human Services	50	15.5	84.5
In-Home Programs			
Iowa Children & Family Services	49	100.0	0
SCAN, Philadelphia, PA	54	100.0	0
Franklin County Children Services, OH	51	98.3	1.7
Intensive Family Services, Multnomah County, OR	50	91.4	8.6
Dakota County Human Services, MN	54	86.3	13.7
Lutheran Social Services, MN	50	82.3	17.7
Total	452	67.6	32.4

Note. Weighted to approximate incidence of placement and nonplacement in the population; *n*'s vary in subsequent tables due to weighting and missing data. Percentages may not total 100 due to rounding.

Since office-based programs were more likely to be located in suburban public agencies providing services to families with juvenile justice problems and in-home programs to be located in private agencies serving younger child maltreatment cases (Table IX–II), four-way analysis of variance was used to attempt to hold constant the effects of population size, auspices, and type of case. The severity of the family's problems has also been found to vary according to auspices and location of service, (Nelson, Emlen, Landsman, & Hutchinson, 1988, ch. 7), so the primary caretaker's level of functioning was controlled by introducing the Parental Disposition subscale of the Child Well-Being Scales as a covariate.

This analysis identified the most important features related to location of service. The tables in this chapter reflect the characteristics, weighted to estimate their actual incidence in the study population, that significantly differentiated in-office from in-home services after the other variables were controlled.

Table IX-II
PROGRAM CHARACTERISTICS BY LOCATION OF
SERVICE DELIVERY TO FAMILIES

Program Characteristics	Home n = 306	Office n = 147
Geographic Location$_a$		
Rural	32.4	37.1
Suburban	19.8	59.4
Urban	47.8	3.5
Auspices$_a$		
Public	36.8	90.5
Private	63.2	9.5
Primary Reason for Referral		
Physical Abuse	10.3	2.9
Sexual Abuse	1.4	4.1
Neglect	13.6	1.5
Delinquency	8.8	22.3
Status Offense	14.4	11.9
Non-Statutory	51.5	57.2

Note. Percentages.
$_a p < .001$.
TIX:II

STUDY FINDINGS

In analyzing the social worker and case record data in this way, significant differences between in-home and in-office family-based services emerged along several dimensions. First looking at worker and caseload characteristics, workers delivering office-based services had nearly one year more education, on average, than those working primarily in the families' homes (Table IX–III). In-home workers, however, had greater access to funds for conferences, continuing education, and books. Only funds for consultation were more readily available to in-office than to in-home workers.

Table IX–III
WORKER EDUCATION AND RESOURCES BY LOCATION OF SERVICE

		Home[a] *n = 47*	*Office* *n = 27*
Education and Training			
Years of Education	*m*	17.6	18.3
	sd	.9	1.5
Funds Generally Available For:			
Conferences	%	61.7**	18.9
Education	%	40.0	16.1
Books	%	33.8*	15.4
Consultants	%	27.7	44.2*

Note. Worker report, weighted by number of cases in sample.
[a]Franklin County excluded due to insufficient response.
*$p < .05$. **$p < .001$.

Both in-office and in-home workers spent about the same proportion of their time in face-to-face contacts with families, but in-home workers spent more time traveling (Table IX–IV). Travel time was strongly related to location and auspices of the program with in-home workers in rural private agencies traveling the most. Increased travel time is also reflected in the lower caseloads of in-home workers. In-home workers coordinated more closely with referring workers than did in-office workers, most often with weekly phone contact and quarterly case plans and reports.

In this study families served in the office had different problems and characteristics than those served in the home (Table IX–V). Without controlling for other differences, the cases most often seen in an office setting concerned delinquency and sexual abuse, while families referred primarily for neglect, physical abuse, and status offenses were much more likely to be seen in their homes.

Generally, families seen in the office more often had two adults in the household, compliant caretakers, and older children (Table IX–VI). Families seen in their homes were more often single parents referred for child abuse or neglect, who had more children at risk of imminent placement, and who were receiving concurrent child protective services. In terms of outcome, there were fewer differences than might be expected. The number of areas of positive change and placement rates did not differ significantly between the different kinds of families seen in the office and the home when other factors were controlled.

Table IX-IV
WORK ALLOCATION BY LOCATION OF SERVICE

Work Allocation		Home[a] n = 47	Office n = 27
Allocation of Time			
In-person Contact	%	44.3	42.0
Travel	%	16.1**	9.3
Average Caseload[b]	m	9.0	16.0**
	sd	4.8	8.7
Coordination With Referring Worker			
Quarterly Case Plan	%	80.3*	39.8
Quarterly Reports	%	94.3**	52.1
Weekly Phone Contact	%	36.5*	3.8

Note. Worker report weighted by number of cases in sample.
[a]Franklin County excluded due to insufficient response. [b]Range: 1–35, 4–35.
*$p < .01$.   **$p < .001$.

Table IX-V
PRIMARY REASON FOR REFERRAL OF FAMILY BY LOCATION OF SERVICE

Reason for Referral[a]	n	Home n = 306 %	Office n = 147 %
Delinquency	63	54.9	45.1
Sexual Abuse	52	60.6	39.4
Physical Abuse	99	76.9	23.1
Status Offenses	63	78.5	21.5
Neglect	66	93.3	6.7

[a]$p < .001$.

Factors Related to Placement

While it is useful to separate out the difference between in-office and in-home interventions without interference from population size, type of case, auspices, and severity of problems, in practice these are intermingled. In looking for predictors of success and failure, therefore, all 150 cases in

Table IX-VI
FAMILY CHARACTERISTICS, SERVICES AND CHANGE BY LOCATION OF SERVICE

		Home $n = 306$	Office $n = 147$
Family Characteristics			
Number of Adults	m	1.8	2.1**
	sd	.6	.6
Caretaker Compliance Score	m	71.7	79.0**
	sd	15.7	17.0
Age of Highest-Risk Child	m	10.2	12.8**
	sd	5.3	3.5
Number at High Risk[a]	m	1.0**	.6
	sd	1.0	.7
Services			
Child Protective Services	%	45.1*	25.0
Information and Referral	%	55.9*	38.4
Change Score[b]	m	4.0*	3.2
	sd	2.8	2.2

[a]Range: 0–5. [b]Range: 0–10, 0–8, measured by Family Systems Change Scale.
*$p < .01$.   **$p < .001$.

which the majority of contacts were in an office were examined in order to highlight this more unusual format for family-based services. A discriminant analysis revealed that the most important factors associated with placement in office-based cases were the compliance of the primary caretaker and the severity of the lowest-functioning child's problems, both measured by the Child Well-Being Scales (see Appendix E). Placement was *less* likely to occur in families with more compliant caretakers and children with less severe problems. Caretaker attendance at most or all the sessions (83% nonplacement vs 61% placement) also contributed to a positive case outcome.

Placement was *more* likely to occur in families with children at greater risk of placement (1 versus .6 children per family), those who had moved in the past year (49% of placement and 19% of nonplacement cases), and those with a second adult in the home (70% of placement and 54% of nonplacement cases). Having a second adult in the home was related to both higher risk and placement in sexual abuse cases, primarily because if the perpetrator was out of the home, the risk to the child decreased dramatically.

Several service characteristics also affected placement in families seen in the office. Case outcomes were more likely to be successful if service objectives included working on marital problems (44% nonplacement versus 15% placement), increasing the family's use of outside counseling (36% nonplacement versus 24% placement), or, after all other differences were accounted for, changing family relationships (38% nonplacement versus 42% placement). Finally, several other characteristics made small contributions to predicting placement: a case manager in another unit in the agency, a female primary caretaker, juvenile offenses, and a case objective of changing parenting all were associated with placement. All together 98 percent of successful case outcomes were correctly predicted by the thirteen variables in the statistical model, but only half of the placements.

In order to compare predictors of case outcome in office settings with those of in-home services, the same set of variables was used to predict placement in cases served primarily in the home. Four of the six strongest predictors were the same, although in a different order of importance. The number of children at high risk of placement, the involvement of the primary caretaker in most of the sessions, the lowest functioning child's Child Well-Being Score, and a move in the prior year were all significant predictors of case outcome regardless of service location. Children with juvenile offenses were at higher risk of placement in families receiving in-home services as well, but neither initial compliance of the primary caretaker nor case objectives involving marital counseling predicted outcome in in-home cases. The in-home model was equally accurate in predicting placement prevention (98%) but even less accurate in predicting placement (19%), indicating that factors not included in this analysis but found to be significant for the types of cases seen in the home, such as previous placements and continuity in caretaking, may be more related to placement in in-home services.

CASE STUDIES

The Intensive Family Therapy Program

To further illustrate the nature of family-based services delivered in an office setting, two cases from a program employing a family treatment model will be presented, illustrating both successful and unsuccessful outcomes.

Agency Description

The Intensive Family Therapy (IFT) program is one of several services designed to offer an alternative to residential placement in Boulder County, Colorado. The program was established in 1980 in response to the statewide Alternative to Out-of-Home Placement Act (SB 26), which in 1979 capped funds available for foster care and residential programs, redirecting them to placement prevention and reunification. Boulder County was one of the first counties in Colorado's state-supervised, county-administered system to utilize the option of diverting foster care funds into placement alternative programs.

The Intensive Family Therapy program is directed at severely disturbed, multiproblem families with the aim of reducing expensive residential placements. More recently it has also been used to reunify families who have a child in an institutional placement. While family-based workers' primary function is to provide therapy, they also make referrals for other services and perform case management functions as necessary. Workers operate primarily in the office to maintain control of the therapeutic environment, to save travel time, and to emphasize to the family that therapy is a professional activity. The main treatment approach is structural family therapy, but workers blend a number of intervention models.

Boulder is the only county in Colorado to have decentralized into three full-service branch offices. IFT workers are part of teams within these district offices. In 1984 a separate IFT supervisor was employed to give the program a representative in the agency administrative structure and in the county Placement Alternatives Commission (PAC). The additional supervision also provides a unifying force for the IFT workers dispersed in the three branch offices.

The IFT supervisor screens all cases referred from the intake or protective service units. If there is a question about the appropriateness of the referral or the workability of the family, IFT will accept the family for four to six assessment sessions, after which a decision is made about continuing services. Workers are expected to serve at least twelve families at a time, but caseloads typically range from fifteen to seventeen. Families are seen weekly for about two hours. The PAC sets a twelve-month limit on services, although this can be extended if there are grounds for doing so.

Site-Specific Findings

Since Boulder County targets adolescents at risk of residential placement, the average ages of both the highest-risk child (13) and primary caretakers (38) were older than the study average (see Appendix F for comparative tables). More than a quarter of the primary caretakers were male, a characteristic shared with other programs serving a high proportion of adolescents. While three-quarters of the primary caretakers were married, only about a third of the highest-risk children in the families were the biological children of the second adult, male or female, in the family. Two-thirds of the primary caretakers were employed.

Although only 26 percent of the highest-risk children were at risk of imminent placement, 22 percent had been placed before and 28 percent were court-ordered into service. Families were referred most frequently for parent-child conflict and treatment focused more on parent-child conflict and family dysfunction than in other programs. Because of their location in a relatively wealthy area near Denver, none of the families received AFDC, although they more often received case management services than in most other sites.

Families in Boulder had more direct contact and received more different kinds of interventions from the family-based program than families in the Midwest or in Oregon. Specifically, in addition to family counseling, Boulder County workers more often used individual counseling, marriage counseling, role modeling, homework assignments, and therapeutic contracts than those in other sites. Families may have received a greater variety of services because their cases were open longer than in other sites. Although the average case was open for about ten months, half the cases were closed within eight months. Families were seen once a week. Teaming was also used more in providing services: over a third of the families were seen by cotherapists or by a single worker in consultation with the team.

Despite coming from a very troubled adolescent population, only 8 percent of the Boulder County cases ended in placement. More than 90 percent of the families showed positive change, and only 20 percent exhibited negative change. More than half the families required no further services at closing, the second highest proportion in the study.

Although both the primary caretakers and the second adults in the families attended a lower proportion of sessions than the study average, more than 80 percent of the primary caretakers cooperated fully with services. The cooperation of the primary caretaker was an important factor in placement prevention in Boulder County as well as for families seen in office settings in general. Also in common with other office-based programs, having a child at risk of imminent placement at the outset was the best predictor of an outcome of placement in the IFT program.

Case Examples

The Johnson Family

The first case example, the Johnson family, consisted of a father, Bob, who was a 50-year-old college graduate employed in a middle-management sales position, and his three children. Bob was divorced four years previously and was granted custody of the children: Bob Jr., 20 years old, 15-year-old Linda, considered the child at risk of placement, and 12-year-old Jack. The children's mother lived in a nearby town and suffered from depression from time to time.

Bob referred himself to the Department of Human Services because of severe conflict with Linda. Linda had been running away and was exhibiting a great deal of hostility at home as well as experimenting with illegal drugs. Linda had been placed briefly in a group home because of behavior problems once before. Bob was very much concerned with avoiding another placement, and from the beginning was very cooperative with the service plan. The case objectives that the family and worker agreed upon focused on reducing conflict between father and daughter, dealing with some unresolved divorce issues, enabling Bob to adapt to the role of single parent, improving family communication, having Linda evaluated by a psychologist for a possible behavior disorder, and arranging for individual counseling for Linda around that issue.

Sue, the social worker on this case, was a 35-year-old single woman, with a doctoral degree in counseling. She had worked for six years in family therapy and had been with this program for about three years at the time she served the Johnsons. Sue carried a caseload of around eleven families, fourteen at most, and believed that the office was the most effective setting for family-based services because it enabled a certain amount of structure which was hard to achieve with in-home therapy. She noted that 60 percent of her time was spent in face-to-face contacts with clients, only about 5 percent in traveling, and the rest in administrative and consultative activities.

The Johnsons were seen for five months, about once a week, sometimes twice in the first couple of months. Meetings were held in the office rather than the home, with both Bob and Linda attending nearly all of the sessions. The mother was invited to and attended a few sessions having to do with resolving divorce issues, and the other children were brought into a few of the sessions as well.

The case ended without a placement, with noted improvements in the behavior of family members and in family dynamics. Although the reason for closure was that service was no longer effective, some case goals had been achieved: reducing conflict, resolving divorce issues, and helping Bob function better in his single-parent role. Linda was following up with individual counseling.

Sue believed that one of the most important factors for effective preventive services was having families establish their own case goals. Her definition of success in family-based services was that a family was able to solve its own problems without outside intervention. In this case, the Johnson family had identified the most important problems and made significant progress toward resolution. While some problems remained, by the end of service they were prepared to work on these problems on their own.

The Smith Family

The second case study is the Smith family, a two-parent blended family that consisted of 35-year-old Jill, employed full-time as a waitress, 35-year-old Steve, who worked seasonally in construction, and five children: 16- and 14-year old boys who were the biological children of Jill and the stepchildren of Steve; a 12-year-old boy, John, who was the biological child of Steve and the stepchild of Jill, the child identified as being at risk of placement; a 4-year-old daughter, the biological child of both parents; and a recently adopted infant daughter of a deceased relative. The Smiths moved to this small city from a rural area within the prior year, and were struggling to support a large family on a very low income.

The Smiths were referred to the child protective services unit by the school for suspected physical abuse of John as well as for John's behavior problems at school. John's score on the Child Well-Being Scales indicated that there were considerable problems in his relationships with peers, parents, and teacher.

When the primary worker for this family, Anne, met with the family, the parents seemed very unmotivated to work on resolving problems with John. They appeared to be rejecting him, were very disapproving of him, and preferred to have him placed out of the home; they were, however, willing to delay placement and use the family-based service which was offered.

Anne, a 40-year-old social worker, married with two children of her own, had fourteen years of family experience (two in this particular agency). She worked primarily with low-income and blended families both in home and office settings, depending on the circumstances of the clients. Like Sue, the social worker in the Johnson case, Anne spent most of her time in direct client contact and carried a similar caseload.

A second worker, Jim, joined as cotherapist, and with the family they established case goals around resolving anger in the family, increasing family members' involvement with John, and assuring safety in the home. After about six months of service including family therapy once or twice weekly, individual therapy and recreational services, John was placed in a residential treatment center with the goal of reunification. Services continued for another couple of months and then the case was closed with the family-based program.

Unfortunately, the only case goals that were achieved were assuring John's safety in the home and assessing his need for placement. Diffusion of anger and increasing the family's positive involvement with John had not been achieved. While the cotherapists had been working toward reunification, this did not occur and services were finally terminated. The family was assessed at termination as having gotten worse in several areas of family functioning, including family structure, behavior, use of available services and community involvement with the family. A follow-up at six months found John still living away from his family, though in a less restrictive setting, a group home. From her years of family therapy experience, Anne believed that timing is an important factor contributing to success and failure: some families were referred too late, some were not ready for the service, and others were simply not motivated to change.

DISCUSSION

Contrary to the general pattern of providing family-based services in the home, several public agencies have established successful office-based placement prevention programs. These differ from in-home programs in that they provide services more often to two-parent families with problems involving the sexual abuse or delinquency of older children. For these kinds of families, it makes little difference whether services are delivered in their homes or in an office setting. Although some in-home workers strongly believe in the necessity of delivering services in family homes, others see benefits in fitting service to the needs of individual families and use in-office services for assessment, to provide structure, to test motivation or to save travel time so that more families can be seen.

These differences are consistent with the descriptions of in-home and in-office services found in the literature and suggest a division of labor in which families with more resources or greater motivation can be seen in the office, reserving home-based services for harder-to-reach families. Through the use of a complementary approach such as that employed by the Iowa agencies described in Chapter Eight, community resources can be used efficiently to provide services to the greatest number of families.

Chapter Ten

THE FUTURE OF FAMILY-BASED SERVICE

Family preservation services cannot be reduced to a single program model or design. More than anything else, this study reveals the richness and diversity in the field. These programs show that no matter what the circumstances of the agency or community, an alternative to immediate placement can be provided. Both statistical analyses and case studies demonstrate that family-based programs can be provided by public as well as private agencies; can be delivered effectively in an office as well as in a family's home; can be designed to meet the needs of urban as well as rural families; and can deal with a wide variety of problems: physical abuse, sexual abuse, neglect, status offenses, and juvenile delinquency.

The variations in the context in which family-based services are provided indicate that all programs should not be expected to be alike. Each agency must adapt its family-based program to the specific community environment, target population, and resources available to it. Hard decisions that affect the type and potential success of the services must be made about eligibility requirements, staff qualifications, caseload sizes, and length of service. Fortunately these choices can be informed by the experiences of earlier programs that creatively met these challenges and prospered. The nine family-based programs described in this study offer guidance for future programs.

One of the benefits of this and other recent studies is the identification of patterns of intervention theory, program structure, and principles of practice that recur in family-based services. These we have grouped in the three models described in the first chapter: the crisis intervention model, typified by Homebuilders (also called Intensive Family Preservation Services); the home-based model, developed in the Midwest; and the family treatment model, which emphasizes therapeutic interventions. The descriptions and analyses of the nine programs in this study can be used in program development by agencies interested in the home-based or family treatment models. Other resources are available for those

160

interested in establishing crisis intervention programs (Whittaker, Kinney, Tracy, & Booth, 1990; Kinney, Haapala, & Booth, 1991; Fraser, Pecora, & Haapala, 1991).

TARGET POPULATIONS

Although programs often served more than one target population, the characteristics and services most predictive of a case outcome of non-placement tended to cluster by reason for referral and to differ for each subgroup. In all types of cases, however, avoidance of placement was strongly associated with positive change in the family. Positive change was found even in families that experienced placement, however, non-placement cases typically changed more and, unlike many placement cases, showed no significant deterioration in any area of functioning measured by the Family Systems Change Scale (Table X–I).

Several predictors of placement were common to most of the groups. In keeping with Belsky's theory that individual characteristics may predispose a parent to maltreatment, the overall level of parental functioning, as measured by the Parental Disposition subscale of the Child Well-Being Scales, was significantly related to placement in all but one of the subgroups, especially in the discriminant analyses of cases involving physical abuse and delinquency. The initial level of compliance with services by the primary caretaker, which is part of the Parental Disposition subscale, was predictive of placement prevention in the discriminant analysis of sexual abuse cases. Conflictual family-child relationships also created a situation more favorable to placement in all types of cases, except those involving delinquency. However, overall child functioning, when considered jointly with other factors, only helped to predict case outcome in status offense cases.

Less than adequate parental functioning, according to Belsky's theory, does not create maltreatment or child behavior problems unless stressors are present in the environment and resources are inadequate to cope with the stress. Poverty, marital problems, health problems, large families, divorce, child behavior problems, school problems, and substance abuse were all stressors that contributed to placement in one or more of the subgroups. Poverty, especially in cases of physical abuse and neglect, and the lack of effective support from a second parent because of absence or conflict also decreased the resources for coping with these stressors for many families.

Table X-I
FACTORS RELATED TO PLACEMENT IN FIVE SUBPOPULATIONS

		Neglect $n = 38$	Physical Abuse $n = 36$	Sexual Abuse $n = 24$	Status Offense $n = 40$	Delinquency $n = 62$
Number of Areas of						
Positive Change[a]	m	1.9***	2.4*	1.6***	1.9***	1.6**
	sd	2.2	2.9	2.2	2.5	2.0
Negative Change[b]	m	1.2***	.7	1.5**	1.8***	1.3***
	sd	1.4	1.2	1.8	1.9	1.8
Child Well-Being Scales						
Parental Disposition	m	59.4***	65.7**	67.0**	66.6	67.4**
	sd	12.9	13.4	12.9	11.2	13.9
Caretaker's Compliance[c]	m	60.6**	66.8†	65.3***	68.0	69.5**
	sd	14.0	17.5	13.6	11.5	15.0
Child's Family Relations	m	57.3***	61.7*	57.9*	49.4†	54.2
	sd	23.7	19.6	22.1	17.2	20.5
Prior Placement of Highest Risk Child	%	41.6*	37.4*	47.7	54.2*	48.9
Number of Children at High Risk[d]	m	1.9**	1.4*	1.2***	1.1	1.1*
	sd	1.3	1.0	.8	.7	.6
Attended Most Sessions						
Primary Caretaker	%	23.0***	54.3*	71.4	65.5	74.1
Highest Risk Child	%	16.7**	44.9	40.4	44.1*	26.0**

Note. Significance tested with two-tail t-tests and chi-square. Scores for placement families only.
[a]Range: 0–8, 0–10, 0–8, 0–8, 0–7. [b]Range: 0–4, 0–4, 0–6, 0–7, 0–6. [c]Motivation, recognition, and cooperation subscales. [d]Range: 0–4, 0–5, 0–3, 0–4, 0–4.
†$p < .10$.　*$p < .05$.　**$p < .01$.　***$p < .001$.

In addition to level of parental functioning and environmental stressors that trigger maltreatment or child behavior problems, a history of prior placement was significantly related to outcome in most of the subgroups, especially in the discriminant analyses of cases involving neglect and status offenses. Unless families are tracked from their first contact with social services, it cannot be determined whether this indicates the presence of more severe and continuing problems in the family, a loosening of family bonds that makes a second or third placement easier than the first, a further deterioration in family relationships and functioning caused by the earlier placement, or some combination of these.

While both parental functioning and prior placements are important determinants of case outcome, the risk of imminent placement at intake, as rated by the case reviewer, was also related to an outcome of placement. This relationship suggests that case characteristics known at the outset of services can be used with some degree of accuracy to predict the outcome of the case. Two alternative explanations are also possible, however. Since case reviewers knew the outcome of the case, it is possible that this knowledge affected their ratings of risk. It is also likely that not all the children were truly at risk of placement and that inaccuracy in targeting services led to lower placement rates among children who were inaccurately referred as at risk of placement and higher placement rates among those who were truly at risk of imminent placement. Assessing risk and targeting services will be discussed later in this chapter as unresolved problems for research and policy.

Although to some extent the dice are weighted towards placement or family preservation before the worker even sees the family, services can have a major impact on case outcome. Some aspect of family-based service had a significant effect on outcome in the statistical models for all the subgroups, with the largest impact in status offense cases.

Given the small sample sizes and the many variables in each analysis, it is encouraging that some services demonstrated a significant effect on outcome, even though most services were not significant on their own and the most effective services differed for each subpopulation. Marital counseling and role modeling had significant positive effects in physical abuse cases as did paraprofessional services in neglect cases. In the discriminant analyses, an objective to increase the family's use of outside counseling, role modeling, and child protective services had positive effects in treating sexual abuse, as did teaching, teaming, and in-home services in status offense cases, and role modeling in neglect cases. None of these services, however, had a significant effect on outcome when considered apart from the other factors in the models.

Across all the service populations studied, among the most important factors for a successful outcome were engaging the primary caretaker and the highest-risk child in services. In the discriminant analyses of cases involving neglect and physical abuse, getting the primary caretaker to participate in most or all of the treatment sessions proved extremely important in averting placement. In the discriminant analyses of juvenile justice cases, involving the highest-risk child in most of the sessions was critical. In the statistical model for sexual abuse cases both the cooperation of the primary caretaker and participation of the child were important. However, the participation of a second adult was predictive of placement of the child, indicating that successful sexual abuse cases included only children and their mothers.

The ability of family-based services to engage and involve hard-to-reach families is, perhaps, their greatest asset. Starting with an attitude of respect for family strengths and immediate attention to the family's expressed needs, and continuing with the ability to muster a variety of concrete and supportive services and perseverance in the face of resistance, family-based workers make it, in the words of one parent, "hard not to change." Workers must, of course, have the time, resources, and support to persist and demonstrate their helpfulness, but given these conditions, most families will respond. Informal follow-ups and even continuing friendships maintain links between workers and families, and many programs encourage families to return for "booster shots" when future crises once again threaten their stability. The goal-focused and time-limited nature of family-based services make it possible to keep an open door while encouraging family independence.

PUBLIC OR PRIVATE AUSPICES?

There has been continuing debate about whether family-based services can be delivered effectively by public agencies. The five public programs described in earlier chapters provide a number of examples of successful public programs. On the one hand we have found a division of labor between public and private programs, such as that described in Chapter Eight between the Family Therapy program of the Iowa Department of Human Services and the private Iowa Children and Family Services program, a division which maximizes the differences between the two services. At the other end of the continuum is the Intensive Family Services program of the Children's Services Division in Oregon described in Chapter Six, which mandates that the same services be delivered by both public and private providers.

Although it may be an accident of sample selection, the public agencies in this study chose to serve families that were on average older, that more often contained at least one employed parent, and that had a narrower range of problems, typically including juvenile offenses and family conflict. These families required and received less intensive and comprehensive services, primarily therapy, which were often provided in an office setting. The private agencies, in contrast, served poorer, multiproblem families in need of intensive outreach and comprehensive services in their own homes and communities.

These programs tended to concentrate their strengths according to the type of families they served. The public agency workers were more experienced, better paid, put more emphasis on therapy, and achieved better therapeutic outcomes. Four of the five public programs followed a family treatment model: the Iowa and Oregon programs mentioned above, the Intensive Services program in Dakota County, Minnesota, and the satellite office-based program in Boulder County, Colorado, which is described in Chapter Nine. The other public program in Franklin County, Ohio, described in Chapter Four, served younger child maltreatment cases in an urban area and followed a home-based model. Whatever the model, the higher salaries, higher morale, and lower turnover in these programs show that it is possible to design and deliver successful service programs in public agencies and to create jobs that professional social workers are happy to have and to keep. These findings suggest that it is not the auspices of the program, but the prevailing working conditions that create the high turnover and low morale characteristic of other services based in public agencies.

The four private programs studied were more responsive and flexible in their services than the public programs, worked more with the community, and helped families to increase their material resources. All but one followed a home-based model. Because private agencies paid much lower salaries, however, they were less able to recruit and retain experienced workers, and they suffered higher turnover and declining morale. Furthermore, the private agencies were held to higher standards of accountability than the public programs. In some cases, the referring worker appears to have dictated case goals, a practice which not only prevented the development of mutual goals between the private agency worker and the family, but was associated with less favorable outcomes.

That private programs tend to be less expensive than public ones is both a strength in times of tight social service budgets and a weakness. Savings stem directly from lower salaries which produce problems of low morale and high turnover. Although the greater focus on therapy in the public programs may require workers with more professional education and higher salaries, the complex service needs of the multiproblem families seen in private agencies cannot all be met by untrained, inexperienced workers. The central role that family conflict, particularly marital conflict, plays in sexual and physical abuse requires that workers be skilled in counseling techniques to address these issues.

Ultimately a responsibility of public agencies, the provision of preventive and reunification services to families has been successfully delegated to private agencies in many areas through purchase-of-service contracts. Whether this approach is best or services are better provided directly by the public agency should be determined by the client population targeted, the community resources available, and the qualifications of existing and future staff, not exclusively by ideological preferences or cost considerations.

OFFICE-BASED AND RURAL SERVICES

Since there is a great deal of variation in families and their problems, family-based services need to be comprehensive and flexible. While the earliest programs stressed in-home services as essential in reaching out to and empowering poor families with multiple needs, successful programs have used office-based services to address more focused issues including sexual abuse and delinquency. For these families there are few differences between in-home and in-office services, other than the obvious one that the family must have the motivation and the means to come into the office for services. Since in-home services require more agency resources in terms of transportation and time, they generally can accommodate fewer families.

Providing a narrower range of direct services, office-based workers also tend to spend more time coordinating with other providers, which may ease the family's transition to other services after they have completed the family-based program. In addition, office-based workers have more access to coworkers for peer supervision, support, and teamed interventions, all of which are important in maintaining worker morale and effectiveness. Ideally, both in-office and in-home interventions and/or programs should be available to meet the needs of individual families and workers.

In-home services appear to be particularly needed in rural and inner city environments in which families face a variety of barriers in accessing services. While more services are available in urban areas, families need assistance in navigating complex service systems that may be less accessible to minority group clients and those with less education. The same persistence in locating and linking families to services is required in an impoverished rural environment. Indeed, there is little evidence that social services, in general, and family-based services, in particular, vary as much in kind as in degree between urban and rural areas. The resources available to the agency and the family, social class, and ethnicity may vary as much within communities as they do between communities. There appear to be few insurmountable difficulties in adapting family-based services to different environments, as successful programs in a wide variety of communities demonstrate.

WHERE HAVE WE BEEN?

Family-based services been developing for the past decade and a half, slowly at first, but at an accelerating pace since the passage of P.L. 96-272 in 1980. With more experience and research, some of the initial magic has worn off, but enthusiasm for this approach continues to grow both within child welfare and in other fields, such as mental health. In a short time the field has accumulated an impressive amount of descriptive and some comparative research. We are now aware of the wide variety of families and problems that are seen by family-based programs, the services that they receive, and the different outcomes they experience. We know some of the factors that affect outcome, and we also know that not all families have equally high chances of success. Several other studies, for example, have also found that cases involving child neglect and delinquency have higher placement rates than those involving other issues (AuClaire & Schwartz, 1986; Yuan & Struckman-Johnson, 1991; and Fraser, Pecora, & Haapala, 1991).

Much of what we have discovered is confirmatory. Families can and do change, and this change can be measured with standard research instruments. Programs in both public and private agencies can engage families with serious problems in finding solutions to those problems and can deliver a variety of counseling and concrete services to that end. Community agencies can work together to provide services to a family. Children can be maintained safely in their own homes.

Other expectations have not been borne out. Despite the importance of concrete services, most of the services provided involve counseling of some kind. Although successful cases include all family members in services, the primary caretaker still receives the most service. Programs in this study that regarded themselves as "intensive" and "time-limited" saw families as little as every other week and for as long as a year. The community is infrequently a target of change. Most families require continuing services after receiving family preservation services.

The earliest research, based on small samples with limited outcome measures and no comparison groups, seemed almost too good to be true, and it was. We now know that it is very hard to predict which families are at risk of imminent placement. Therefore, we can no longer claim that without family preservation services all would experience placement. We also know that in addition to improvement in family functioning and parenting, a variety of individual, agency, and community factors influence placement decisions and that many of these are beyond the reach of family preservation workers. It should have come as no surprise that placement is harder to prevent in families with more severe and long-lasting problems and that not all placements represent the failure of services. In short, in exchange for knowledge, we have lost our innocence, but not our enthusiasm and conviction that family preservation services are an essential part of the service continuum.

WHERE DO WE GO FROM HERE?

Practice Issues

What remains after our first decade and a half is a set of increasingly sharply focused questions involving treatment, research, and policy issues. While we can better describe family preservation services, the most typical models of service, and the client populations they most frequently address, there are still many treatment issues that remain to be clarified. Research and training in interventions associated with both a social learning approach and a family systems approach provide the basic skills necessary for family-based practice.[1] Yet we still do not know the appropriate mix of hard and soft services or of therapeutic counseling and skill development for different types of cases. Like over-the-counter drugs, most programs provide an array of active ingredients, hoping that one or more will be effective. While family-based workers must artfully apply a variety of skills, they must also know which services are necessary and which are optional, what level of service is sufficient and what is optimal, in order to efficiently serve as many families as possible.

Family-based services must also be constantly adapting to the needs of different kinds of families. While some progress has been made in developing services for black and Native American families (American Public Welfare Association, 1986; Legatski, 1990; Mannes & Yuan, 1988; Maryland Department of Human Resources, 1987; Mitchell, Tovar, & Knitzer, 1989), little has been written on Hispanic and Asian families. Family-based services are well suited to the needs of single-parent families, but stepparent, adoptive, foster, and extended families have received less attention. The special needs of gay and lesbian parents are just beginning to be addressed (Deutelbaum, 1991; Faria, 1991).

While many of the values necessary to family-based services have been identified and training has been developed that helps workers to acquire them (Pecora, Delewski, Booth, Haapala, & Kinney, 1985), we have not yet figured out what empowering families means, or with any certainty, how to do it. What we do for the most part, by seeing families' strengths as well as their problems, by taking their goals seriously, and by instilling hope for a better future is to try not to *disempower* them. How workers can remain authoritative without being authoritarian in serving families under legal mandates, how families can be partners in a relationship that is inherently unequal in many respects, and how they can be empowered in a social context that is profoundly disempowering are hard questions we have not yet begun to answer.

We also do not know how much our agencies will have to change to support this new kind of child welfare practice. Can the agency investigate charges against parents and at the same time offer affirming help and support to families, or do we need to separate these functions? What kind of administrative support and teamwork are necessary to maintain staff morale and encourage the personal development of workers? Do family-based workers *have* to disappear from the scene when placements are made, or can they continue providing services toward reunification or some other permanent plan for the child? Can a family-based service survive in an agency that is oriented to individual interventions or to a primary focus on the child? As more agencies adopt family-based services, these are questions that must be answered.

Research Issues

Many of these questions can be addressed through evaluation research, perhaps not as quickly as policymakers and practitioners might hope, but with patience, eventually. A major controversy, however, is brewing within the expanding field of family preservation research. Reacting to the inadequacies in design of the earliest research in the field, some evaluators are advocating that a large-scale, multi-site, longitudinal research project be fielded by a large research enterprise (Rossi, 1991a). Arguing that useful research must employ random assignment to control and experimental groups, must have sufficient numbers of cases to detect modest treatment effects, and must cover the full range of services and families seen in family preservation services, some evaluators are seeking federal funding for a "grand evaluation" that could answer many of the remaining questions about family preservation services once and for all (American Enterprise Institute, 1991; Rossi, 1991b).

While it is certainly possible to imagine the perfect study that would give definitive answers about the effectiveness of family-based services with different treatment populations, it will surely prove much more difficult to carry out such a perfect study. The few studies that have already, with much difficulty, randomly assigned cases to family preservation services and control groups have raised as many questions as they have answered. The studies had difficulty obtaining sufficient referrals to maintain sample sizes in both control and experimental groups; could not maintain control of referral criteria or the study population targeted; could not identify what services had been received by control group families; and could not track services received after termination from family preservation programs or their impact on placement rates measured months after termination. Further, sample sizes were not sufficient, nor the programs homogeneous enough, to detect the typically modest effects of clinical interventions (Bickman, 1990; Nelson, 1990; Gershenson, 1990).

As in earlier social experiments, these experiences have demonstrated that the intrusiveness of an experimental design ultimately changes the service and client population under study (Manski, 1990). The validity of experimental approaches is further clouded by the fact that while it is easiest to secure compliance with random assignment when a program is new and limited in scope, this is the worst time to assess its effectiveness.

Because of these limitations, many researchers believe that more modest studies repeated in different types of programs with different client populations will ultimately yield more useful knowledge. While most agencies are loathe to deny a valued service to a family assigned to a control group, they are more likely to agree to experiment with a single program element. Families can be randomly assigned to be seen in an office rather than in their homes, to receive or not receive emergency funds, to be served by a single worker or a professional/paraprofessional team, or, as the National Resource Center on Family Based Services is doing in a study currently underway, to six-month rather than three-month service contracts. These designs do not raise the social, legal and ethical questions which are potentially broached if families are denied the service outright. A modest experiment that randomly assigns families to alternative interventions can greatly increase our knowledge of what kind of intervention is most effective with what kind of problem. Single subject designs that carefully track interventions and family change can also help to identify effective interventions.

Regardless of the type of research undertaken, clarity must be achieved on several questions. First, how and why are certain families selected to receive family preservation services and how do they differ from families not selected? This needs to be determined to clarify the appropriate timing and expectations of family preservation services. Second, how should placement be defined? Should it include informal placement with relatives or friends or only formal agency placements? How long must a placement last to be counted as an outcome of this service? Should placement data be collected from agency information systems, families, or both? How long and under what circumstances must placement be avoided for family preservation services to be regarded as successful? A year after case closure, how much credit or blame can be placed on family preservation services for long-term outcomes and how much on follow-up services? While each study may not ask these questions in the same way, the definitions and expectations in each study and program must be made explicit.

Policy Issues

The answers to the many questions that remain about family-based services surely will not come fast enough to determine their fate. Whether family preservation services become just another good idea in the past depends on legislation and policy decisions that will be made long before all the data are in. Currently, Congress is considering several bills that would greatly expand the financing available for services providing an alternative to placement, while at the same time the executive branch is attempting to restrict funds that are being used to finance programs now. The outcome of these contradictory directions will depend on political and economic forces and on accidents of history, not on research findings.

Whether family preservation services continue to be narrowly construed as another categorical service that has as its main benefit the saving of taxpayer dollars by averting expensive long-term placements or whether they become an entitlement, a "reasonable effort" that must be made before a child can be removed from home is a political decision. This decision will determine how much importance is placed on the ability to precisely target preventive services, thereby guaranteeing that placement dollars will be saved. If it is decided that every family is owed a chance to resolve its problems and preserve its integrity, cost-savings and placement prevention are not appropriate measures of success.

While the value and place in the service continuum of family preservation services will not be determined by research, it can answer many questions important in policy formulation. Certainly cost is always an issue in public social services. The timing, targets, and length of service as well as staff qualifications, caseloads, and teaming have important effects on the cost of services. Cost-effectiveness research can help identify the most efficient delivery structure and conserve scarce resources. Furthermore, realistic appraisals of the costs and benefits of family preservation services can solidify support for them. Regardless of federal policy, decisions made at the state level in terms of both legislation and funding have a direct and substantial impact on the availability of family preservation services statewide (Tyler, 1990).

Perhaps the most important effect of family-based services remains the most elusive. After 150 years of removing children from their homes in response to a range of family problems, the wisdom of this approach is being questioned. This questioning reflects at once a new understanding of the importance to children and parents of family ties and a new tolerance for diverse family forms and family styles. On a less idealistic level it is also a continuation of a fiscally-motivated trend toward deinstitutionalization that began in the 1970s. The experience of the mental health field has shown that placements cannot be safely and humanely decreased without an increase in community-based services for the people who have been deinstitutionalized and those who follow. For generations the policy in the United States has been one of "rugged individualism" towards families and child rearing. Under this policy families have been left to struggle with their problems as best they could. If they failed and if their children began to suffer grievously at their hands, the children were removed. Whether this policy will be replaced by one of "shared responsibility" between parents and the larger society for the well-being of children remains to be seen (Moroney, 1986).

Even if family preservation services are a harbinger of a paradigm shift in child welfare services toward a more benign and supportive stance toward families with problems, they will remain only a stopgap measure unless the structural problems that contribute to family stress and parental dysfunction are addressed. Even with the provision of material resources and supportive services, family preservation services remain, in essence, a social service that relies heavily on counseling. While this can be extremely helpful for families experiencing communication breakdowns, crises in confidence, interpersonal conflicts, or a shortage of skills, it cannot substitute for training and jobs for unemployed parents, health and mental health care for ill family members, adequate income and housing for economically deprived families, child care for working parents, or equal opportunity for oppressed minorities. Family-based services are well founded and defensible as effective and practical services that address a range of family problems. They are not a panacea for all the problems that confront families in an increasingly polarized society.

Endnote

1. Both the Homebuilders Program in Federal Way, Washington, and the National Resource Center on Family Based Services at the University of Iowa School of Social Work in Iowa City, Iowa, offer extensive training programs.

APPENDICES

Appendix A

SUCCESS AND FAILURE
IN FAMILY-BASED SERVICES

Although placement or nonplacement is by far the most common measure of failure and success in family-based services, it is by no means the only measure, or even an adequate one. Funders and administrators concerned with "the bottom line" often regard preventing expensive placements as the only persuasive argument for family-based services. Clinicians, on the other hand, argue for the importance of an array of interrelated outcomes. Placement is not a failure when it protects a child from serious harm; conversely, keeping a family together is not a success unless some change has occurred in the circumstances that brought the family into service.

In order to establish more refined, practice-based definitions of success and failure, administrators, supervisors, and workers were asked during on-site interviews to define success and failure in family-based services. Their responses formed the basis both for the series of questions about success and failure in the Family Based Services Inventory, completed by all workers in the study, and for the outcome measures used in the case review instrument.

To establish empirically-based definitions of success and failure, nineteen possible case outcomes were generated from the on-site interviews and then included in the social worker questionnaire. In response to the following question, "Thinking about the cases you regarded as successes, how often did the families have the following outcomes?", workers were asked to rate each of the possible outcomes on a six-point scale ranging from "never" to "always." A factor analysis of their responses, weighted by the number of their cases which were included in the sample and using a principle-components solution and quartimax rotation, identified three factors underlying the nineteen outcomes. The first factor was by far the strongest and accounted for 38 percent of the variance. It included ten of the nineteen possible outcomes, in the following order:

- The adults felt more competent in their roles.
- Positive change in the family's interactions, behavior or communication occurred.
- The family was stabilized and no longer in crisis.
- The family achieved its own goals.
- The family was together at the time services were terminated.
- The children's needs were being appropriately met.
- The family felt better about themselves.
- The family was able to solve its own problems without further outside help.
- All or most case objectives were met.

- The family told you they no longer needed your services.

As can be readily observed, this "success" factor included a variety of possible outcomes, all of which were closely associated in the workers' minds with keeping the family together, that is, nonplacement.

The remaining two factors were much weaker, explaining only 16 percent and 9 percent of the variance, but gave some support to the idea that placement can be seen as a successful outcome as can the family's asserting independence from the worker by actively or passively "firing" him or her. The placement-as-success factor included four of the nineteen possible case outcomes:

- The child was protected from further harm by placement.
- Parental rights were terminated.
- The child at risk was placed but other children were maintained in the home.
- The child was placed with a relative.

The "firing" factor included an additional four of the nineteen outcomes:

- The family stopped keeping appointments.
- The family told you they no longer needed your services.
- The family was able to solve its own problems without further outside help.
- (Negative) All or most case objectives were met.

Fifteen possible outcomes that represented failure were also generated from the on-site interviews, included in the social worker questionnaire, and rated in the same fashion. A factor analysis of these items yielded five factors. The first, which accounted for 26 percent of the variance, included, in order: placement in a group or foster home, termination of parental rights, placement in an institution or for short term or respite care, inappropriate parenting, maintenance of all but the placed child in the home, and lack of a permanency plan. The second factor explained 17 percent of the variance and reflected unfavorable treatment outcomes including inappropriate parenting, continued instability, need for outside help, and lack of change. Placement with a relative loaded negatively on this factor.

Finally, the items in the "firing-as-success" factor mentioned above, that the family stopped keeping appointments or said services were no longer needed, combined with lack of goal achievement and a continued need for outside help explain 11 percent of the variance and indicate that being "fired" can also be seen as a sign of failure. Two additional factors contained the same items with smaller loadings and represented, primarily, the individual variables, "the child at risk was placed but other children were maintained in the home" and "a permanent plan was not achieved for the child at risk." These latter two factors accounted for 9 percent and 7 percent of the variance, respectively.

The strength of the general "success" factor and the predominance of the placement-as-failure factor suggest that placement or nonplacement is, indeed, a fairly good definition and of success and failure, from a practitioner's as well as a legislator's or administrator's point of view. For this reason, it is used as the major dependent variable in the study. It was not, however, the only case outcome studied and its relationship to the other measures of outcome deserves a brief exploration.

Most studies of family-based services have not differentiated placement as a temporary intervention during service from placement as an outcome at the end of service, regarding, instead, any instance of placement as "failure." In this study, if a child entered placement during the service period and moved before termination to another type of placement or back home, it was counted as a temporary placement, not as an outcome. This clarification did not change the fact that temporary placement was highly related to terminal placement. Indeed, nearly half the highest risk children in placement cases had been placed temporarily, while only 13 percent in nonplacement cases were out of the home during service. This significant difference was maintained for all types of temporary placement including placement with relatives. Respite care was too infrequent to test since only three families received this service.

Table A-I
RELATION OF OTHER OUTCOME VARIABLES
TO PLACEMENT/NON-PLACEMENT

	Placement $n = 81$	Non-Placement $n = 375$	Total $n = 456$
Outcome Measures			
Goals Achieved$_a$			
None	16.9	13.5	14.1
1–50%	22.3	16.7	17.7
51–75%	18.7	11.1	12.4
76–100%	42.1	58.7	55.9
Positive Change in Family Functioning$_b$			
None	42.8	12.9	18.2
Moderate	44.5	41.9	42.2
High	13.7	45.1	39.6
Negative Change in Family Functioning$_b$			
None	50.9	85.3	79.3
Worse	49.1	14.7	20.7
No Additional Services After Closing$_b$	6.2	25.9	22.5

Note. Percentages. Weighted to represent estimated incidence of placement and non-placement based on sampling lists.
$_a p < .05$. $_b p < .001$.

Goal achievement, a common indicator of outcome, was measured in this study by dividing the number of family's case objectives which were assessed by the case readers as partially or completely achieved by the total number of case objectives for which a level of achievement was indicated. The majority of families in both placement and nonplacement categories achieved at least half their case objectives. Nonplacement cases showed a higher level of goal achievement, however, with the majority fulfilling three-quarters or more of their objectives at least partially.

Perhaps of even greater importance in determining success or failure, nonplacement cases also demonstrated a high level of change in family functioning. Since no measure of family functioning was found that could be applied to case record data, the Family Systems Change Scale, a brief scale that listed ten areas of family functioning and family-community interaction, was developed for this study (see Appendix D). Case readers rated each scale as to whether the family got worse, stayed the same, or improved in that area, or indicated that there was insufficient data in the case record to make such a judgment.

The number of areas of positive and negative change were aggregated into separate overall measures that were strongly related to placement and nonplacement. Forty percent of the placement cases showed no positive change and half got worse in at least one area. Only 13 percent of nonplacement families failed to show any positive change and only 21 percent changed for the worse in any area. This does not mean that outcomes for the placement families were completely negative, however, since they achieved a relatively high proportion of their goals and about the same proportion as nonplacement families achieved a moderate level of change in family functioning.

One final outcome indicator highly related to placement or nonplacement was the service status of families at termination. Less than a tenth of placement families were expected to be independent of services at termination, whereas a quarter of nonplacement families were not scheduled for further service. That three quarters of "successful" cases require continuing resources from the human services system is not surprising, given the severity of the cases referred to family-based services and the relative brevity of the service. For the most part, these preventive family-based services were successful at what they set out to do—avert placement of children from families in crisis. Placement rates ranged from 4 percent to 25 percent in the programs studied, with an average placement rate of 18 percent projected from the sampling lists. Family-based programs do not seek to, nor could they be reasonably asked to help families solve all their problems.

Appendix B

RELIABILITY ANALYSIS

Two types of reliability were calculated in this study, the interrater reliability of key variables (Table B–I) and the interitem reliability (Cronbach's Alpha) of additive scales. Interrater reliability was calculated from a sample of twenty cases, two cases in each of ten sites in which a second coder was available. The cases were coded later during the review to assure that coders were thoroughly familiar with the coding system. Reliability was calculated using Pearson Product Moment Correlations and, for variables in which a zero was frequently recorded, percent agreement between coders. Means of the variables in the original and recoded sample were also compared.

Because the coders were working from lengthy case records using a complex instrument, some unreliability was expected. Table B–I gives the Pearson's r and sample means for selected variables. Of the 25 variables tested, nine were correlated at .70 or above including a number of the variables that were found to be related to placement across sites. An additional six variables were correlated at .48 or better, again including several important predictors of placement. Ten of the variables were correlated at well below .50, the level considered acceptable for studies of this type (Magura & Moses, 1986, p. 185). Comparing means on the least reliable variables shows little substantive difference, however, so averages may be safely compared among sites for most variables.

The percentage of agreement between coders for variables for which a zero was frequently recorded showed some of them to be more reliable than the correlation coefficient indicated, including the number of children at high risk of placement. Several variables had unacceptably low reliability by either method, including the percentage of goals achieved and the level of stress the family experienced in the year before termination.

Clearly there was disagreement about what constituted goal achievement and stress. Coding of these involved identifying both the occurrence of the variable in the case narrative and the number of times it occurred. Since low reliability reduces the relationships and significance of the variables affected, it can be surmised that these would have shown more consistent relationships to outcome if they had been coded reliably (Magura & Moses, 1986, pp. 192–193). They were probably coded more reliably at the few sites in which they were related to placement.

Interitem reliability was calculated for the longer additive scales. Of the scales computed from the case review data, the Family Systems Change Scale proved most reliable at .94. Both the Child Well-Being Scales for the oldest child and the Parental Disposition subscale also had high reliability at .84 and .73 respectively. The Holmes

181

Table B-I
INTERRATER RELIABILITY OF SELECTED VARIABLES
$(N = 20)$

Variable	Correlation[a]	Mean A	Mean B
Age of Oldest Child	.99	13.6	12.9
Total Visits in First Month	.89	5.8	4.5
Total Number of Support Services	.82	.7	.8
Number of Areas of Positive Change	.78	2.6	2.8
Lowest Child CWBS[b]	.75	69.1	72.4
Additional Services After Closing	.74	1.7	1.7
Length of Service	.73	169.0	146.0
Number of Areas of Negative Change	.59	.9	.8
Primary Caretaker CWBS[b]	.51	62.0	63.9
Total Number of Problems	.49	7.4	6.7
Percent of Goals Achieved	.44	38.0	25.0
Stress	.40	96.9	80.9
Number of Children at High Risk	.37	.6	.9
Total Number of Family-Based Services	.32	5.7	5.4

[a]Pearson product moment correlation. [b]Child Well-Being Score (Magura & Moses, 1986).

Schedule of Recent Experience (stress scale), which also had a low interrater reliability, was the least reliable with an alpha of .50; however, it still meets the minimum criterion for reliability (Magura & Moses, 1986, p. 187).

Despite the problems of using case record data and multiple coders at multiple sites, both the interrater and interitem reliability of most items tested were relatively high. Only the Homes scale proved unsuitable for this type of methodology. Particularly encouraging was the high reliability of the Family Systems Change Scale and the Child Well-Being Scales. Both can be seen as promising measures of outcome in family-based services research. The Family Systems Change Scale was developed for this study and needs to be tested in direct practice. The Child Well-Being Scales were designed to be completed by workers and, although they proved their applicability to case record data in this study, they could be used only to assess the family's functioning at intake because there was too little information about the family at the time the case was closed to rate the scales and compute change scores.

Appendix C

DEFINITION OF TERMS

This section provides operational definitions of the key variables in the National Resource Center's study. These are taken, for the most part, from the coding manual used in the study.

ACCOMPANYING: Going with family member(s) to meetings or appointments to provide support and encouragement, to make sure appointment is kept, or to teach family member to negotiate with service systems.

ADVOCACY: Intervening in the community or agency on behalf of the family; family members may or may not be present.

CASE MANAGEMENT: Arranging for and coordinating services to a family.

DELINQUENCY: Child has committed an offense which would be a crime if committed by an adult.

HIGHEST-RISK CHILD: Refers to the oldest child at the highest risk of placement in the family (see imminence of risk).

HOMEWORK ASSIGNMENTS: Specific assigned activities between appointments or face-to-face contacts for one or more family members.

IMMINENCE OF RISK: An assessment, at intake to family-based services, of the degree to which each child was likely to be placed out of the home. This assessment was made by the case reviewer based on material in the written case record and included low risk (no indication of possible placement); moderate risk (discussion of possible placement, but not imminent); high risk (placement seemed imminent without family based-services, or a child just returned from placement); or temporary placement (a child was actually in a short-term placement of less than one month with a goal of reunification at the time family-based services began). To code high risk, some action toward making a placement must have been recorded.

INFORMATION AND REFERRAL: Giving information about available resources or making referrals for needed services with no continuing responsibility for coordination.

NEGLECT: Failure to provide minimally adequate or essential food, shelter, clothing, health care, or supervision.

NON-PLACEMENT CASES: Families in which none of the children involved in the current referral were in or recommended for out-of-home care at the time family-based services were terminated.

OBJECTIVE: Most specific statement of what is to be achieved during service, according to the case or service plan. This does not include standard goals such as Title XX goals, but is specific to the family.

OTHER ADULT: A household member related to the primary caretaker by birth,

183

adoption, or marriage; a live-in boyfriend or girlfriend; surrogate kin (unrelated "aunt" or "grandmother," "spouse" of same sex, etc.); or a significant other (adult child, relative or friend) who plays an important role in the family but does not live in the household.

PHYSICAL ABUSE: Nonaccidental physical injury to a child by a caretaker.

PLACEMENT CASES: Families who, at the termination of family-based services, had at least one child living out of the home, either through a formal placement in foster or residential care, or an informal living arrangement with friends or relatives or for whom such a placement was recommended by the family-based worker.

PRIMARY CARETAKER: The adult with legal or major responsibility for all or most of the children in a family and with whom the children primarily reside.

PRIVATE AGENCY: An agency which contracts with a public agency with primary responsibility for child welfare services to provide family-based services; typically an agency controlled by a board of directors of private citizens rather than by a governmental unit.

PUBLIC AGENCY: A unit of government legally charged with the responsibility of providing mandated child welfare services.

RECREATION: Accompanying family member(s) on recreational or social outings or providing fun experiences.

ROLE MODELING: Demonstrating parenting, household or interpersonal skills by doing with family member present in an actual or simulated situation as part of the intervention plan.

SEXUAL ABUSE: Using or allowing a child to be used for sexual gratification.

STATUS OFFENSE: Child has committed an offense which would not be a crime if committed by an adult (e.g., running away, truancy, ungovernable behavior).

STRESS: Score on the Holmes' Schedule of Recent Experience (1981), which sums and weights the number of specific events which occurred in the family in the twelve months prior to termination of family-based services (e.g., death of spouse, pregnancy, moving to a new location, being fired from a job, eviction, major personal injury or illness, etc.).

TEACHING: Presentation of material or information on parenting, budgeting, coping, social, or self-help skills.

TEMPORARY PLACEMENTS: Placements, either formal or informal, which occurred during the family-based service period, but by case closure were no longer in effect.

Appendix D

FAMILY SYSTEMS CHANGE SCALE

Summary of changes from intake to termination:
1. Has become worse since intake
2. No change—remains the same
3. Has improved since intake

_____ 1. Behavior of family members
E.g., for adults: discipline, physical care, age-appropriate care, nurturance, drug/alcohol use, home or financial management, etc.
For child: destructive, violent, uncooperative, withdrawn, truancy, poor grades, conflict with adults, disruption, delinquency, status offense, petty offenses and misdemeanors, etc.

_____ 2. Family structure/hierarchy
E.g., age and generational boundaries, coalition between parents, "parenting" child, etc.; addition or loss of members.

_____ 3. Dynamics/relationships within family
E.g., clear messages, open communication, reduction of blame, constructive problem solving, conflict, sexual relationship between adults.

_____ 4. Family's affect or emotional climate
E.g., problems with self-esteem, depression, anger, separation, differentiation, guilt, blame, feelings of powerlessness vs. personal growth, fun, enjoyment.

_____ 5. Family's perception/definition of problem
Definition as family problem rather than identified patient's problem; reframing as positive rather than negative.

_____ 6. Family's material resources or circumstances
E.g., housing, income, employment, household furnishings, etc.

_____ 7. Use of available services
Appropriate use of, e.g., medical care, day care, counseling, homemaker, transportation, etc.

_____ 8. Community's perception of/reaction to family
Understanding, acceptance, tolerance on part of neighbors, officials, agencies, etc.

_____ 9. Informal support network of family

Friends, neighbors, community persons other than agency representatives, officials, etc.

_____ 10. Degree of community involvement with family

Reports, complaints, number of persons, agencies involved in family.

Appendix E

INTRODUCTION TO
THE MULTIVARIATE ANALYSES

A number of multivariate procedures were utilized in this study. Because of the nonnormal distribution of the continuous dependent variables (goal achievement and family change as measured by the Family Systems Change Scale), standard multiple regression techniques could not be employed.

Four-way analysis of variance, with the Parental Disposition subscale of the Child Well-Being Scales as a covariate, was used to identify the most distinctive features of rural as compared to urban and suburban programs, public as opposed to private programs, and in-office versus in-home services. Type of case (juvenile justice or child maltreatment), was also entered as a factor to control for differences in target population. Standard ANOVA procedures available in SPSSX were employed using hierarchical entry of factors.

The primary multivariate technique, however, was discriminant analysis, an application of canonical correlation analysis, "the most general case of the general linear model" (Thompson, 1984, p. 7). This was selected because it was appropriate for a dichotomous dependent variable (placement versus nonplacement) and because, at the time of the initial analysis, a fully developed logistical regression package was not available in SPSSX. Discriminant analysis sorts interval level independent variables into factors based on the categories of the dependent variable, maximizing the differences between them in a procedure similar to factor analysis (Thompson, 1984, p. 23).

For these analyses, nominal and ordinal variables were recoded as dummy variables (1,0) and treated as interval level data. The variables in the final models were selected in three ways:

1. Important predictors identified in prior research were included, to the extent that they were able to be measured in this study. Because case record data were employed, several family history and family environment variables were not available.

2. Variables significantly correlated with placement at the bivariate level were included, to the extent that equal variance assumptions were met. Widely divergent variances excluded certain variables such as psychiatric/psychological evaluation which was commonly sought when a placement was being planned. Variables with high correlations to placement, such as change in family functioning and goal achievement, were excluded because they masked the contributions of demographic and service variables.

3. Predictors identified in preliminary discriminant analyses of all variables that met statistical assumptions (juvenile justice cases) or of domains of variables (child maltreatment cases) were also tested. Discriminant analyses of the same set of variables were also used to identify the differences in predictors for in-office and in-home services and placement of adolescent as compared to younger children in physical abuse cases. The results of these analyses are not included in this volume, but are available from the authors.

A standard, stepwise discriminant analysis procedure using forward and backward selection, available in SPSSX, was employed using Wilks lambda to guide the inclusion and deletion of variables and Box's M (at $p < .05$) to test equality of variances. Since approximately equal numbers of placement and nonplacement cases were used in the analyses, many of the problems in identifying predictors of infrequent events were avoided.

The increased number of placement cases, however, inflated the capacity of the derived statistical models to correctly classify placement cases, so classification procedures were adjusted by assigning prior probabilities in accordance with estimated placement rates (based on sampling frames) for each subpopulation (Klecka, 1980, p. 46). This resulted in a lower rate of accurate predictions for placement cases, but a higher rate for nonplacement cases, since they are more frequent. It did not affect the identification or weighting of predictor variables in the statistical models. Since sufficient cases were not available to reserve a subset to test the models on cases other than those from which they were derived, the models' ability to predict placement and nonplacement using these variables is overestimated.

The tables in this Appendix represent the best-fitting canonical discriminant functions identified for each subpopulation. Bivariate F values and significance levels are reported as well as standardized canonical discriminant function coefficients (analogous to standardized beta weights in multiple regression analysis [Thompson, 1984, p. 14]) and pooled within-group correlations between each discriminating variable and the canonical discriminant function (identical to Pearson product-moment correlations [Klecka, 1980, p. 37]). The most important variables were identified by looking at both their within-group correlations (structure coefficients) and their bivariate significance with placement, following Klecka's observation that "the structure coefficients are a better guide to the meaning of the canonical discriminant functions than the standardized coefficients are" (1980, p. 34).

Generally, the standardized discriminant function coefficients were similar in magnitude and direction to the structure coefficients, but, occasionally, overlapping variance created divergence. Statistics reported for the canonical discriminant function include the canonical correlation with placement/nonplacement, chi-square, and statistical significance for the discriminant function, and the percentage of cases that were correctly classified by the statistical model. In all models nonplacement was more accurately predicted than placement.

Individual case examples were selected from the agency used in the case study for each chapter, generally an agency that served a large proportion of cases with the feature under study. Cases were chosen to include key characteristics of families and services that were predictive of placement and nonplacement in the discriminant models. While some of them represented "average" cases in terms of the group centroids, others were more extreme cases, selected for the particular combination of variables they included. All were correctly classified by the discriminant function.

Table E-I
DISCRIMINANT ANALYSIS: NEGLECT CASES
$n = 54$

Variables	Coefficients[a]	Correlations[a]	F
Caretaker Attended Most Sessions	.58	.44	17.03**
Number of Children at High Risk	−.63	−.42	14.96**
Prior Placement	−.63	−.35	10.75**
Continuity in Caretakers	.25	.30	7.88**
Number of Problems	−.28	−.28	6.57*
Paraprofessional Services	.70	.18	2.73
Number of Children	.31	−.07	.42
Caretaker's Age at Birth of Highest-Risk Child	.22	.01	.47
Total Model[b]		.79	46.67**

Correctly Classified (%)   83.9
   Placement   73.4
   Non-placement   94.7
Note. Missing data = 13 (unweighted).
[a]Positive = Non-placement. [b]Canonical correlation and chi-square.
*$p < .05$. **$p < .001$.

Table E-II
DISCRIMINANT ANALYSIS: PHYSICAL ABUSE CASES
$n = 79$

Variables	Coefficient[a]	Correlation[a]	F
Caretaker Child Well-Being Score	.24	.42	12.51***
Marital Counseling	.54	.33	7.41**
Caretaker Attended Most Sessions	.66	.32	7.13**
Role Modeling	.49	.28	5.47*
Child Protective Services	−.51	−.25	4.18*
Additional Abuse Reports	−.37	−.25	4.18*
Substance Abuse	−.33	−.17	2.10
Accompanied to Appointment	−.38	−.12	.96
Parent Education	.36	.08	.50
Caretaker's Age at Birth of Highest-Risk Child	.23	.08	.50
Individual Counseling	.35	.02	.26
Total Model[b]		.69	45.46***

Correctly classified (%)   76.0
   Placement   48.1
   Non-Placement   96.6
Note. Missing data = 12 (unweighted).
[a]Positive = Non-placement. [b]Canonical correlation and chi-square.
*$p < .05$. **$p < .01$. ***$p < .001$.

Table E-III
DISCRIMINANT ANALYSIS: SEXUAL ABUSE CASES
$n = 46$

Variables	Coefficient[a]	Correlation[a]	F
Number of Children at High Risk	−.58	−.25	9.40**
Caretaker's Compliance Score	.78	.22	7.23**
Second Adult Attended Most Sessions	−.78	−.21	6.64**
Caretaker Employed	−.58	−.21	6.44**
Second Adult Employed	−.24	−.17	4.26*
Referred Out for Services	−.68	−.17	3.99*
Use of Counseling Objective	.62	.15	3.46
Prior Placement	−.30	.11	1.73
Highest-Risk Child Attended Most Sessions	.63	.11	1.69
Role Modeling	.30	.08	.85
Child Protective Services	.62	.03	.12
Total Model[b]		.88	56.27***

Correctly classified (%)   87.8
   Placement   75.3
   Non-Placement   100.0
Note. Missing data = 4 (unweighted).
[a]Positive = Non-placement.   [b]Canonical correlation and chi-square.
*$p < .05$.   **$p < .01$.   ***$p < .001$.

Table E-IV
DISCRIMINANT ANALYSIS: DELINQUENCY CASES
$n = 83$

Variables	Coefficient[a]	Correlation[a]	F
Substance Abuse	−.65	−.37	7.89**
Involvement of Highest-Risk Child	.30	.36	7.39**
Caretaker's Child Well-Being Score	.31	.30	5.25*
Imminent Risk of Placement	−.35	−.28	4.59*
Child in Regular School	.43	.27	4.36*
Stress Score	−.46	−.27	4.26*
Use of Counseling Objectives	.50	.22	2.79
Two Adults in Household	.28	.15	1.32
Male Primary Caretaker	−.43	−.15	1.23
Total Model[b]		.64	41.76***

Correctly classified (%)   76.5
   Placement   70.8
   Non-placement   87.8
Note. Missing data = 5 (unweighted).
[a]Positive = Non-placement.   [b]Canonical correlation and chi-square.
*$p < .05$.   **$p < .01$.   ***$p < .001$.

Table E-V
DISCRIMINANT ANALYSIS: STATUS OFFENSE CASES
$n = 67$

Variables	Coefficient[a]	Correlation[a]	F
Prior Placement	−.83	−.27	5.29*
Involvement of Highest-Risk Child	.29	.23	3.98*
Parenting Change Objective	−.38	−.23	3.97*
Lowest Child's Child Well-Being Score	.75	.21	3.50
Number in Household	−.39	−.21	3.23
Child in Regular School	.43	.17	2.02
Teaching	.36	.16	1.86
Teaming	.48	.13	1.31
Family Relationship Change Objective	−.67	−.12	1.01
Outside Case Manager	−.74	−.09	.54
Child Behavior Change Objective	−.40	−.08	.51
In-Home Services	.28	.02	.33
Total Model[b]		.73	44.62**

Correctly classified (%)   83.9
  Placement   83.8
  Non-Placement   84.3

Note. Missing data = 4 (unweighted).
[a]Positive = Non-placement. [b]Canonical correlation and chi-square.
*$p < .01$.   **$p < .001$.

Table E-VI
DISCRIMINANT ANALYSIS: RURAL CASES
$n = 147$

Variables	Coefficient[a]	Correlation[a]	F
Number of Children at High Risk	.28	.41	12.29***
Prior Placement	.38	.33	8.30**
Juvenile Offense	.30	.32	7.43**
Case Management	.55	.29	6.38*
Age of Child at Highest Risk	.24	.29	6.21*
Marital Problems	−.33	−.26	4.97*
Caretaker's Compliance Score	−.34	−.24	4.45*
Marriage Counseling	−.17	−.24	4.16*
Substance Abuse	.25	.20	3.08
Divorce	.49	.20	3.06
Psychological Evaluation	.28	.20	2.97
Family Relationship Problems	.23	.19	2.75
Other Social Services	−.32	.05	.22
Second Adult in Home	.31	−.05	.20
Increase Use of Supportive Services Objective	.23	.03	.52
Total Model[b]		.58	57.00***

Correctly classified (%) 66.3
  Placement 92.4
  Non-Placement 42.9

Note. Missing data = 4 (unweighted).
[a]Positive = Placement. [b]Canonical correlation and chi-square.
*$p < .05$. **$p < .01$. ***$p < .001$.

Table E-VII
DISCRIMINANT ANALYSIS: IN-OFFICE CASES
$n = 121$

Variables	Coefficient[a]	Correlation[a]	F
Caretaker's Compliance Score	−.35	−.40	17.91***
Lowest Child's Child Well-Being Score	−.17	−.34	12.69***
Number of Children at High Risk	.46	.30	10.33**
Marital Change Objective	−.29	−.28	8.84*
Moved in Last Year	.40	.25	7.02**
Primary Caretaker Attended Most Sessions	−.17	−.22	5.60*
Increase Use of Counseling Objective	−.45	−.20	4.64*
Second Adult in Home	.66	.19	4.09*
Case Manager in Another Unit	.33	.16	2.89
Female Primary Caretaker	.30	.15	2.48
Family Change Objective	−.46	−.15	2.41
Juvenile Offense	.37	.12	1.77
Parenting Change Objective	.22	.08	.73
Total Model[b]		.70	74.68***

Correctly classified (%)   70.8
   Placement   49.8
   Non-Placement   98.1
Note. Missing data = 30 (unweighted).
[a]Positive = Placement. [b]Canonical correlation and chi-square.
*$p < .05$. **$p < .01$. ***$p < .001$.

Appendix F

COMPARATIVE SITE TABLES

Alternative Models of Family Preservation

Table F-I
DEMOGRAPHIC CHARACTERISTICS OF FAMILIES BY SITE

		Franklin County n = 50	SCAN n = 54	ICFS n = 48	IDHS n = 50	Dakota County n = 50	LSS n = 54	Boulder County n = 48	CSD n = 50	Mult-nomah County n = 50	Totals N = 454
Primary Caretaker											
Age	m	29.3	26.8	30.9	36.4	39.4	36.8	38.5	38.4	37.5	34.7*
	sd	6.8	11.2	7.4	7.0	7.2	6.9	5.0	4.7	8.4	8.5
Female	%	89.8	95.1	96.6	88.0	97.5	67.9	72.1	87.5	79.4	85.9*
Married	%	33.0	11.8	49.6	53.0	52.8	63.2	75.1	39.5	45.1	47.5*
Divorced	%	23.5	24.2	32.0	26.7	32.1	19.8	16.7	43.1	40.1	28.7
Non-white	%	17.4	82.2	5.0	8.3	1.7	0.0	4.2	4.1	17.2	16.5*
Employed	%	20.9	6.3	27.5	35.5	69.2	68.9	64.1	69.8	33.1	43.7*
Below Poverty Level	%	82.4	90.0	75.6	56.2	38.1	38.6	0.0	N/A	N/A	57.9*
AFDC	%	75.7	83.9	59.5	50.6	3.2	18.1	0.0	16.0	6.8	35.3*
Child Well-Being Score	m	73.0	77.7	79.2	75.7	73.3	72.0	74.2	77.7	64.8	73.3*
	sd	12.6	15.4	9.6	10.1	9.1	12.3	16.3	12.8	12.6	13.1
Highest Risk Child[a]											
Age	m	7.7	5.2	9.0	13.2	13.2	12.5	13.0	12.3	14.1	11.8*
	sd	5.6	4.3	4.4	3.6	3.2	4.0	3.3	3.4	2.9	4.9
Biological Child of 2nd Adult[b]	%	56.7	57.9	55.0	47.8	50.9	46.4	35.1	65.6	48.1	51.3
Prior Placement	%	27.0	6.1	17.5	22.8	26.7	35.1	22.2	28.5	68.1	28.1*
At High Risk of Placement	%	87.4	25.7	48.8	56.8	65.9	80.0	25.7	70.3	79.3	60.0*
Court-Ordered Into Program	%	17.7	3.8	20.3	42.1	4.0	17.8	24.6	8.0	12.0	16.4*
Child Well-Being Score	m	75.8	81.9	84.9	75.4	74.9	74.1	66.0	65.2	52.1	72.1*
	sd	12.1	13.0	10.7	10.0	11.7	12.5	13.0	13.4	15.7	15.6

Note. Data weighted to represent estimated incidence of placement and non-placement based on sampling lists. Significance based on F test.
[a]Oldest child at highest risk of placement. [b]n = 345.
*p < .001.

Table F-II
PROBLEMS IDENTIFIED BY REFERRAL SOURCE
AND BY ALL SOURCES BY SITE

	Franklin County $n = 50$	SCAN $n = 54$	ICFS $n = 48$	IDHS $n = 50$	Dakota County $n = 50$	LSS $n = 54$	Boulder County $n = 48$	CSD $n = 50$	Mult- nomah County $n = 50$	Totals $n = 454$
Most Common Reasons for Referral (%)										
Abuse	39.0	27.2	23.3	25.4	32.0	25.7	27.3	5.0	16.0	24.6**
Sexual Abuse	10.7	6.2	7.5	16.5	8.8	3.7	8.3	20.0	29.6	12.3**
Neglect	55.9	44.3	13.0	7.5	7.2	8.4	.9	8.5	10.2	17.6***
Delinquency	6.2	0.0	6.9	23.5	21.0	34.8	18.1	36.5	24.2	19.0***
Status Offense	3.9	0.0	4.8	8.0	53.0	16.1	13.3	11.5	45.8	17.2***
Adult Substance Abuse	23.7	12.4	15.0	18.1	11.2	8.4	4.4	3.1	16.0	12.5*
Child Substance Abuse	0.0	0.0	0.0	.5	12.8	12.4	5.3	2.1	20.6	6.0***
Adult Health/ Mental Health	25.4	29.6	15.0	5.9	3.2	8.4	4.2	5.0	18.2	12.9***
Adult Relationships	20.9	12.3	27.4	40.6	44.6	9.7	16.3	12.5	19.4	22.4***
Parent-Child Conflict	14.7	8.7	24.7	46.4	88.8	63.5	75.4	52.5	65.2	48.6***
Family Relationships	29.4	39.5	34.3	21.0	10.3	6.4	23.8	8.0	28.4	22.3***
Child Behavior	25.9	3.7	26.1	21.4	10.5	71.9	67.9	45.4	39.0	34.6***
With Problem (%)										
Abuse	49.7	29.6	28.8	24.5	5.7	26.1	28.2	13.0	24.8	25.7***
Sexual Abuse	14.7	11.1	10.9	17.0	12.0	8.7	8.3	37.0	50.8	18.8***
Neglect	64.4	56.7	19.8	8.5	6.3	16.7	5.0	5.0	22.2	23.1***
Delinquency	19.7	3.7	12.4	16.5	2.5	36.2	19.2	42.5	52.0	23.0***
Status Offense	14.6	2.5	13.1	24.0	5.7	29.8	36.1	33.0	64.6	24.6***
Child Substance Abuse	5.6	0.0	3.5	5.4	3.2	15.4	18.9	17.0	25.8	10.5***
Adult Substance Abuse	37.8	21.0	21.9	15.0	0.0	26.4	8.6	33.6	37.8	22.6***
Adult Relationships	50.2	33.3	61.6	49.1	31.2	60.8	73.3	59.5	57.4	52.7***
Parent-Child Conflict	51.3	22.2	44.6	59.8	8.0	89.0	84.0	72.5	81.8	56.9***

Table F-II (Continued)

		Franklin County n = 50	SCAN n = 54	ICFS n = 48	IDHS n = 50	Dakota County n = 50	LSS n = 54	Boulder County n = 48	CSD n = 50	Mult- nomah County n = 50	Totals n = 454
With Problem (%) (Continued)											
Family Relationships Adult		69.5	88.9	63.7	40.5	12.0	31.1	58.2	39.0	80.0	53.7***
Health/ Mental Health Child		68.9	48.0	40.4	17.9	7.2	41.8	24.3	25.0	35.4	34.6***
Behavior Total # of		55.8	22.2	51.4	54.4	.8	89.3	92.0	80.9	92.6	59.8***
Problems	m	6.2	7.1	4.0	2.3	.7	3.8	2.9	3.7	4.7	4.0***
	sd	2.9	2.6	2.4	2.2	.9	2.4	1.5	2.4	2.4	2.9

[a]Data weighted to represent estimated incidence of placement and non-placement based on sampling lists. Significance based on F test.

*$p < .05$. **$p < .01$. ***$p < .001$.

Table F-III
CASE OBJECTIVES AND SERVICES BY SITE

		Franklin County n = 50	SCAN n = 54	ICFS n = 48	IDHS n = 50	Dakota County n = 50	LSS n = 54	Boulder County n = 48	CSD n = 50	Mult-nomah County n = 50	Totals n = 454
Case Objectives (%)											
Use Outside Counseling		48.6	54.3	12.3	19.5	12.0	10.0	16.6	78.3	60.0	34.7***
Use Supportive Services		38.5	55.6	16.4	16.0	12.0	14.7	8.3	33.9	44.0	26.9***
Change in Parenting		79.1	82.7	98.6	88.5	72.2	88.0	62.0	2.1	0.0	64.0***
Change in Adult Behavior		36.2	55.5	41.1	23.4	8.8	17.7	4.4	3.5	0.0	21.4***
Change in Adult/ Marital Relationship		11.8	6.2	63.6	41.6	54.8	11.8	51.7	11.0	5.6	31.4***
Total Number of Objectives	m	7.3	9.9	9.4	6.7	5.2	9.0	6.3	3.8	3.4	6.8***
	sd	3.9	3.1	3.2	3.7	1.1	4.1	4.1	2.2	2.2	3.9
FBS Services (%)											
Individual Counseling		97.7	91.4	47.4	55.0	55.8	95.3	84.3	25.6	21.6	64.3***
Marriage Counseling		27.1	18.5	26.0	22.6	40.6	50.2	63.2	17.6	13.2	30.9***
Role Modeling		36.2	63.0	34.3	18.1	23.2	19.1	55.2	.5	3.4	28.2***
Teaching		59.4	85.2	26.8	27.5	59.0	34.8	46.9	63.0	10.4	46.2***
Homework		37.3	28.4	47.9	51.0	64.0	57.9	59.9	11.0	3.4	40.0***
Accompany to Appointment		28.8	79.0	46.6	14.9	3.4	13.4	18.1	.5	8.0	24.0***
Advocacy		29.9	96.3	28.1	30.9	4.0	15.7	35.8	7.5	14.2	29.6***
Case Management		52.5	95.0	46.6	47.8	86.5	3.7	59.0	62.1	23.4	52.9***
Information & Referral		60.5	100.0	43.2	29.9	65.0	39.8	39.1	44.5	26.2	30.2***
Recreation		31.6	11.1	25.3	1.0	0.0	23.1	6.8	0.0	0.0	11.1***
Outreach		13.5	54.3	.7	3.5	0.0	1.3	1.5	4.0	6.8	9.9***

Table F-III (Continued)

		Franklin County	SCAN	ICFS	IDHS	Dakota County	LSS	Boulder County	CSD	Mult-nomah County	Totals
		$n = 50$	$n = 54$	$n = 48$	$n = 50$	$n = 50$	$n = 54$	$n = 48$	$n = 50$	$n = 50$	$n = 454$
Collateral Services (%)											
Protective Services School		96.1	66.6	29.5	36.0	47.2	12.0	29.4	15.5	11.0	38.3***
Social Work Community Mental		40.0	33.3	24.0	13.0	32.0	29.8	17.8	17.0	34.2	26.9*
Health Psychologi-cal Testing Substance		47.9	44.4	14.4	21.9	10.3	10.1	.6	19.5	9.8	20.1***
		53.6	44.4	12.3	16.5	13.0	18.4	19.8	6.1	1.8	20.9***
Abuse Counseling Para-professional		15.2	3.7	15.7	11.5	7.2	8.7	13.3	2.6	9.8	9.7
Services Public		98.3	16.0	19.8	13.0	10.5	2.3	0.0	8.0	6.8	19.4***
Health Nurse Parent		23.8	19.7	4.1	0.0	0.0	3.7	3.9	0.0	0.0	6.3***
Education Support Group/		81.4	64.2	15.7	18.6	13.5	6.0	8.3	11.0	7.4	25.5***
Volunteer Money Management		31.1	13.6	14.3	23.0	15.8	16.1	9.5	5.0	29.6	17.6**
Counseling		54.8	39.5	10.9	0.0	6.3	8.4	.6	1.0	0.0	13.8***
AFDC		75.7	83.9	59.5	50.6	3.2	18.1	0.0	16.0	6.8	35.3***
Food Stamps		73.5	79.0	70.5	39.0	6.3	5.0	0.0	1.6	0.0	30.8***
Medicaid Emergency		71.2	81.5	10.9	28.0	0.0	1.3	18.6	.5	0	24.0***
Financial Aid Trans-		42.9	22.3	3.4	.5	0.0	4.7	0.0	0.0	0.0	8.4***
portation Total Number of		74.0	19.6	27.4	1.0	3.2	6.0	.9	4.0	3.4	15.6***
Services	m	20.1	20.4	9.9	8.4	8.9	8.0	8.8	5.1	4.1	10.5***
	sd	9.0	5.6	3.6	4.9	4.1	4.5	5.9	2.4	2.7	7.6
Home Visits in First 3 Months	m	19.0	8.6	19.5	1.0	8.4	8.9	2.3	.8	5.3	8.3***
	sd	10.6	3.9	8.2	1.7	4.5	9.0	5.5	1.6	2.6	8.9

Table F-III (Continued)

		Franklin County	SCAN	ICFS	IDHS	Dakota County	LSS	Boulder County	CSD	Mult-nomah County	Totals
		$n = 50$	$n = 54$	$n = 48$	$n = 50$	$n = 50$	$n = 54$	$n = 48$	$n = 50$	$n = 50$	$n = 454$
Office Visits in First 3 Months	m	.7	0.0	.1	4.0	.6	0.0	9.8	5.6	.7	2.3***
	sd	1.1	.2	.3	2.8	1.7	.1	5.8	4.6	1.2	4.1
Length of Services (Months)	m	7.0	11.1	7.6	5.1	2.9	4.9	10.4	4.2	5.2	6.4***
	sd	3.9	6.5	4.0	4.1	1.2	2.7	8.7	1.3	3.6	5.3
Teamed Services (%)		100.0	35.8	.7	.5	99.2	2.3	34.4	33.0	55.8	40.0***

Note. Data weighted to represent estimated incidence of placement and non-placement based on sampling lists. Significance based on F test.

*$p < .05$.   **$p < .01$.   ***$p < .001$.

Table F-IV
CASE OUTCOMES BY SITE

	Franklin County n = 50	SCAN n = 54	ICFS n = 48	IDHS n = 50	Dakota County n = 50	LSS n = 54	Boulder County n = 48	CSD n = 50	Mult-nomah County n = 50	Totals n = 454
Estimated Placement Rate[a] (%)	25.2	23.2	18.2	12.0	21.0	22.9	7.3	13.0	15.0	17.7
Restrictiveness of Final Placement (Highest-Risk Child[b]) (%)										
Relatives	50.0	38.9	30.8	4.2	0.0	17.6	12.0	8.7	4.3	21.8
Foster Home	7.1	33.3	34.6	75.0	40.0	29.4	32.0	13.0	52.2	32.9
Institution	0.0	0.0	23.1	12.5	24.0	29.4	44.0	21.7	21.7	17.1
% Attending Most or All Sessions										
Caretaker	64.0	59.7	90.9	83.0	69.7	81.9	60.3	92.3	79.4	75.5***
Other Adult[c]	30.9	26.8	39.3	70.3	62.5	66.4	40.1	59.3	58.6	51.1**
Highest-Risk Child	52.8	40.7	36.1	47.3	55.2	32.1	68.0	79.0	55.3	51.3***
% of Caretakers Cooperating Fully with Services	58.9	47.0	60.7	52.9	59.2	54.5	83.3	60.9	40.6	57.1***
% Positive Change										
Behavior	88.5	48.8	67.7	63.2	67.6	54.6	78.0	86.9	71.6	69.6***
Material Resources	53.7	30.2	8.7	8.7	4.3	35.7	32.5	0.0	18.7	23.6***
Family Hierarchy	47.5	19.1	35.6	56.2	66.5	58.2	57.6	76.3	62.0	53.1***
Family Relationships	62.8	46.8	65.7	54.3	62.8	66.0	71.1	85.8	69.4	65.0*
Use of Services	92.1	72.1	41.9	18.1	11.5	52.4	53.9	45.1	52.2	51.4***
Emotional Climate	71.3	62.4	45.0	49.4	56.4	47.2	95.5	80.5	68.1	62.7***
Perception of Problem	81.5	71.6	34.3	39.0	49.7	51.4	74.4	88.7	62.9	60.4***
% with Positive Change	100.0	76.6	86.2	75.2	73.3	65.5	92.1	88.4	80.8	81.8***
% Negative Change in at Least One Area	7.3	25.8	23.4	11.8	27.6	36.8	20.1	13.0	19.2	20.7**
Overall % of Goals Achieved	89.6	85.5	80.2	60.2	68.2	73.8	88.6	27.1	47.8	69.3***

Table F-IV (Continued)

	Franklin County $n = 50$	SCAN $n = 54$	ICFS $n = 48$	IDHS $n = 50$	Dakota County $n = 50$	LSS $n = 54$	Boulder County $n = 48$	CSD $n = 50$	Mult-nomah County $n = 50$	Totals $n = 454$
% With a Long Range Plan[b]	66.7	10.5	34.6	48.0	0.0	35.3	88.0	0.0	0.0	28.8***
% With No Additional Services After Closing	4.3	5.1	13.3	37.5	18.1	14.4	54.7	23.8	32.3	22.4***

Note. Data weighted to represent estimated incidence of placement and non-placement based on sampling lists. Significance based on F test.
[a]By family; estimated from sampling lists of placement prevention cases provided by agencies. Does not include assessment or reunification cases. [b]Placement cases only. [c]Includes only adult living in household; $n = 345$.
*$p < .05$. **$p < .01$. ***$p < .001$.

REFERENCES

Foreword

Bradbury, D. E. (1962). *Five decades of action for children: A history of the Children's Bureau.* Washington, D.C.: U.S. Department of Health, Education, and Welfare, Children's Bureau.

National Resource Center on Family Based Services. (1991). *Annotated directory of selected family-based services programs* (7th ed.). Iowa City, IA: The University of Iowa, School of Social Work.

State Charities Aid Association. (1960). *"Multi-problem families": A new name or a new problem?* New York: State Charities Aid Association, Social Research Service.

Chapter One

AuClaire, P., & Schwartz, I. M. (1986). *An evaluation of the effectiveness of intensive home-based services as an alternative to placement for adolescents and their families.* Minneapolis: University of Minnesota, Hubert H. Humphrey Institute of Public Affairs.

Balmer, J. U., Kogan, L., Voorhees, C., Levin-Shaw, W., & Shapiro, F. (1979). High impact family treatment: A progress report. *Juvenile and Family Court Journal, 30,* 3–7.

Barth, R. P. (1988). Theories guiding home-based intensive family preservation services. In J.K. Whittaker, J. Kinney, E.M. Tracy, and C. Booth (Eds.), *Improving practice technology for work with high-risk families: Lessons from the Homebuilders' social work education project* (pp. 9–13). Seattle: University of Washington School of Social Work, Center for Social Welfare Research.

Bryce, M. E. (1982). Preplacement prevention and family reunification: Direction for the 80's. In Ellen S. Saalberg (Ed.), *A dialogue on the challenge for education and training: Child welfare issues in the 80's* (pp. 77–84). Ann Arbor: Child Welfare Training Center.

Bryce, M., & Lloyd, J. (1981). *Treating families in the home: An alternative to placement.* Springfield, IL: Charles C Thomas.

Carter, E., & McGoldrick, M. (Eds.). (1980). *The family life cycle: A framework for family therapy.* New York: Gardner.

de Shazer, S. (1985). *Keys to solution in brief therapy.* New York: Norton.

de Shazer, S. (1988). *Clues: Investigating solutions in brief therapy.* New York: Norton.

Frankel, H. (1988). Family-centered, home-based services in child protection. *Social Service Review, 62,* 137–157.

Fraser, D., & Haapala, D. (1987–88). Home-based family treatment: A quantitative-qualitative assessment. *The Journal of Applied Social Sciences, 12,* 1–23.

Fraser, M. W., Pecora, P. J., & Haapala, D. A. (1989). *Families in crisis: Findings from the family-based intensive treatment project* (Vols. 1–2). Salt Lake City: University of Utah, Graduate School of Social Work, Social Research Institute.

Goldstein, H. (1973). Providing services to children in their own homes: An approach that can reduce foster placement. *Children Today, 2*(4), 2–7.

Haapala, D., & Kinney, J. (1979). Homebuilders approach to the training of in-home therapists. In S. Maybanks & M. Bryce (Eds.), *Home-based services for children and families* (pp. 248–259). Springfield, IL: Charles C Thomas.

Hartman, A. (1978). Diagrammatic assessment of family relationships. *Social Casework, 59*, 465–476.

Hartman, A., & Laird, J. (1983). *Family-centered social work practice.* New York: Free Press.

Hutchinson, J. R., Lloyd, J. C., Landsman, M., Nelson, K., & Bryce, M. (1983). *Family-centered social services: A model for child welfare agencies.* Iowa City: The University of Iowa School of Social Work, National Resource Center on Family Based Services.

Hutchinson, J. R., & Nelson, K. (1985). How public agencies can provide family-centered services. *Social Casework, 66*, 367–371.

Janzen, C., & Harris, O. (1986). *Family treatment in social work practice* (2nd. ed.). Itasca, IL: Peacock.

Jones, M. A., Neuman, R., & Shyne, A. W. (1976). *A second chance for families: Evaluation of a program to reduce foster care.* New York: Child Welfare League of America.

Kinney, J., Haapala, D., Booth, C., & Leavitt, S. (1988). The Homebuilders model. In J. K. Whittaker, J. Kinney, E. M. Tracy, and C. Booth (Eds.), *Improving practice technology for work with high-risk families: Lessons from the Homebuilders' social work education project* (pp. 37–67). Seattle: University of Washington School of Social Work, Center for Social Welfare Research.

Lahti, J., Green, K., Emlen, A., Zadny, J., Clarkson, Q., Kuehnel, M., & Casciato, J. (1978). *A follow-up study of the Oregon project.* Portland: Portland State University, Regional Research Institute for Human Services.

Leverington, J., & Wulff, D. [Erroneously attributed to L. Woods]. (1988). Home-based family therapy. *Social Work, 33*, 211–214.

Lloyd, J. C., & Bryce, M. E. (1984). *Placement prevention and family reunification.* Iowa City, IA: The University of Iowa School of Social Work, National Resource Center on Family Based Services.

Maas, H., & Engler, R. (1959). *Children in need of parents.* New York: Columbia University Press.

Magura, S., & DeRubeis, R. (1980). *The effectiveness of preventive services for families and abused, neglected and disturbed children: Second-year evaluation of the Hudson County Project.* Trenton, NJ: Division of Youth and Family Services, Bureau of Research.

Maybanks, S., & Bryce, M. (1978). *Home-based services for children and families: Policy, practice and research.* Springfield, IL: Charles C Thomas.

McGoldrick, M., & Gerson, R. (1985). *Genograms in family assessment.* New York: Norton.

McGowan, B. (1988). Family-based services and public policy: Context and implications. In J. K. Whittaker, J. Kinney, E. M. Tracy, and C. Booth (Eds.), *Improving practice technology for work with high-risk families: Lessons from the Homebuilders' social work education project* (pp. 69–89). Seattle: University of Washington School of Social Work, Center for Social Welfare Research.

Minuchin, P. (1985). Families and individual development: Provocations from the field of family therapy. *Child Development, 56,* 289–302.

Minuchin, S. (1974). *Families and family therapy.* Cambridge: Harvard University Press.

Minuchin, S., & Fishman, C. (1981). *Family therapy techniques.* Cambridge: Harvard University Press.

Napier, A., & Whitaker, C. (1978). *The family crucible.* New York: Harper & Row.

Nelson, K., Emlen, A., Landsman, M., & Hutchinson, J. (1988). *Factors contributing to success and failure in family-based child welfare services.* Iowa City: The University of Iowa, National Resource Center on Family Based Services.

Nelson, K., Landsman, M., & Deutelbaum, W. (1990). Three models of family-centered placement prevention services. *Child Welfare, 69,* 3–21.

Satir, V. M. (1982). *Conjoint family therapy* (3rd. rev. ed.). Palo Alto, CA: Science and Behavior Books.

Stanton, M. D. (1981). An integrated structural/strategic approach to family therapy. *Journal of Marital and Family Therapy, 7:*427–439.

Stroul, B. A. (1988). *Series on community-based services for children and adolescents who are severely emotionally disturbed: Vol. 1. Home-based services.* Washington, DC: Georgetown University Child Development Center, CASSP Technical Assistance Center.

Tavantzis, T. N., Tavantzis, M., Brown, L. G., & Rohrbaugh, M. (1985). Home-based structural family therapy for delinquents at risk of placement. In M. P. Mirkin & S. Koman (Eds.), *Handbook of adolescent and family therapy* (pp. 69–88). New York: Gardner Press.

Tyler, M. (1990). *State survey on placement prevention and family reunification programs: Final report.* Iowa City: The University of Iowa School of Social Work, National Resource Center on Family Based Services.

Watzlawick, P. (1974). *Change; Principles of problem formulation and problem resolution.* New York: Norton.

Wells, K. (In press). Family preservation services in context: Origins, practices and current issues. In I. Schwartz (Ed.), *Family and home-based services.* Lincoln: University of Nebraska Press.

Whittaker, J. K., & Tracy, F. M. (1988). Family preservation services and education for social work practice: Stimulus and response. In J. K. Whittaker, J. Kinney, E. M. Tracy, and C. Booth (Eds.), *Improving practice technology for work with high-risk families: Lessons from the Homebuilders' social work education project* (pp. 9–18). Seattle: University of Washington School of Social Work, Center for Social Welfare Research.

Wiltse, K. T. (1985). Foster care: An overview. In J. Laird & A. Hartman (Eds.), *A handbook of child welfare: Context, knowledge, and practice.* New York: The Free Press.

Chapter Two

Alexander, J. F., & Parsons, B. V. (1982). *Functional family therapy.* Monterey, CA: Brooks/Cole.

AuClaire, P., & Schwartz, I. M. (1986). *An evaluation of the effectiveness of intensive home-based services as an alternative to placement for adolescents and their families.* Minneapolis: University of Minnesota, Hubert H. Humphrey Institute of Public Affairs.

Barton, C., Alexander, J. F., Waldron, H., Turner, C. W., & Warburton, J. (1985). Generalizing treatment effects of functional therapy: Three replications. *The American Journal of Family Therapy, 13,* 16–26.

Berry, M. (1990). *Keeping families together: An evaluation of an intensive family preservation program.* Unpublished doctoral dissertation, School of Social Welfare, University of California, Berkeley.

Bryce, M. E. (1978). *Client and worker comparison of agency organizational design and treatment techniques in an intensive home-based social service program for families.* Unpublished doctoral dissertation. College of Education, The University of Iowa.

Callister, J., Mitchell, L., & Tolley, G. (1986). Profiling family preservation efforts in Utah. *Children Today, 15* (6), 23–25, 36–37.

Feldman, L. (1991). *Assessing the effectiveness of family preservation services in New Jersey within an ecological context.* Trenton: New Jersey Division of Youth and Family Services, Bureau of Research, Evaluation and Quality Assurance.

Fraser, M. W., Pecora, P. J., & Haapala, D. A. (1989). *Families in crisis: Findings from the family-based intensive treatment project* (Vols. 1–2). Salt Lake City: University of Utah, Graduate School of Social Work, Social Research Institute.

Gordon, D. A., Arbuthnot, J., Gustafson, K. E., & McGreen, P. (1988). Home-based behavioral-systems family therapy with disadvantaged juvenile delinquents. *The American Journal of Family Therapy, 16,* 243–255.

Haapala, D., & Kinney, J. (1988). Avoiding out-of-home placement of high-risk status offenders through the use of intensive home-based family preservation services. *Criminal Justice and Behavior, 15,* 334–348.

Halper, G., & Jones, M. A. (1981). *Serving families at risk of dissolution: Public preventive services in New York City.* New York: Human Resources Administration.

Hinckley, E. (1984). Homebuilders: The Maine experience. *Children Today, 13* (5), 14–17.

Hinckley, E. C., & Ellis, W. F. (1985). An effective alternative to residential placement: Home-based services. *Journal of Clinical Child Psychology, 14,* 209–213.

Holmes, T. H. (1981). *The Schedule of Recent Experience.* Seattle, WA: University of Washington Press.

Hutchinson, J. R., Lloyd, J. C., Landsman, M., Nelson, K., & Bryce, M. (1983). *Family-centered social services: A model for child welfare agencies.* Iowa City: The University of Iowa, School of Social Work, National Resource Center on Family Based Services.

Jayaratne, S., & Chess, W. A. (1984). Job satisfaction, burnout, and turnover: A national study. *Social Work, 29,* 448–455.

Jones, M. A., Neuman, R., & Shyne, A. W. (1976). *A second chance for families: Evaluation of a program to reduce foster care.* New York: Child Welfare League of America.

Jones, M. A. (1985). *A second chance for families: Five years later.* New York: Child Welfare League of America.

Kinney, J., Haapala, D., Booth, C., & Leavitt, S. (1988). The Homebuilders model. In J. K. Whittaker, J. Kinney, E. M. Tracy, and C. Booth (Eds.), *Improving practice technology for work with high-risk families: Lessons from the Homebuilders' social work education project* (pp. 37–67). Seattle: University of Washington, School of Social Work, Center for Social Welfare Research.

Kinney, J., Haapala, D., Madsen, B., & Fleming, T. (1977). Homebuilders: Keeping families together. *Journal of Counseling and Clinical Psychology, 14,* 209–213.

Landsman, M. J. (1985). *Evaluation of fourteen child placement prevention projects in Wisconsin, 1983-1985.* Iowa City: The University of Iowa School of Social Work, National Resource Center on Family Based Services.

Lantz, B. K. (1985). Keeping troubled teens at home. *Children Today, 14* (3), 8–12.

Lawder, E. A., Poulin, J. E., & Andrews, R. G. (1984). *Helping the multi-problem family: A study of services to children in their own homes.* Philadelphia: Children's Aid Society of Pennsylvania.

Leeds, S. (1984). *Evaluation of Nebraska's intensive services project.* Iowa City, IA: The University of Iowa School of Social Work, National Resource Center on Family Based Services.

Lyle, C. G., & Nelson, J. (1983). *Home-based vs traditional child protection services: A study of the home-based services demonstration project in the Ramsey County Community Human Services Department.* St. Paul, MN: Ramsey County Community Human Services.

Magura, S., & DeRubeis, R. (1980). *The effectiveness of preventive services for families and abused, neglected and disturbed children: Second-year evaluation of the Hudson County Project.* Trenton, NJ: Bureau of Research, Division of Youth and Family Services.

Magura, S., & Moses, B. S. (1986). *Outcome measures for child welfare services: Theory and applications.* Washington, DC: Child Welfare League of America, Inc.

Magura, S., Moses, B. S., & Jones, M. A. (1987). *Assessing risk and measuring changes in families: The family risk scales.* Washington, DC: Child Welfare League of America.

Maslach, C., & Jackson, S. (1981). *The human services survey.* Palo Alto: Consulting Psychologists Press.

Mitchell, C., Tovar, P., & Knitzer, J. (1989). *The Bronx Homebuilders program: An evaluation of the first 45 families.* New York: Bank Street College of Education.

Montayne, M. P. (1986). *The clinician's view of success in comprehensive family-centered services.* Unpublished master's thesis, The University of Iowa, School of Social Work.

Nelson, K. (1990, Fall). How do we know that family based services are effective? *Prevention Report,* pp. 1–3. (Available from the National Resource Center on

Family Based Services, School of Social Work, The University of Iowa, Iowa City, IA.)

Nelson, K. E. (1989). [Review of Protecting abused and neglected children]. *Children and Youth Services Review, 11,* 185–200.

Nelson, K., Emlen, A., Landsman, M., & Hutchinson, J. (1988). *Factors contributing to success and failure in family-based child welfare services.* Iowa City: The University of Iowa School of Social Work, National Resource Center on Family Based Services.

Paschal, J., & Schwahn, L. (1986). Intensive counseling in Florida. *Children Today, 15* (6), 12–16.

Pearson, C. L., & King, P. A. (1987). *Intensive family services: Evaluation of foster care in Maryland: Final report.* Baltimore: Maryland Department of Human Resources.

Pecora, P., Delewski, C., Booth, C., Haapala, D., & Kinney, J. (1985). Home-based family-centered services: The impact of training on worker attitudes. *Child Welfare, 64,* 529–540.

Reid, W. J., Kagan, R. M., & Schlosberg, S. (1988). Prevention of placement: Critical factors in program success. *Child Welfare, 67,* 25–36.

Showell, W. H. (1985). *1983–1985 biennial report of CSD's intensive family services.* Salem: Oregon Department of Human Resources, Children's Services Division.

Showell, W. H., Hartley, R., & Allen, M. (1988). *Outcomes of Oregon's family therapy programs: A descriptive study of 999 families.* Salem: Oregon Department of Human Resources, Children's Services Division.

Stroul, B.A. (1988). *Series on community-based services for children and adolescents who are severely emotionally disturbed: Vol. 1. Home-based services.* Washington, DC: Georgetown University Child Development Center, CASSP Technical Assistance Center.

Szykula, S., & Fleischman, M. (1985). Reducing out-of-home placements of abused children: Two controlled field studies. *Child Abuse and Neglect, 9,* 277–283.

Tavantzis, T. N., Tavantzis, M., Brown, L. G., & Rohrbaugh, M. (1985). Home-based structural family therapy for adolescents at risk. In M.P. Mirkin & S. Koman (Eds.), *Handbook of adolescent and family therapy* (pp. 69–88). New York: Gardner Press.

Thieman, A. A., Fuqua, R., & Linnan, K. (1990). *Iowa family preservation three year pilot project: Final evaluation report.* Ames: Iowa State University, Child Welfare Research and Training Project.

Virginia Department of Social Services. (1985). *Report on the preplacement preventive services grant evaluation.* Richmond: Virginia Department of Social Services.

Wald, M. S., Carlsmith, J. M., & Leiderman, P. H. (1988). *Protecting abused and neglected children.* Stanford, CA: Stanford University Press.

Yoshikama, R. T. (1984). *Assessing the implementation of federal policy to reduce the cost of foster care.* Portland, OR: Portland State University, Regional Research Institute for Human Services.

Yuan, Y., McDonald, W., Wheeler, C., Struckman-Johnson, D., & Rivest, M. (1990). *Evaluation of AB 1562 in-home care demonstration projects: Final report* (Contract No. KED6012). Sacramento, CA: Office of Child Abuse Prevention.

Chapter Three

American Humane Association. (1988). *Highlights of official child abuse and neglect reporting: 1986.* Denver: American Humane Association.

Aragona, J., & Eyberg, S. (1981). Neglected children: Mothers' report of child behavior problems and observed verbal behavior. *Child Development, 52,* 596–602.

Ayoub, C., & Jacewitz, M. M. (1982). Families at risk of poor parenting: A descriptive study of sixty at risk families in a model prevention program. *Child Abuse and Neglect, 6,* 413–422.

Belsky, J. (1981). Child maltreatment: An ecological integration. In S. Chess & A. Thomas (Eds.), *Annual progress in child psychiatry and child development* (pp. 637–665). New York: Brunner-Mazel.

Belsky, J. (1984). The determinants of parenting: A process model. *Child Development, 55,* 83–96.

Belsky, J., & Vondra, J. (1989). Lessons from child abuse: The determinants of parenting. In D. Cicchetti & V. Carlson (Eds.), *Child maltreatment: Theory and research on the causes and consequences of child abuse and neglect* (pp. 153–202). New York: Cambridge.

Berry, M. (1990). *Keeping families together: An evaluation of an intensive family preservation program.* Doctoral dissertation, School of Social Welfare, University of California, Berkeley.

Bousha, D. M., & Twentyman, C. T. (1984). Mother-child interactional style in abuse, neglect, and control groups: Naturalistic observations in the home. *Journal of Abnormal Psychology, 93,* 106–114.

Brunk, M., Henggeler, S. W., & Whelan, J. B. (1987). Comparison of multisystemic therapy and parent training in the brief treatment of child abuse and neglect. *Journal of Consulting and Clinical Psychology, 55,* 171–178.

Burgess, R., & Conger, R. (1978). Family interaction in abusive, neglectful, and normal families. *Child Development, 49,* 1163–1173.

Colon, F. (1980). The family life cycle of the multiproblem poor family. In E. Carter & M. McGoldrick. *The family life cycle: A framework for family therapy* (pp. 343–377). New York: Gardner Press.

Dale, P., & Davies, M. (1985). A model of intervention in child-abusing families: A wider systems view. *Child Abuse and Neglect, 9,* 449–455.

Daro, D. (1988). *Confronting child abuse.* New York: Free Press.

Daro, D., & Cohn, A. H. (1988). Child maltreatment evaluation efforts: What have we learned? In G. T. Hotaling, D. Finkelhor, J. T. Kirkpatrick, & M. A. Straus (Eds.), *Coping with family violence: Research and policy perspectives* (pp. 275–287). Newbury Park, CA: Sage Publications.

Gaines, R., Sandgrund, A., Green, A., & Power, E. (1978). Etiological factors in child maltreatment: A multivariate study of abusing, neglecting, and normal mothers. *Journal of Abnormal Psychiatry, 87,* 531–540.

Giovannoni, J. (1989). Definitional issues in child maltreatment. In D. Cicchetti & V. Carlson (Eds.), *Child maltreatment: Theory and research on the causes and consequences of child abuse and neglect* (pp. 1–37). New York: Cambridge.

Giovannoni, J., & Billingsley, A. (1970). Child neglect among the poor: A study of parental adequacy in families of three ethnic groups. *Child Welfare, 49,* 196–204.

Gold, N. (1990). Motivation: The crucial but unexplored component of social work practice. *Social Work, 35,* 49–56.

Green, A. H., Power, E., Steinbook, B., & Gaines, R. (1981). Factors associated with successful and unsuccessful intervention with child abusive families. *Child Abuse and Neglect, 5,* 45–52.

Gutierrez, L. M. (1990). Working with women of color: An empowerment perspective. *Social Work, 35,* 149–153.

Hartley, R., Showell, W., & White, J. (1989, September). *Outcomes of Oregon's family treatment programs: A descriptive study of 1752 families.* Paper presented at the Intensive Family Preservation Services Research Conference, Cleveland, OH.

Herrenkohl, R., Herrenkohl, E., & Egolf, B. (1983). Circumstances surrounding the occurrence of child maltreatment. *Journal of Consulting and Clinical Psychology, 51,* 424–431.

Herzberger, S. (1990). The cyclical pattern of child abuse. *American Behavioral Scientist, 33,* 529–545.

Horowitz, B., & Wolock, I. (1981). Material deprivation, child maltreatment, and agency interventions among poor families. In L. Pelton (Ed.), *The social context of child abuse and neglect* (pp. 137–184). New York: Human Sciences Press.

Jean-Gilles, M., & Crittenden, P. M. (1990). Maltreating families: A look at siblings. *Family Relations, 39,* 323–329.

Jones, J., & McNeely, R. (1980). Mothers who neglect and those who do not: A comparative study. *Social Casework, 61,* 559–567.

Kagan, R., & Schlosberg, S. (1989). *Families in perpetual crisis.* New York: W.W. Norton.

Kaplan, L. (1986). *Working with multiproblem families.* Lexington, MA: Lexington Books.

National Center on Child Abuse and Neglect. (1988). *Study findings: Study of incidence and prevalence of child abuse and neglect: 1988.* Washington, D.C.: U.S. Department of Health and Human Services.

Nelson, K., Saunders, E., and Landsman, M. (1990). *Chronic neglect in perspective: A study of chronically neglecting families in a large metropolitan county.* Iowa City, IA: The University of Iowa School of Social Work, National Resource Center on Family Based Services.

Orenchuk-Tomiuk, N., Matthey, G., & Pigler-Christensen, C. (1990). The resolution model: A comprehensive treatment framework in sexual abuse. *Child Welfare, 69*(5), 417–431.

Ory, M., & Earp, J. (1980). Child maltreatment: An analysis of familial and institutional predictors. *Journal of Family Issues, 1,* 339–356.

Polansky, N., Ammons, P., & Gaudin, J. (1985). Loneliness and isolation in child neglect. *Social Casework, 66,* 38–47.

Polansky, N., Chalmers, M., Williams, D., & Buttenweiser, E. (1981). *Damaged parents: An anatomy of neglect.* Chicago: University of Chicago Press.

Polansky, N., Gaudin, J., Ammons, P., & Davis, K. (1985). The psychological ecology of the neglectful mother. *Child Abuse and Neglect, 9,* 265–275.

Twentyman, C., & Plotkin, R. (1982). Unrealistic expectations of parents who maltreat their children: An educational deficit that pertains to child development. *Journal of Clinical Psychology, 38,* 497–503.

Weitzman, J. (1985). Engaging the severely dysfunctional family in treatment: Basic considerations. *Family Process, 24,* 473–485.

Wolock, I., & Horowitz, B. (1979). Child maltreatment and material deprivation among AFDC-recipient families. *Social Service Review, 53,* 175–194.

Yuan, Y. T., & Struckman-Johnson, D. L. (1991). Placement outcomes for neglected children with prior placements in family preservation programs. In K. Wells & D. A. Biegel (Eds.), *Family preservation services: Research and evaluation* (pp. 92–118). Newbury Park, CA: Sage.

Zuravin, S. (1988). Child abuse, child neglect, and maternal depression: Is there a connection? *Child neglect monograph: Proceedings from a symposium* (pp. 20–43). Washington, D.C.: U.S. Department of Health and Human Services, National Center on Child Abuse and Neglect.

Zuravin, S., & Greif, G. L. (1989). Normative and child-maltreating AFDC mothers. *Social Casework, 70,* 76–84.

Chapter Four

American Humane Association. (1988). *Highlights of official child abuse and neglect reporting: 1986.* Denver: American Humane Association.

Belsky, J. (1981). Child maltreatment: An ecological integration. In S. Chess & A. Thomas (Eds.), *Annual progress in child psychiatry and child development* (pp. 637–665). New York: Brunner-Mazel.

Belsky, J., & Vondra, J. (1989). Lessons from child abuse: The determinants of parenting. In D. Cicchetti & V. Carlson (Eds.), *Child maltreatment: Theory and research on the causes and consequences of child abuse and neglect* (pp. 153–202). New York: Cambridge.

Brunk, M., Henggeler, S. W., & Whelan, J. B. (1987). Comparison of multisystemic therapy and parent training in the brief treatment of child abuse and neglect. *Journal of Consulting and Clinical Psychology, 55,* 171–178.

Burgess, R. L. & Youngblade, L. M. (1988). Social incompetency and the inter-generational transmission of abusive parental behavior. In R. J. Gelles, G. Hotaling, D. Finkelhor, & M. Strauss (Eds.), *New directions in family violence research* (pp. 38–60). Beverly Hills, CA: Sage.

Burgess, R. L., Anderson, E., Schellenbach, C., & Conger, R. (1981). A social interactional approach to the study of abusive families. In J. P. Vincent (Ed.), *Advances in family intervention, assessment and theory: An annual compilation of research* (Vol. 2). Greenwich, CT: JAI Press.

Cicchetti, D., & Carlson, V. (Eds.). (1989). *Child maltreatment: Theory and research on the causes and consequences of child abuse and neglect.* New York: Cambridge.

Conger, R. D., Burgess, R. L., & Barrett, C. (1979). Child abuse related to life change and perceptions of illness: Some preliminary findings. *The Family Coordinator, 28,* 73–78.

Dale, P., & Davies, M. (1985). A model of intervention in child-abusing families: A wider systems view. *Child Abuse and Neglect, 9,* 449–455.

Engfer, A., & Schneewind, K. A. (1982). Causes and consequences of harsh parental punishment: An empirical investigation in a representative sample of 570 German families. *Child Abuse and Neglect, 6,* 129–139.

Famularo, R., Barnum, R., & Stone, K. (1986). Court-ordered removal in severe child maltreatment: An association to parental major affective disorder. *Child Abuse and Neglect, 10,* 487–492.

Famularo, R., Stone, K., & Barnum, R. (1986). Alcoholism and severe child maltreatment. *American Journal of Orthopsychiatry, 56,* 481–485.

Fraser, M. W., Pecora, P. J., & Haapala, D. A. (1989). *Families in crisis: Findings from the family-based intensive treatment project* (Vols. 1–2). Salt Lake City: University of Utah, Graduate School of Social Work, Social Research Institute.

Garbarino, J. (1989). The dynamics of adolescent maltreatment. In D. Cicchetti & V. Carlson (Eds.), *Child maltreatment: Theory and research on the causes and consequences of child abuse and neglect* (pp. 685–706). New York: Cambridge.

Garbarino, J., Schellenbach, C. J., Sebes, J., & Associates (1986). *Troubled youth, troubled families.* New York: Aldine de Gruyter.

Garbarino, J., Sebes, J., & Schellenbach, C.J. (1984). Families at risk for destructive parent-child relations in adolescence. *Child Development, 55,* 174–183.

Gelles, R. J., & Cornell, C. P. (1990). *Intimate violence in families* (2nd ed.). Newbury Park, CA: Sage.

Gelles, R. J., & Maynard, P. E. (1987). A structural family systems approach to intervention in cases of family violence. *Family Relations, 36,* 270–275.

Green, A. H., Power, E., Steinbook, B., & Gaines, R. (1981). Factors associated with successful and unsuccessful intervention with child abusive families. *Child Abuse and Neglect, 5,* 45–52.

Hartley, R., Showell, W., & White, J. (1989, September). *Outcomes of Oregon's family treatment programs: A descriptive study of 1752 families.* Paper presented at the Intensive Family Preservation Services Research Conference, Cleveland, OH.

Herzberger, S. (1990). The cyclical pattern of child abuse. *American Behavioral Scientist, 33,* 529–545.

Justice, B., & Justice, R. (1982). Etiology of physical abuse of children and dynamics of coercive treatment. *Family Therapy Collections, 3,* 1–20.

Justice, B., & Justice, R. (1990). *The abusing family* (rev. ed.). New York: Plenum Press.

Kaufman, K. L. & Rudy, L. (1991). Future directions in the treatment of physical child abuse. *Criminal Justice and Behavior, 18,* 82–97.

Meddin, B. (1984). Criteria for placement decisions in protective services. *Child Welfare, 63,* 367–373.

Oldershaw, L., Walters, G. C., Hall, D. K. (1989). A behavioral approach to the classification of different types of physically abusive mothers. *Merrill-Palmer Quarterly, 35,* 255–279.

Ory, M., & Earp, J. (1980). Child maltreatment: An analysis of familial and institutional predictors. *Journal of Family Issues, 1,* 339–356.

Panaccione, V. F., & Wahler, R. G. (1986). Child behavior, maternal depression, and social coercion as factors in the quality of child care. *Journal of Abnormal Child Psychology, 14,* 263–278.

Pianta, R., Egeland, B., & Erickson, M. F. (1989). The antecedents of maltreatment: Results of the Mother-Child Interaction Research Project. In D. Cicchetti & V. Carlson (Eds.), *Child maltreatment: Theory and research on the causes and consequences of child abuse and neglect* (pp. 203–253). New York: Cambridge.

Reid, J.B., Taplin, P.S., & Lorber, R. (1981). A social interactional approach to the treatment of abusive families. In R.B. Stuart (Ed.), *Violent behavior: Social learning approaches to prediction, management, and treatment* (pp. 83–101). New York: Brunner/Mazel.

Rodgers, R. H. (1987). Postmarital reorganization of family relationships: A propositional theory. In D. Perlman & S. Duck (Eds.), *Intimate relationships: Development, dynamics and deterioration* (pp. 239–268). Newbury Park, CA: Sage.

Rutter, M. (1989). Intergenerational continuities and discontinuities in serious parenting difficulties. In D. Cicchetti & V. Carlson (Eds.), *Child maltreatment: Theory and research on the causes and consequences of child abuse and neglect* (pp. 317–348). New York: Cambridge.

Straus, M., Gelles, R., & Steinmetz, S. (1980). *Behind closed doors: Violence in the American family.* Garden City, NJ: Doubleday.

Straus, M., & Gelles, R. J. (1988). Violence in American families: How much is there and why does it occur? In E. W. Nunnally, C. Chilman, & M. Cox (Eds.), *Troubled relationships* (pp. 141–162). Newbury Park, CA: Sage.

Susman, E. J., Trickett, P. K., Iannotti, R. J., Hollenbeck, B. E., & Zahn-Waxler, C. (1985). Child-rearing patterns in depressed, abusive, and normal mothers. *American Journal of Orthopsychiatry, 55,* 237–251.

Trickett, P. K. & Susman, E. J. (1989). Perceived similarities and disagreements about childrearing practices in abusive and nonabusive families: Intergenerational and concurrent family processes. In D. Cicchetti & V. Carlson (Eds.), *Child maltreatment: Theory and research on the causes and consequences of child abuse and neglect* (pp. 280–301). New York: Cambridge.

Webster-Stratton, C. (1985). Comparison of abusive and non-abusive families with conduct-disordered children. *American Journal of Orthopsychiatry, 55,* 59–69.

Wolfe, D. A. (1985). Child-abusive parents: An empirical review and analysis. *Psychological Bulletin, 97,* 462–482.

Yuan, Y. T., & Struckman-Johnson, D. L. (1991). Placement outcomes for neglected children with prior placements in family preservation programs. In K. Wells & D. A. Biegel (Eds.), *Family preservation services: Research and evaluation* (pp. 92–118). Newbury Park, CA: Sage.

Chapter Five

Coleman, H., & Collins, D. (1990). Treatment trilogy of father-daughter incest. *Child and Adolescent Social Work, 7,* 339–355.

Cornille, T. A. (1989). Family therapy and social control with incestuous families. *Contemporary Family Therapy, 1,* 101–118.

Daro, D. (1988). *Confronting child abuse.* New York: Free Press.

Everson, M. D., Hunter, W. M., Runyon, D. K., Edelsohn, G. A., & Coulter, M. L. (1989). Maternal support following disclosure of incest. *American Journal of Orthopsychiatry, 59,* 197–207.

Finkelhor, D. (1984). *Child sexual abuse: New theory and research.* New York: Free Press.

Finkelhor, D. (1990). Early and long-term effects of child sexual abuse: An update. *Professional Psychology: Research and Practice, 21,* 325–330.

Fish, V., & Faynik, C. (1989). Treatment of incest families with the father temporarily removed: A structural approach. *Journal of Strategic and Systemic Therapies, 8,* 53–63.

Garbarino, J. (1989). The dynamics of adolescent maltreatment. In D. Cicchetti & V. Carlson (Eds.), *Child maltreatment: Theory and research on the causes and consequences of child abuse and neglect* (pp. 685–706). New York: Cambridge.

Giaretto, H. (1982). *Integrated treatment of child sexual abuse: A treatment and training manual.* Palo Alto, CA: Science and Behavior Books.

Glaser, D., & Frosh, S. (1988). *Child sexual abuse.* London: Macmillan.

Gomes-Schwartz, B., Horowitz, J. M., & Cardarelli, A. P. (1990). *Child sexual abuse: The initial effects.* Newbury Park, CA: Sage.

Green, A. H. (1988). Child maltreatment and its victims: A comparison of physical and sexual abuse. *Psychiatric Clinics of North America, 11,* 591–610.

Hoke, S. L., Sykes, C., & Winn, M. (1989). Systemic/strategic interventions targeting denial in the incestuous family. *Journal of Strategic and Systemic Therapies, 8,* 44–51.

Hunter, W. M., Coulter, M. L., Runyan, D. K., & Everson, M. D. (1990). Determinants of placement for sexually abused children. *Child Abuse and Neglect, 14,* 407–417.

Kaufman, K. L. & Rudy, L. (1991). Future directions in the treatment of physical child abuse. *Criminal Justice and Behavior, 18,* 82–97.

Keller, R. A., Cicchinelli, L. F., & Gardner, D. M. (1989). Characteristics of child sexual abuse treatment programs. *Child Abuse and Neglect, 13,* 361–368.

Orenchuk-Tomiuk, N., Matthey, G., & Pigler-Christensen, C. (1990). The resolution model: A comprehensive treatment framework in sexual abuse. *Child Welfare, 69,* 417–431.

Pellegrin, A. & Wagner, W. G. (1990). Child sexual abuse: Factors affecting victims' removal from home. *Child Abuse & Neglect, 14,* 53–60.

Russell, D. E. J. (1986). *The secret trauma: Incest in the lives of girls and women.* New York: Basic Books.

Sever, J., & Janzen, C. (1982). Contradictions to reconstitution of sexually abusive families. *Child Welfare, 61,* 279–288.

Singer, M. I., Petchers, M. K., & Hussey, D. (1989). The relationship between sexual abuse and substance abuse among psychiatrically hospitalized adolescents. *Child Abuse and Neglect, 13,* 319–325.

Sirles, E. A. & Lofberg, C. E. (1990). Factors associated with divorce in intrafamily child sexual abuse cases. *Child Abuse & Neglect, 14,* 165–170.

Tzeng, O. C. S., & Schwarzin, H. J. (1990). Gender and race differences in child sexual abuse correlates. *International Journal of Intercultural Relations, 14,* 135–161.

Weiss, R. S. (1984). The impact of marital dissolution on income and consumption in single-parent households. *Journal of Marriage and the Family, 46,* 115–127.

Chapter Six

Alexander, J., & Parsons, B. V. (1973). Short-term behavioral intervention with delinquent families: Impact on family process and recidivism. *Journal of Abnormal Psychology, 81,* 219–225.

Alexander, J. F., & Parsons, B. V. (1982). *Functional family therapy.* Monterey, CA: Brooks/Cole.

AuClaire, P., & Schwartz, I. M. (1986). *An evaluation of the effectiveness of intensive home-based services as an alternative to placement for adolescents and their families.* Minneapolis: University of Minnesota, Hubert H. Humphrey Institute of Public Affairs.

Balmer, J. U., Kogan, L., Voorhees, C., Levin-Shaw, W., & Shapiro, F. (1979). High impact family treatment: A progress report. *Juvenile and Family Court Journal, 30,* 3–7.

Barton, C., Alexander, J. F., Waldron, H., Turner, C. W., & Warburton, J. (1985). Generalizing treatment effects of functional therapy: Three replications. *The American Journal of Family Therapy, 13,* 16–26.

Blomberg, T. G. (1983). Diversion's disparate results and unresolved questions: An integrative evaluation perspective. *Journal of Research in Crime and Delinquency, 20,* 24–38.

Dadds, M.R. (1987). Families and the origins of child behavior problems. *Family Process, 26,* 341–357.

Friedman, A. S., Tomko, L. A. & Utada, A. (1991). Client and family characteristics that predict better family therapy outcome for adolescent drug users. *Family Dynamics of Addiction Quarterly, 1,* 77–93.

Garbarino, J., Schellenbach, C. J., Sebes, J., & Associates (1986). *Troubled youth, troubled families.* New York: Aldine de Gruyter.

Geismar, L. L., & Wood, K. (1986). *Family and delinquency: Resocializing the young offender.* New York: Human Sciences Press.

Glueck, S., & Glueck, E. (1950). *Unraveling juvenile delinquency.* London: Routledge and Kegan Paul.

Gordon, D. A., Arbuthnot, J., Gustafson, K. E., & McGreen, P. (1988). Home-based behavioral systems therapy with disadvantaged juvenile delinquents. *The American Journal of Family Therapy, 16,* 243–255.

Haapala, D., & Kinney, J. (1988). Avoiding out-of-home placement of high-risk status offenders through the use of intensive home-based family preservation services. *Criminal Justice and Behavior, 15,* 334–348.

Hartley, R., Showell, W., & White, J. (1989, September). *Outcomes of Oregon's family treatment programs: A descriptive study of 1752 families.* Paper presented at the Intensive Family Preservation Services Research Conference, Cleveland, OH.

Johnstone, J. W. C. (1978). Juvenile delinquency and the family: A contextual interpretation. *Youth and Society, 9,* 299–313.

Kagan, R. M., Reid, W. J., Roberts, S. E., & Silverman-Pollow, J. (1987). Engaging families of court-mandated youth in an alternative to institutional placement. *Child Welfare, 66,* 365–376.

Landsman, M. J. (1985). *Evaluation of fourteen child placement prevention projects in Wisconsin, 1983-1985.* Iowa City: The University of Iowa School of Social Work, National Resource Center on Family Based Services.

Landsman, M. J., Leung, P., & Hutchinson, J. (1987). *Preventive services to families in four states: Subcontractor's final report for the New Jersey performance contracting study.* Iowa City: The University of Iowa School of Social Work, National Resource Center on Family Based Services.

Lantz, B. K. (1985). Keeping troubled teens at home. *Children Today, 14* (3), 9–12.

Leeds, S. (1984). *Evaluation of Nebraska's intensive services project.* Iowa City: The University of Iowa School of Social Work, National Resource Center on Family Based Services.

Mann, B. J., Borduin, C. M., Henggeler, S. W., & Blaske, D. M. (1990). An investigation of systemic conceptualizations of parent-child coalitions and symptom change. *Journal of Consulting and Clinical Psychology, 58,* 336–344.

Nelson, K. (1990). Family-based services for juvenile offenders. *Children and Youth Services Review, 12,* 193–212.

Norland, S., Shover, N., Thornton, W. E., & James, J. (1979). Intrafamily conflict and delinquency. *Pacific Sociological Review, 22,* 223–240.

Nugent, W.R. (1991). *Correlates of family preservation and family reunification.* Unpublished manuscript. Nashville, TN: University of Tennessee, College of Social Work.

Olweus, D. (1980). Familial and temperamental determinants of aggressive behavior in adolescent boys: A causal analysis. *Developmental Psychology, 16,* 644–660.

Parsons, B.V. & Alexander, J.F. (1973). Short-term family intervention: A therapy outcome study. *Journal of Consulting and Clinical Psychology, 41,* 195–201.

Roberts, A. R. (1989). *Juvenile justice: Policies, programs, and services.* Chicago: Dorsey.

Sarri, R. (1983). Paradigms and pitfalls in juvenile justice diversion. In A. Morris & H. Giller (Eds.), *Providing criminal justice for children* (pp. 52–73). London: Edward Arnold.

Schwartz, I. M. (1989). *(In)justice for juveniles.* Lexington, MA: Lexington Books.

Showell, W., Hartley, R., & Allen, M. (1988). *Outcomes of Oregon's family therapy programs: A descriptive study of 99 families.* Salem, OR: Oregon Department of Human Resources.

Showell, W., & White, T. (1990, Spring). In-home and in-office intensive family services. *Prevention Report,* pp. 6 & 10. (Available from the National Resource Center on Family Based Services, School of Social Work, The University of Iowa, Iowa City, IA.)

Simcha-Fagan, O. (1979). The prediction of delinquent behavior over time: Sex-specific patterns related to official and survey-reported delinquent behavior. In R.G. Simmons (Ed.), *Research in community and mental health: An annual compilation of research, 1,* 163–181.

Simons, R. L., Robertson, J. F., & Downs, W. R. (1989). The nature of the association between parental rejection and delinquent behavior. *Journal of Youth and Adolescence, 18,* 297–310.

Spaid, W. M. & Fraser, M. (1991). The correlates of success/failure in brief and intensive family treatment: Implications for family preservation services. *Children and Youth Services Review, 13,* 77–99.

Stroul, B. A. (1988). *Series on community-based services for children and adolescents who are severely emotionally disturbed: (Vol. 1). Home-based services.* Washington, DC: Georgetown University Child Development Center, CASSP Technical Assistance Center.

Tavantzis, T. N., Tavantzis, M., Brown, L. G., & Rohrbaugh, M. (1985). Home-based structural family therapy for adolescents at risk. In M. P. Mirkin & S. Koman (Eds.), *Handbook of adolescent and family therapy* (pp. 69–88). New York: Gardner.

Tolan, P. H., Cromwell, R. E., & Brasswell, M. (1986). Family therapy with delinquents: A critical review of the literature. *Family Process, 25,* 619–649.

Ulrici, D.K. (1983). The effects of behavioral and family interventions on juvenile recidivism. *Family Therapy, 10,* 25–36.

Wells, L. E. & Rankin, J. H. (1991). Families and delinquency: A meta-analysis of the impact of broken homes. *Social Problems, 38,* 71–93.

Wodarski, J. S. (1981). Comprehensive treatment of parents who abuse their children. *Adolescence, 16,* 959–972.

Chapter Seven

AuClaire, P., & Schwartz, I. M. (1986). *An evaluation of the effectiveness of intensive home-based services as an alternative to placement for adolescents and their families.* Minneapolis: University of Minnesota, Hubert H. Humphrey Institute of Public Affairs.

Buffum, V. (1984). Choosing a rural service delivery design. *The Journal of Applied Social Sciences, 8,* 187–203.

Coward, R. T. (1983). Serving families in contemporary rural America. In R. T. Coward & W. M. Smith, Jr. (Eds.), *Family services: Issues and opportunities in contemporary rural America* (pp. 3–25). Lincoln: University of Nebraska Press.

Coward, R. T., & Smith, W. M., Jr. (Eds.). (1983). *Family services: Issues and opportunities in contemporary rural America.* Lincoln: University of Nebraska Press.

Craig, B., & Hurry, D. (1981). Rural multi-problem families. *Journal of Family Therapy, 3,* 91–99.

Elkin, B., & Boyer, P. A. (1987). Practice skills and personal characteristics that facilitate practitioner retention in rural mental health settings. *Journal of Rural Community Psychology, 8* (2), 30–39.

Fraser, M. W., Pecora, P. J., & Haapala, D. A. (1989). *Families in crisis: Findings from the family-based intensive treatment project* (Vols. 1–2). Salt Lake City: University of Utah, Graduate School of Social Work, Social Research Institute.

Glenn, N. D., & Hill, L., Jr. (1977). Rural-urban differences in attitudes and behaviors in the United States. *Annals of the American Academy of Political Science, 123,* 36–50.

Gross, C. J. (1990). The status of the rural status offender. *Human Services in the Rural Environment, 14* (1), 35–39.

Heyman, S. R. (1986). Addressing preventive interventions in rural community psychology. *Journal of Rural Community Psychology, 7*(2), 7–15.

Hurn, J. (1990). Rural single father families: Emerging issues and needs. *Human Services in the Rural Environment, 14*(2), 19–22.

Jayaratne, S., & Chess, W. A. (1984). Job satisfaction, burnout, and turnover: A national study. *Social Work, 29,* 448–455.

Jerrell, J. M. (1983). Work satisfaction among rural mental health staff. *Community Mental Health Journal, 19,* 187–200.

Jurich, A. P., & Russell, C. S. (1987). Family therapy with rural families in a time of farm crisis. *Family Relations, 36,* 364–367.

Kamerman, S. B., & Kahn, A. J. (1990). Social services for children, youth and families in the United States. *Children and Youth Services Review, 11,* 1–184.

Nelson, K., Emlen, A., Landsman, M. J., & Hutchinson, J. (1988). *Factors contributing to success and failure in family-based child welfare services.* Iowa City: The University of Iowa School of Social Work, National Resource Center on Family Based Services.

Pecora, P. J., Delewski, C., Booth, C., Haapala, D., & Kinney, J. (1985). Home-based family-centered services: The impact of training on worker attitudes. *Child Welfare, 64,* 529–540.

Perlman, B., Hartman, E. A., & Bosak, J. (1984). A study of mental health administrators and systems using a four-part rural/urban taxonomy. *Community Mental Health Journal, 20,* 202–211.

Pulakos, J., & Dengerink, H. A. (1983). Comparison of mental health services in rural and urban Washington. *Community Mental Health Journal, 19,* 164–172.

Stefl, M. E., & Prosperi, D. C. (1985). Barriers to mental health service utilization. *Community Mental Health Journal, 21,* 167–177.

Tremblay, K. R., Walker, F. S., & Dillman, D. A. (1983). The quality of life experienced by rural families. In R.T. Coward & W. M. Smith, Jr. (Eds.), *Family services: Issues and opportunities in contemporary rural America* (pp. 26–40). Lincoln: University of Nebraska Press.

Wagenfeld, M. O., & Buffum, W. E. (1983). Problems in, and prospects for, rural mental health services in the United States. *International Journal of Mental Health, 12*, 89–107.

Weeks, E. C., & Drencacz, S. (1983). Rocking in a small boat: The consequences of economic changes in rural communities. *International Journal of Mental Health, 12*, 62–75.

Whitaker, W. H. (1986). A survey of perceptions of social work practice in rural and urban areas. *Human Services in the Rural Environment, 3*(6), 12–19.

York, R. O., Denton, R. T., & Moran, J. R. (1989). Rural and urban social work practice: Is there a difference? *Social Casework, 70*, 201–209.

Chapter Eight

Gibelman, M. (1981). Are clients served better when services are purchased? *Public Welfare, 39*(4), 26–34.

Gronbjerg, K. A. (1987). Patterns of institutional relations in the welfare state. Public mandates and the nonprofit sector. In S. A. Ostrander & S. Langton (Eds.), *Shifting the debate: Public/private sector relations in the modern welfare state.* New Brunswick, NJ: Transaction Books.

Gronbjerg, K. A. (1990). Poverty and nonprofit organizational behavior. *Social Service Review, 64*, 208–243.

Hall, P. D. (1987). Abandoning the rhetoric of independence: Reflections on the nonprofit sector in the post-liberal era. In S.A. Ostrander & S. Langton (Eds.), *Shifting the debate: Public/private sector relations in the modern welfare state* (pp. 11–28). New Brunswick, NJ: Transaction Books.

Hart, A. F. (1988). Contracting for child welfare services in Massachusetts: Emerging issues for policy and practice. *Social Work, 33*, 511–515.

Hurl, L. F. (1986). Keeping on top of governmental contracting: The challenge to social work educators. *Journal of Social Work Education, 22*(2), 6–18.

Hutchinson, J., & Nelson, K. (1985). How public agencies can provide family-centered services. *Social Casework, 66*, 367–371.

Iowa Department of Human Services. (1985). *Family-centered services employees manual.* (Available from the National Resource Center on Family Based Services, School of Social Work, The University of Iowa, Iowa City, IA.)

Kramer, R. M. (1985, August). *The future of the voluntary agency in a mixed economy.* Paper presented at the Annual Meeting of the Society for the Study of Social Problems, Washington, D.C.

Kramer, R. M., & Grossman, B. (1987). Contracting for social services: Process management and resource dependencies. *Social Service Review, 61*, 32–55.

Pecora, P. J., Delewski, C., Booth, C., Haapala, D., & Kinney, J. (1985). Home-based family-centered services: The impact of training on worker attitudes. *Child Welfare, 64*, 529–540.

Pecora, P. J., Kinney, J. M., Mitchell, L., & Tolley, G. (1990). Selecting an agency auspice for family preservation services. *Social Service Review, 64*, 288–307.

Reagen, M. V., & Musser, M. J. (1984). A quiet revolution comes to Iowa. *Public Welfare, 42* (Winter), 12–16.

Salamon, L. M. (1987). Of market failure, voluntary failure, and third-party government: Toward a theory of government-nonprofit relations in the modern welfare state. In S. A. Ostrander & S. Langton (Eds.), *Shifting the debate: Public/private sector relations in the modern welfare state* (pp. 29–49). New Brunswick, NJ: Transaction Books.

Smith, S. R. (1989). The changing politics of child welfare services: New roles for the government and the nonprofit sectors. *Child Welfare, 68,* 289–299.

Terrell, P., & Kramer, R. M. (1984). Contracting with nonprofits. *Public Welfare, 42* (Winter), 31–37.

Chapter Nine

Bryce, M. (1979). Home-based care: Development and rationale. In S. Maybanks & M. Bryce (Eds.), *Home-based services for children and families: Policy, practice, and research* (pp. 13–26). Springfield, IL: Charles C Thomas.

Compher, J. (1983). Home services to families to prevent child placement. *Social Work, 28,* 360–364.

Hartley, R., Showell, W., & White, J. (1989, September). *Outcomes of Oregon's family treatment programs: A descriptive study of 1752 families.* Paper presented at the Intensive Family Preservation Services Research Conference. Cleveland, OH.

Horejsi, C. R. (1981). The St. Paul family-centered project revisited: Exploring an old gold mine. In M. Bryce & J. Lloyd (Eds.), *Treating families in the home: An alternative to placement* (pp. 12–23). Springfield, IL: Charles C Thomas.

Hutchinson, J. R., & Nelson, K. (1985). How public agencies can provide family-centered services. *Social Casework, 66,* 367–371.

Kagan, R., & Schlosberg, S. (1989). *Families in perpetual crisis.* New York: W.W. Norton.

Kaplan, L. (1986). *Working with multiproblem families.* Lexington, MA: Lexington Books.

Kinney, J., Haapala, D., Booth, C., & Leavitt, S. (1988). The Homebuilders model. In J. K. Whittaker, J. Kinney, E. M. Tracy, and C. Booth (Eds.), *Improving practice technology for work with high-risk families: Lessons from the Homebuilders' social work education project* (pp. 37–67). Seattle: University of Washington School of Social Work, Center for Social Welfare Research.

Leverington, J., & Wulff, D. [Erroneously attributed to Wood, L.] (1988). Home-based family therapy. *Social Work, 33,* 211–214.

Nelson, K., Emlen, A., Hutchinson, J., & Landsman, M. (1988). *Factors contributing to success and failure in family-based child welfare services.* Iowa City: The University of Iowa School of Social Work, National Resource Center on Family Based Services.

Rabin, C., Rosenbaum, H., & Sens, M. (1982). Home-based marital therapy for multiproblem families. *Journal of Marital and Family Therapy, 8,* 451–461.

Reynolds-Mejia, P., & Levitan, S. (1990). Countertransference issues in the in-home treatment of child sexual abuse. *Child Welfare, 69,* 53–61.

Showell, W., & White, T. (1990, Spring). In-home and in-office intensive family services. *Prevention Report,* pp. 6 & 10. (Available from the National Resource Center on Family Based Services, School of Social Work, The University of Iowa, Iowa City, IA.)

Webster-Stratton, C. (1985). Comparisons of behavior transactions between conduct disordered children and their mothers in the clinic and at home. *Journal of Abnormal Child Psychology, 13,* 169–184.

Chapter Ten

American Enterprise Institute (1991, February). *Conference on Child Welfare Evaluation,* Washington, D.C.

American Public Welfare Association. (1986). *The Supportive Child Adult Network (SCAN) of Philadelphia: Program documentation.* Iowa City: The University of Iowa, School of Social Work, National Resource Center on Family Based Services.

AuClaire, P., & Schwartz, I. M. (1986). *An evaluation of the effectiveness of intensive home-based services as an alternative to placement for adolescents and their families.* Minneapolis: University of Minnesota, Hubert H. Humphrey Institute of Public Affairs.

Bickman, L. (1990). Study design. In Y. Yuan & M. Rivest (Eds.), *Preserving families: Evaluation resources for practitioners and policymakers* (132–166). Beverly Hills, CA: Sage.

Deutelbaum, W. (1991, December). *Not all families are straight: Working with gay and lesbian families.* Paper presented at the Empowering Families Conference, 5th Annual Meeting of the National Association for Family-Based Services, St. Louis, MO.

Faria, G. (1991, December). *Educating students for family based practice with lesbian families.* Paper presented at the Empowering Families Conference, 5th Annual Meeting of the National Association for Family-Based Services, St. Louis, MO.

Fraser, M., Pecora, P., & Haapala, D. (1991). *Families in crisis.* New York: Aldine de Gruyter.

Gershenson, C. P. (1990). Observations on family preservation services evaluations. *Frontline Views, 1,* 6–7. (Available from the Center for the Study of Social Policy, Washington, D.C.)

Kinney, J., Haapala, D., & Booth, C. (1991). *Keeping families together: The Homebuilders model.* New York: Aldine de Gruyter.

Legatski, P. (1990). Urban American Indians: Strengthening the family. *Empowering families: Papers from the third annual conference on family based services.* Riverdale, IL: National Association for Family-Based Services.

Mannes, M. & Yuan, Y. (1988). Keeping Indian families together: The potential of family based placement prevention services. *American Indian Law Newsletter, 21,* 20–47.

Manski, C. M. (1990). Where are we in the evaluation of federal social welfare programs? *Focus, 12*(4), 1–5.

Maryland Department of Human Resources. (1987). *Intensive family services: A family preservation service delivery model.* Baltimore: Maryland Department of Human Resources.

Mitchell, C., Tovar, P., & Knitzer, J. (1989). *The Bronx Homebuilders program: An evaluation of the first 45 families.* New York: Bank Street College of Education.

Moroney, R. M. (1986). *Shared responsibility: Families and social policy.* New York: Aldine de Gruyter.

Nelson, K. (1990, Fall). How do we know that family based services are effective? *Prevention Report,* pp. 1–3. (Available from the National Resource Center on Family Based Services, School of Social Work, The University of Iowa, Iowa City, IA.)

Pecora, P. J., Delewski, C., Booth, C., Haapala, D., & Kinney, J. (1985). Home-based family-centered services: The impact of training on worker attitudes. *Child Welfare, 64,* 529–540.

Rossi, P. H. (1991a, February). *A strategy for evaluating family preservation programs.* Paper presented at the American Enterprise Institute Conference on Child Welfare Reform Evaluation, Washington, D.C.

Rossi, P. H. (1991b). *Evaluating family preservation programs: A report to the Edna McConnell Clark Foundation.* New York: Edna McConnell Clark Foundation.

Tyler, M. (1990). *State survey on placement prevention and family reunification programs: Final report.* Iowa City: The University of Iowa School of Social Work, National Resource Center on Family Based Services.

Whittaker, J. K., Kinney, J., Tracy, E. M., & Booth, C. (Eds.). (1990). *Reaching high-risk families: Intensive family preservation in human services.* New York: Aldine de Gruyter.

Yuan, Y. T., & Struckman-Johnson, D. L. (1991). Placement outcomes for neglected children with prior placements in family preservation programs. In K. Wells & D. A. Biegel (Eds.), *Family preservation services: Research and evaluation* (pp. 92–118). Newbury Park, CA: Sage.

Appendices

Holmes, T. H. (1981). *The schedule of recent experience.* Seattle: University of Washington Press.

Klecka, W. R. (1980). *Discriminant analysis.* Beverly Hills, CA: Sage.

Magura, S., & Moses, B. S. (1986). *Outcome measures for child welfare services: Theory and applications.* Washington, DC: Child Welfare League of America, Inc.

Thompson, B. (1984). *Canonical correlation analysis: Uses and interpretation.* Beverly Hills, CA: Sage.

AUTHOR INDEX

SUBJECT INDEX